Zapotec Oral Literature

El Folklore de San Lorenzo Texmelucan

Summer Institute of Linguistics
Language Data Amerindian Series

Publication 13

Folklore Texts in Mexican
Indian Languages 4

LANGUAGE DATA is a serial publication of the Summer Institute of Lingusitics, Inc. The series is intended as an outlet for data-oriented papers authored by members of the Institute. All volumes are issued as microfiche editions, while certain selected volumes are also printed in off-set editions.

Series Editor

Charles H. Speck

Volume Editor

Bonnie Brown

Production Staff

Laurie Nelson, Production Manager
Judy Benjamin, Compositor
Hazel Shorey, Graphic Artist

Zapotec Oral Literature

El Folklore de San Lorenzo Texmelucan

Charles H. Speck

A Publication of
The Summer Institute of Linguistics
Dallas

©1998 by the Summer Institute of Linguistics, Inc.
Library of Congress Catalog No: 98-61276
ISBN: 1-55671-058-5
ISSN: 1040-1113

Printed in the United States of America
All Rights Reserved

08 07 06 05 04 03 02 01 00 99 10 9 8 7 6 5 4 3 2 1

Copies of this and other publications of the Summer Institute of Linguistics may be obtained from

International Academic Bookstore
Summer Institute of Linguistics
7500 W. Camp Wisdom Road
Dallas, TX 75236-5699
Voice: 972-708-7404
Fax: 972-708-7433
Email: academic_books@sil.org
Internet: http://www.sil.org

Contents

Preface ix

Prólogo xi

Introduction to Texmelucan Zapotec Culture xiii

1. The Seven Kinds of Rain 1
   A man from San Lorenzo is swallowed by an alligator and taken to
   the other side of the seventh ocean where he meets the rain maker.

2. Matlaziwa, the Mountain Fairy 25
   In the mountains a man from San Lorenzo meets a fairy, who is a
   seducer of men.

3. The Poisonous Tuber and a Young Man 47
   With the help of a poisonous tuber, a young man turns the tables on
   an old man who wants to eat him.

4. The Skunk Takes a Compadre 57
   A skunk asks a mountain lion to be his compadre with tragic
   results.

5. Peter Deceives the King 65
The trickster Pedro de Urdemalas demonstrates that his
intelligence is superior to that of the king.

6. The Foolish Man 77
An inept and foolish man proves to have more wisdom than his
clever brother.

7. Lucecita 97
Lucecita uses feminine wisdom to help her inept husband succeed.

8. Cuerposulal 135
A man goes to the other side of the seventh ocean to get his wife
back from Cuerposulal, a personification of death.

9. The World of the Dead 153
A man goes into the world of the dead to bring his deceased wife
back.

10. An Elderly Woman Discovers the Sun and the Moon 171
An elderly woman finds two orphans who become the ones who
carry the sun and moon through the sky.

11. Lovers 189
A young man and a young woman allude to their love for each
other as they talk about pretty birds.

12. The Vampire 191
A man from San Lorenzo spends the night at the house of a woman
who is a vampire.

13. Zapotec Proverbs 199
Zapotec wisdom is portrayed in short traditional expressions
about life, vices, virtues, and human relationships.

14. Ashes 213
A Zapotec poet communicates his world view.

Los Zapotecos de San Lorenzo Texmelucan 217

Appendix 1: The Archive 223

Contents

Apéndice 2: El archivo de español 227

Índice 231

References 233

Preface

The purpose of this collection of tales is to present a small sampling of
the oral literature of the Zapotec people who live in the municipality of
San Lorenzo Texmelucan, district of Sola de Vega, Oaxaca, Mexico. With
this goal in mind, tales were carefully selected from materials collected between 1972 and the present to represent a number of different genres
given by both men and women of a variety of ages. Most of the tales presented here are widely known throughout the community; I collected a
number of versions of some of them. In each case I include the most com-
plete version in this collection. An introduction to each tale provides addi-
tional information on how the tale was collected as well as information
that might help in understanding the tale, or its function in society.

In order to make the tales accessible to the Zapotec people who gave
them, I include the original Zapotec in practical orthography, as well as
Spanish and English translations. Information on phonology and orthography are available in publications cited in the references. The only con-
straint placed on the translations, was that they be sentence by
sentence. Since language and culture are so closely related, I opted for a
fairly literal English translation. I departed from the literal translation in
the following ways. I followed the most natural English word order. Zapotec does not have infinitives. I did not try to avoid them. I did not translate
all parts of some fixed expressions, like the quote formula. I translated
nouns as pronouns or pronouns as nouns when the rules of English required it. I did not translate intransitive verbs as intransitive verbs when

doing so would result in unnatural English. The Spanish translation was produced by a native Zapotec speaker in collaboration with a native Spanish speaker.

A considerable amount of linguistic information for each tale is available from the Archive Project of the Mexico Branch of the Summer Institute of Linguistics and an electronic copy will be available on the internet. This information includes a technical transcription with tone, a morphophonemic transcription, morpheme glosses in English and Spanish, word glosses in English and Spanish, and literal English and Spanish translations. A sample of this information occurs in the appendix.

I began my field work in San Lorenzo in 1972 under the sponsorship of the Instituto Lingüístico de Verano, and the Secretary of Public Education in Mexico. Between 1972 and 1980 I had the opportunity to spend a considerable amount of time living in San Lorenzo. I never spoke anything but Zapotec in the community even during early stages of language learning. I collected much of this material during that time. In 1981 I moved to Tucson, Arizona, where I continued to work on Texmelucan Zapotec.

Like all of my work with the Zapotec language, this project is the result of a partnership between myself and a number of other people. Two men have made an especially significant contribution to this collection. First, I have worked with Claudio Martinez Antonio since 1973 when he and I first studied the phonology and morphology of Texmelucan Zapotec together. As a result of this collaboration Claudio learned to read, write, and type his language accurately. Consequently, he was able to transcribe from the tape recorder over a thousand pages of texts that I collected on a wide range of subjects. His discussions of these texts greatly improved my understanding of the Zapotec language and culture. Some of these texts occur here. Secondly, I have worked with Alvaro Marcial López since 1980. Alvaro also reads, writes, and types Zapotec. He likes to think about his culture, and he took an interest in helping me to understand it. I have benefited from many long conversations with him. Alvaro has a good understanding of translation principles. The Spanish translation that is included here is primarily his work in collaboration with Sara Arjona de Watson.

Tales by both of these men are included in this collection, as well as tales by some others. Claudio's mother Juana Antonio was an enthusiastic supporter of my work, and would occasionally have her son tape her tales for me. Antonia Marcial de Sumano and her husband Querino Martinez frequently invited my wife and myself to their home to talk. Policarpo Martinez and his family not only let us study in their home, but frequently dropped in to talk and see if he would help. During the years that we lived in San Lorenzo, we were warmly received by many people. Any progress I have made in studying Zapotec, I owe to their support and friendship.

Prólogo

El propósito de esta colección de cuentos es presentar una pequeña muestra del folklore oral zapoteca de la gente que vive en la municipalidad de San Lorenzo Texmelucan, distrito de Sola de Vega, Oaxaca, México. Con esta meta en mente, se seleccionaron cuentos de los materiales coleccionados desde 1972 hasta el presente para representar una variedad de típos de cuentos típicos dados tanto por hombres como por mujeres de distintas edades. La mayoría de los cuentos que se presentan aquí son muy conocidos en toda la comunidad, y coleccioné varias versiones de algunos de ellos. De todas las versiones escogí las más completas para poner en esta colección. Una introducción en cada cuento provee de información adicional acerca de cómo se coleccionó el cuento, y algunos datos que pueden ayudar a entender mejor el cuento y su función en la sociedad.

Para poder hacer los cuentos más accesibles a los zapotecas que nos los dieron, incluyo el zapoteca original escrito en ortografía práctica, así como la traducción en inglés y en español. La única restricción que hubo en las traducciones fue que se hicieran oración por oración.

En el archivo electrónico del Instituto Lingüístico de Verano hay información de naturaleza lingüística disponible para los que deseen usarla. Para cada historia, esta información incluye una adaptación técnica con tono, transcripciones morfofonémicas, glosas de morfemas en inglés y en español, y glosas de palabras en inglés y en español. En el apéndice se encuentra una muestra de esta información.

Comencé mi trabajo en el campo en 1972 bajo la dirección del Instituto Lingüístico de Verano y la Secretaría de Educación Pública de México. Durante los años de 1972 a 1980 tuve la oportunidad de vivir en San Lorenzo por un período considerable de tiempo. Desde el principio procuré no hablar más que zapoteco en el pueblo, aunque todavía estaba aprendiendo la lengua. Mucho de mi material lo coleccioné durante este tiempo. En 1981 me pasé a vivir a Tucson, Arizona, donde continué mi trabajo en el zapoteco de Texmelucan.

Como todos mis trabajos en la lengua zapoteca, este proyecto es el resultado de una colaboración entre un grupo de personas y yo. Dos personas han prestado una muy especial y significativa contribución a esta colección de cuentos. Primero, Claudio Martínez Antonio, con quien trabajé desde principios de 1970, cuando él y yo estudiamos juntos la fonología y morfología del zapoteca de Texmelucan. Como resultado de esta colaboración Claudio aprendió a leer, a escribir su lengua correctamente y a escribir a máquina. Como resultado, él fue capaz de transcribir del cassette más de 1000 páginas de una extensa variedad de temas que yo había coleccionado. Sus discusiones sobre estos textos aumentaron grandemente mi entendimiento de la cultura y la lengua zapoteca; algunos de estos textos se mencionan aquí.

En 2.o lugar, he trabajado con Álvaro Marcial López desde 1980. Álvaro también lee y escribe su lengua a mano y a máquina. Le gusta pensar acerca de su cultura, y tuvo gran interés en ayudarme a entenderla. Me han beneficiado las largas pláticas que he tenido con él. Álvaro entiende bien los principios de traducción; la traducción de los cuentos al español, que se incluye con estos datos es trabajo suyo, corregido por la Sra. Sara Arjona de Watson.

Las historias relatadas por estas dos personas están incluidas en esta colección, así como algunas historias de otros. La madre de Claudio, Juana Antonio, prestó un apoyo entusiástico a mi trabajo, y de vez en cuando pedía a su hijo grabar cuentos para mí. Antonia Sumano y su esposo, Querino Martínez, frecuentemente nos invitaban a platicar en su casa. Policarpo Martínez y su familia no sólo nos permitían estudiar en su casa, sino que a menudo pasaban a platicar y preguntar si podían ayudar. Durante los años que vivimos en San Lorenzo fuimos recibidos calurosamente por mucha gente. Todo el progreso que logré en el estudio del zapoteca lo debo a su apoyo y amistad.

Introduction to Texmelucan Zapotec Culture

San Lorenzo Texmelucan, *shcyeey,* is a small Zapotec town southwest of Oaxaca City in the district of Sola de Vega. It is a municipal center and has six smaller settlements, called *rancherías,* within its administration: El Río Nube, El Carrizal, Palo de Lima, Rancho de Talea, El Zuchil, and El Arador. People who live in all of these settlements commonly refer to San Lorenzo simply as *gyedz* 'town', as it is the political and religious center for them all. They go to "town" to do community and military service, to pay taxes, for legal settlements, to go to mass, to celebrate the Catholic feasts, to get married, to be baptized, and to be buried.[1] Thus, San Lorenzo is the focal point for community activity for all of the surrounding area, and it is not surprising that all of the people of the municipality simply refer to themselves as the people of San Lorenzo, *mbecy shcyeey.*

The people of San Lorenzo constitute a linguistic as well as a cultural unit. Linguistically, they all speak a variety of Zapotec that has been referred to as "Papabuco" in literature (Upson and Longacre 1965; Harvey 1968; Rendón 1971, 1976). Other communities where people speak Papabuco include Santa Maria Zaniza, San Juan Elotepec, Santiago Textitlán, and Santiago Xochiltepec. Texmelucan Zapotec shares a large number of

---

[1]When I lived in San Lorenzo, the only church was in the town. In recent years churches have been built at some of the *rancherías.*

close cognates with the languages spoken in these communities, but it is mutually unintelligible with them. Egland (1978) reports only a ten percent score for intelligibility of the Zaniza Zapotec text played in San Lorenzo Texmelucan. Other Zapotecan languages are much more distant.

Almost all of the speakers of the Texmelucan Zapotec live in the municipality of San Lorenzo Texmelucan and no Spanish speakers live among them, except for the government school teachers. Most inhabitants of the area are functionally monolingual and Zapotec is used in every aspect of life.

The cultural unity of the people of San Lorenzo is reflected in the distinction they make between themselves—*mbecy shcyeey* 'the people of San Lorenzo' and everyone else—whom they call "John" *wan.* This last expression contrasts with the name *waa* 'John'; it denotes class membership rather than individual identity. Among those people who are called "John," there are also unique words that further distinguish other Papabuco speakers, *waan,* and for the Chatinos, *chok.*

Social patterns of the people of San Lorenzo have many characteristics that are similar to those found in other Zapotec communities. Marriage is contracted through a go-between, *chigool.* After the engagement celebration, *lagyez* (which means literally 'cigarette'), the groom goes to live with the bride's family to do a bride service. Such is not the case with "John." He gets his wife for free.

During the time of the bride service, the groom's father-in-law gives him his wife. Also, during this time they are married in the Catholic Church, if neither party has a living spouse by a previous marriage. A marriage celebration, *fandang,* follows.

When the bride service is over, the newlyweds go to live with the family of the groom. They live with the man's family until the next younger son is grown, and then, ideally, the man's father sets his son up with a house and land, thus establishing a new residence. The man is no longer said to be living with his father, and is no longer considered under his authority; in the view of the community, "he has left his father."

The youngest son remains with his father until he dies, and then inherits his remaining wealth. Thus, inheritance is typically from a man to his sons, part of it being distributed during the man's lifetime. Women do not inherit equally with the men as in some Zapotec communities. A man may leave something to his daughters. But their brothers or uncles are likely to take it away.

As in other areas, it is common for a man to have "bush wives" *mñaa gyish.* He considers them to be as much his property as his legal wife, although he does not consider himself to be responsible for providing for them or his children (called *gyid lab* 'the skin of his foot') by them.

The *compadrinazco* is a voluntary association that exists in San Lorenzo in much the same form as it does in other Zapotec communities. Ravicz (1967) refers to the two dimensions of this association as the "compadrazco" and the "padrinazco." The "compadrazco," the relationship between a man and his children's godparents, is characterized by respect and mutual aid. Respect is shown by the special terms of address and reference used for one's compadres. In greeting one's compadre, one must call to him *shnur compadre* 'hello compadre' and never refer to him by first name. In referring to one's compadre one must always say, "my compadre Peter" *(mbalya bed)* and never simply, "Peter."

As has been noted by others, the relationship is not symmetrical. The father of a child is thought to be beholding to his compadre, the child's godfather. Mutual aid is shown by performing the labor exchange together, by helping each other when one puts on a feast, and by helping during house building.

The "padrinazco," the relationship between godparent and godchild, is characterized by respect and mutual obligation. When a godchild meets his godfather, he greets him as he would his father: *shnur tat, doo yaar ca ru'* 'Hello dad, give me your hand to kiss' and he bows to him. The godfather says, *shnup num ru* 'God bless you', and holds his hand over the godchild's head. The child takes gifts to his godfather during All Saints. The godfather gives advice to his godchild concerning his marriage and helps the godchild's father put on the feed. Should the godchild die, the godfather also has responsibilities in burying him.

As in other Zapotec communities, the political life of the community centers around a system of compulsory unpaid service. This system consists of a series of ranked political and religious offices, called "cargos," through which every man is expected to pass. All men from the time they are sixteen years old are required to give service for one year followed by at least one year of rest. Since only one man per family gives service at any one time, this period of rest will vary depending on the size of the family. The cargos are ranked so that, theoretically, a man should take on each cargo in order of rank. The cargos are listed in order of rank as follows: *ga* 'topil', *hef* 'boss', *mayoor* 'mayora', *gulab* 'colaco', *bacyer* 'cowboy', and *mayordom* 'mayordomo'. Once a person has been a *mayordomo*, he is no longer required to take on a cargo. He is said to have left off being a topil, and he can be elected to office on the town council.

All town services are performed without pay and are considered a hardship. The Zapotec expression for being appointed to a cargo is literally *dugyi* 'to be hit' with it. When the people vote for the town authorities they say that they *cub dey yu* 'capture them'. The office of the town president is considered to be the greatest hardship, since the president cannot work in his fields for three years, but must sit daily in the town hall to perform the

duties of his office. So after a person serves as president, he is no longer required to do town work. It is said that "town work has passed him up."

In addition to the cargos that people perform, there is community work,
riiñ gyedz, that is participated in by everyone not currently giving other
service. At the first of every year (*ña'n cub*) everyone cooperates in clean-
ing the trails. And everyone cooperates in working the town corn field
(*gyel riiñ*). Participation in the cargos and in community activities like
town work and the Catholic feasts reinforces the cultural unity of the people of San Lorenzo and distinguish them from "John."

The people of San Lorenzo are all agriculturists. They live in a moun-
tainous area of Oaxaca, the altitude varying from 4,000 feet to 6,000 feet.
In the lower altitudes they grow corn, beans, bananas, pineapples, citrus
fruits, sugar cane, *mamé*, avocados, chiles, tomatoes, and coffee. In the
higher altitudes they grow corn, beans, squash, and tomatoes. The corn,
beans, and brown sugar they produce are consumed locally. The main cash
crops are bananas, pineapples, and coffee.

In the early 1970s the only means of marketing these cash crops was by
carrying them on their backs or by pack animals a day's hike over the trail
to the market town of Sola de Vega. In more recent years, roads have been
built to each of the settlements. People now have easier access to markets
in Sola de Vega and Oaxaca using hired trucks. Regular trips to the market
are necessary, to buy basic commodities such as farm implements, cloth,
soap, rice, sugar, extra corn, etc. Thus, many continue to take their produce over the trail to Sola de Vega.

Although there is a general demand for labor, hired hands are hard to
come by. This is due partially to a negative value they put on working for
other people, and partially due to a general lack of capital. Alternatives to
hiring help are similar to those that occur elsewhere in Oaxaca. There is
the labor exchange, called *riiñ lo'* 'fence work', *riiñ coz cyaal* 'share crop
farming', labor payment for the use of animals, bride service, adoption of a
relative where a couple does not have children to help run the family farm,
and, rarely, borrowing a topil from the authorities.

Beside agricultural pursuits, secondary means of making money include
dalhez 'business ventures', like raising and selling animals and going to
work on the outside for short periods of time, *cha nap tiiñ.*

As in other Mexican Indian communities, there are negative feelings
about accumulating wealth. These feelings are expressed in a number of
ways. Wealthy people never display their wealth in their lifestyle, but
adopt the same lifestyle as the majority of the community. They are often
the object of criticism, witchcraft, and sometimes of vandalism from their
neighbors. Some occupations, like that of storekeeper, are not considered
appropriate for the people of San Lorenzo.

In 1972 there were no stores in town. With great difficulty, two people soon after started selling some general merchandise. Aside from soft drinks, beer, mescal, and cheap cloth, however, they were not very successful because most people prefer to save money by shopping in Sola de Vega. In more recent years the town began operating a government sponsored store which sells basic commodities. The men who work in the store are appointed in the same way men are appointed to other political office. They are not thought of as storekeepers. Thus, the people of San Lorenzo participate in and share a common outlook on their economy, thus reinforcing their identity as "the people of San Lorenzo."

The people of San Lorenzo view the world as being made up of unpredictable, potentially harmful beings of a number of different types. Two supernatural types are distinguished by the words *ñgyoozh* 'god' and *doo* 'fairy'. The term "god" is applied to the God of the Catholic church, to Jesus, to the saints, the cross, and the virgins who are further identified by the term *gyishnazh*. The term "fairy" translates a word that refers to a second type of supernatural being. Unlike spirits, they are not to be thought to be disembodied. They are sometimes referred to as the "people who were not created by God." They are *doo gyi'* 'the mountain fairy', or Matlaziwa, *doo guyu'* 'the local fairy' or Chaneque, *doo be'y* 'the fairy of the hallucinatory mushroom', *doo gyee ñaa* 'the fairy of the morning glory', or *doo lyuky, doo gyee yon* 'the fairy of the floripondio', *doo gyech* 'the fairy of the jimsum weed', *doo guzii* 'the thunder fairy', or Cosijo, and *doo güidz* 'the sun'. Of these beings, only the sun is ever called "god."

The people of San Lorenzo seek to maintain harmony with these supernatural beings by participating in the activities of the Catholic church, offering sacrifices (*chu' dey presen*) and enlisting the aid of various practitioners.

Whenever this harmony is disturbed, they may go to a diviner. There are three kinds of diviners: the fortune teller (*yu rboo cuen*), the spiritualist (*yu sin*), and the person who divines using wax and water (*yu nu rboo nab lo nis za*). A sick person may also go to an herb doctor (*yu ricy guñaa*), or to the one who removes unclean elements (*yu rboo toop*) that have been supernaturally inserted into the body of the sick person. There are also specialists (*yu rgu' presen*) in offering sacrifices to the local fairy, who is a major cause of sickness, and there are specialists (*yu rboo nab*) in reversing the effects of witchcraft.

Mankind is also viewed as unpredictable and potentially harmful. The people of San Lorenzo believe that witchcraft is wide spread. As in other Zapotec communities, however, there are no practitioners. Selby (1974) considers the Zapotec term *tu'* 'witch' to be a way of labeling people as "outsiders" and formalizing suspicion. Witchcraft is thought to be performed by inserting harmful elements into an image of the victim that is often manufactured using a piece of his clothing. The image is then hidden. The cure is affected by a specialist who knows how to find the image.

Other evil influences men may exert include the evil eye, and the *byee* 'vampire'. Both of these influences have an evil force, the air, associated with them. The evil eye is literally the "air of a person's eye" *(bi lo mbecy)*. The sickness caused by the vampire is called *bi dañ* 'the harmful air'. Air may exert an evil influence on people in a number of other ways. It may enter a person causing pain. It is the cause of epileptic seizures *(ricy ñi bi)*. The air of a corpse is thought to harm plants and people. The people of San Lorenzo say that they do not have familiar spirits *(nan dey bañcyug)* as do the Chatinos and some other Zapotec groups (MacLaury 1970:23). They differ in this respect also from a number of other Zapotec communities.

In a cultural sketch of this nature, it is not possible to treat any cultural pattern in detail, but rather I have attempted to highlight some of the patterns that characterize the people of San Lorenzo as a cultural unit. It is because of their participation in common social, political, economic, and religious patterns, as illustrated in this sketch, that they view themselves as one people distinct from "John."

1

The Seven Kinds of Rain

Once Alvaro asked me, "Do you know how many kinds of rain there are? Because the people of San Lorenzo have the custom that there are seven kinds of rain." He then told me the story of "The Seven Kinds of Rain."

This folktale, however, talks about things that are a lot more important to the people of San Lorenzo than the different kinds of rain. For one thing, it confirms their belief in a supernatural rainmaker. The people of San Lorenzo believe that *doo guzii* causes rain. They refer to him as "the lord of the corn field." And some people sacrifice chickens to him in order to insure a good corn crop.

doo is a word that refers to a number of indigenous supernatural beings. They are not God. They are referred to as "the people who were not created by God." Human beings were created by God. The *doo's* like God have always existed. Further information on these beings is given in the introduction to the *Matlaziwa* tale.

The second word, *guzii*, means 'thunder'. It is cognate with *cosijo*, the term which often appears in anthropological literature for *doo guzii*. Thunder is referred to with a masculine pronoun in men's speech. And one says "it thundered," by saying, *mnii guzii* 'thunder spoke'.

doo guzii is never referred to by name in the story. But the old woman's son, to whom God has given the responsibility of causing rain, is a clear reference to him.

The story begins with a trail driver from San Lorenzo being swallowed by an alligator. There are no alligators near San Lorenzo, but it is interesting to note that there is an indigenous word for them, *be'n*. Historically in Zapotecan mythology, *cosijo* was sometimes pictured as a lizard or alligator in the sky (Parsons 1936:212–13; Whitecotton 1977:296). The alligator takes the trail driver to the other side of the seventh ocean. There he pulls out his knife and cuts himself free. The seventh ocean occurs in Zapotecan and Mixtecan mythology as the end of the world, the home of the gods. There the trail driver meets an old man (a recurrent motif in Zapotec folktales), who tells him where to go. The trail driver then meets an old lady. She hides him because she is concerned that her son might eat him. According to Zapotec world view, supernatural beings are potentially harmful and unpredictable (Kearney 1972:44). But the woman's son, the rain maker, treats him well. He lives in a paradise for a while. But through disobedience, he causes a great destruction, and so is put out—another familiar motif. The rainmaker returns him home in a bolt of lightning, and that is how he knows that there are seven kinds of rain.

This text was given to me by Alvaro Marcial, age 35, in 1981. I recorded it on the tape recorder and later he transcribed it in practical orthography. As he was transcribing it he edited it considerably.

Los siete tipos de lluvia

Una vez Álvaro me preguntó: "¿Sabes cuántas clases de lluvia hay? Porque la gente de San Lorenzo cree que hay siete clases de lluvia." Luego me contó la historia de las siete clases de lluvia.

Sin embargo, este cuento habla de cosas que para la gente de San Lorenzo son mucho más importantes que las diferentes clases de lluvia. En primer lugar, confirma su creencia de un ser sobrenatural que hace que llueva. La gente de San Lorenzo cree que *doo guzii* hace que llueva. Se refieren a él como "el señor de la milpa" y algunos le sacrifican pollos para asegurarse de tener buena cosecha.

doo es una palabra que se refiere a varios seres sobrenaturales indígenas. No son dioses. Se refieren a ellos como "la gente que no fue creada por Dios." Los *doo,* como Dios, siempre han existido. Se da más información acerca de estos seres sobrenaturales en la introducción de Matlaziwa.

La segunda palabra en *doo guzii* quiere decir "trueno." Es pariente de cosijo, el término que con frecuencia aparece en literatura antropológica para *doo guzii.* En el habla de los hombres el trueno tiene pronombre masculino. Dicen "tronó," con las palabras *mnii guzii* 'el trueno habló'.

En la historia nunca se le menciona a *doo guzii* con ese nombre. Pero el hijo de la vieja, a quien Dios dio la responsabilidad de causar la lluvia, es una clara referencia a él.

La historia comienza con un guía de San Lorenzo, que es tragado por un cocodrilo. En San Lorenzo no hay cocodrilos, pero es interesante notar que hay una palabra indígena para referirse a ellos—*be'n*.

Históricamente, en la mitología zapoteca el cosijo se presenta algunas veces como una lagartija en el cielo (Parsons 1936:212–13: Whitecotton 1977:296). El cocodrilo lleva al hombre al otro lado del séptimo océano. Ahí, él saca su cuchillo y corta lo que le ata para libertarse. El séptimo océano en la mitología zapoteca y mixteca es como el fin del mundo, la casa de los dioses. Ahí el guía encuentra a un viejito (una situación que se presenta repetidas veces en los cuentos zapotecas), que le dice a dónde ir. El guía luego se encuentra con una viejita. Ella lo esconde porque tiene miedo de que su hijo se lo coma. Según el punto de vista zapoteca del mundo, los seres sobrenaturales son dañinos y nunca se sabe que van a hacer (Kearney 1972:44). Pero el hijo de la mujer, el que hace llover, lo trata bien. Vive en un paraíso por un tiempo, pero por desobediente causa una gran destrucción, así que lo echan a la calle: un cuadro familiar. Y así regresa a su casa con el cuento de cómo sabe que hay siete clases de lluvia.

Este texto me lo dio Álvaro Marcial, de 35 años, en 1981. Lo grabé en una cinta magnética y más tarde él lo escribió. Al escribirlo, hizo un considerable número de correcciones.

1 Now I will tell you a story, the story of the seven kinds of rain that the people of San Lorenzo say exist. 2 It happened once a long time ago. 3 There were two trail drivers. 4 They went to some other town 5 to buy some animals. 6 When they were on the way there, their trip went well. 7 But when they returned home, as they passed by a lagoon, 8 they thought that they *would like to* drink some water. 9 So they went to the shore of the lagoon to get a drink. 10 When they arrived at the shore of the lagoon, they began to drink. 11 Now at the shore of the lagoon there was an alligator. 12 It swallowed one of them. 13 The other one ran away.

1 Te voy a contar un cuento: el cuento de los siete tipos de lluvia que los de San Lorenzo dicen que hay. 2 Porque sucedió hace mucho tiempo. 3 Habían dos arreadores 4 que fueron a otro pueblo. 5 Fueron a comprar animales. 6 Cuando se fueron ellos, entonces les fue bien. 7 Pero cuando regresaron, pasaron por la orilla de una laguna. 8 Entonces pensaron en tomar agua. 9 Se fueron a tomar agua en la laguna. 10 Cuando llegaron a la orilla de la laguna, empezaron a tomar agua. 11 Pero a la orilla de la laguna estaba un cocodrilo. 12 Ese animal se tragó a uno de ellos. 13 Entonces el otro corrió.

Rishtoo ni gagy lo gyey

1 Na nee tub rishtoo lor: rishtoo ni gagy lo gyey nu rnii mbecy Shcyeey nu yu'ñ. 2 Gun guc ñi tub tiem gulas. 3 Bzu cyup areadoor. 4 Orze' yu ze' guay tuuba' gyedz. 5 Gua ziiy bañcyug. 6 Ornu za dey, orze' nap la zay. 7 Ze' ornu bish cya dey nu yeed yu, orze' bded dey ru' tub lagun. 8 Orze' mnii too dey nu go'y nis. 9 Orze' za dey za to'y nis ru' lagun ze'. 10 Na ornu bru'ña dey ru' lagun, orze' brugyi' ro' dey nis. 11 Ze' ru' lagun ze' mbish tub be'n. 12 Orze' ma ze' bdab ma tub yu. 13 Orze' tuubay gush yu carer.

14 After the alligator had swallowed one of them, it went deep down into the lake. 15 It went all along the bottom of the water. 16 It didn't emerge *from the water* until *it was at* the other side of the seventh ocean.[1] 17 People say that the alligator crossed seven oceans.

18 When it arrived at the other side *of the seventh ocean*, it came out into the sunlight on the shore. 19 The person who was in it was alive. 20 He had not died. 21 He remembered that he had a knife on him. 22 So he put his hand to his waist,[2] drew out his knife, and split the alligator open. 23 Then he came out *of it*.

---

[1] The word for ocean means literally "the water where the *doo* live." *doo* is a very old word for god.

[2] Men traditionally wear a scarf called a *bay nañ* wrapped tightly around their waist.

14 Cuando el cocodrilo ya se había tragado a uno de ellos, se fue al fondo de la laguna. 15 Entonces se fue por todo el fondo del agua. 16 Y no salió, sino hasta el otro lado del séptimo mar.[1] 17 Se dice que cruzó siete mares.

18 Cuando llegó al otro lado, entonces el animal salió a asolearse en la playa. 19 La persona que estaba en el vientre del animal estaba viva. 20 No había muerto. 21 Entonces, recordó que llevaba un cuchillo. 22 Entonces se metió la mano en la cintura[2] para sacar el cuchillo y abrirle el estómago al animal. 23 Entonces salió del estómago del cocodrilo

---

[1] La palabra océano quiere decir literalmente "el agua donde vive el *doo.*" *doo* es una palabra muy antigua para dios.

[2] Los hombres llevan por tradicion un pañuelo atada fuertemente alrededor de la cintura.

14 Na be'n ze', ornu bi bdab ma tub yu ze', orze' ya ma ze' nu gyi ni lagun ze'. 15 Orze' ya ma dub iiñ nis la. 16 Orze' briib ma gashtal tub la' ga' ru' nisyudoo gagy. 17 Be'n ze', rnii dey nu bded ma gagy nisyudoo.

18 Na ornu bru'ña ma tub la' ga', orze' bruu ma lo ba lat yu uzh. 19 Orze' mbecy nu ri nañ ma ze' mbañ yu. 20 Wagat yu. 21 Orze' byeza' lagy yu nu nuuy gyiscyiib. 22 Orze' mne' yaay ru' bay yu nu blooy gyiscyiib niy nu cshalay nañ ma. 23 Orze' bruuy.

24 Now after he emerged *from inside the alligator*, he looked all around. 25 The ocean appeared blue everywhere. 26 The sand was also very wide. 27 He thought, "How unfortunate I am![3] 28 Where should I go? 29 What *direction* should I take?"

30 He set out walking along the beach. 31 He saw someone's footprints. 32 He followed them. 33 He followed them for a long way.

34 When it was late, he met an old man. 35 The old man said to him,

"Where are you going? 36 And where did you come from?"

---

[3]When people speak to themselves, they always use first person plural inclusive.

24 Cuando salió, entonces miró alrededor. 25 Solo se veía el azul del mar por todas partes. 26 Y también la anchura de la arena. 27 Entonces él pensó: "Pobre de mí![3] 28 ¿A dónde iré? 29 ¿Qué dirección debo de tomar?" decía.

30 Entonces cogió su camino y se fue él por la playa. 31 Entonces vio que había huellas de una persona. 32 Y se fue siguiéndolas. 33 Caminó él mucho siguiendolas.

34 Cuando ya era tarde, se encontró con un viejo. 35 Ese viejo le dijo:

—¿A dónde vas? 36 Y ¿de dónde saliste? —dijo.

---

[3]La gente se refiere a si misma en la 1a persona de plural cuando est pensando.

---

24 Na ornu briib yu, orze' bgüiiy dub yub la. 25 Se nu ca' zi'l rabee nisyudoo. 26 Ze' yu uzh ni' she zañ. 27 Orze' mnii tooy «¡Lashta ub na! 28 ¿Ca par chan? 29 ¿Ca par rush na?» nay.

30 Orze' gush nez yu zay dub lat yu uzh la. 31 Orze' bzaac yu nu ta' gyi' mbecy. 32 Orze' zay za cay dub ich gyi' mbecy la ze'. 33 Tona' la tuñ bzay nu za cay ich gyi' mbecy ze'.

34 Na ornu bi gudze, orze' bdzeel yu tub mbecy bel. 35 Orze' yu bel ze' nay rab yuy:

«¿Ca char? 36 Nunu ¿ca bruur?» nay.

37 He said to the old man,
"Let's not mention it.
38 Something bad happened to
me. 39 I am out of luck. 40 First,
an alligator swallowed me.
41 Then I killed it when it came
out *of the water* into the sunlight. 42 And now I don't know
where I am, and *I don't know*
what direction I should take."
43 The old man spoke to him.
44 He said,

"Don't be afraid, because you
are not in an uncertain place
here. 45 You are at a safe place
here. 46 Only, you will never go
home again, because this place
is the very farthest *from your
home*. 47 Now I will give you a
piece of advice. 48 Follow this
person's footprints. 49 When
dusk comes, look for a light.
50 Go straight toward the light.
51 And exert yourself to arrive
at the place where the light is even
if it has already dawned."

52 "Okay," said the trail
driver.

37 Entonces le dijo él al abue-
lito:
—No digas nada. 38 Me sucedió una desgracia. 39 Me aban-
donó la suerte. 40 Un cocodrilo
me tragó. 41 Pero lo maté
cuando salió a asolearse. 42 Pero
ahora no sé dónde estoy, y por
dónde debo ir —le dijo él al viejo.

43 Entonces el viejo le habló y
44 le dijo:
—No tengas miedo, porque no
estás en el lugar inseguro aquí
—le dijo—. 45 Estás en un lugar
seguro. 46 Sólo que ya no
volverás a tu tierra otra vez,
porque este lugar es el más lejano
de tu hogar. 47 Pero ahora, yo te
doy un consejo: 48 Anda por
donde están las huellas de esa
persona. 49 Entonces cuando llegue la noche, fíjate en donde hay
una luz. 50 Entonces ve derecho
para allá. 51 Y haz un esfuerzo
por llegar, aunque esté amaneciendo—.

52 —Bueno —dijo.

37 Orze' nay rab yu yu bel ze':
«Cue' la niir. 38 Ya bzaca tub gyel zi. 39 Bzaan yaa suert ya.40 Tub be'n
bdab ma ya. 41 Se na bduta ma ornu bruu ma lo ba. 42. Se na wagad lagya
ca lugaar zu nunu ca par rusha», nay rab yu yu bel ze'.
43 Orze' yu bel ze' nay rab yuy. 44 Orze' na yu bel:
«Cue' dzib ru, gun walab nu lugaar nu cyup ridz zur ii», nay rab yuy.
45 «Ii lugaar segur zur. 46 Nomaas nu warii ga'r ledz ru, gun ii tub lugaar
nu blaazh la zet. 47 Tees na ya grica tub consef nir. 48 Na gua dub ze' nu ta'
la gyi' mbecy ii. 49 Na ornu gyecheñ, orze' cu' cuen ru ca gal ze' nu rca tub
gyi 50 Orze' li laa ze' char. 51 Nunu gyicy ru fers nu grir, mas bi rza' yu»,
nay.
52 Orze' «O», nay.

53 He left the old man 54 and went on his way. 55 When it was evening, he began to look for where there might be a light, just like the old man said. 56 Then he saw a small light. 57 But it was very far away. 58 He went straight toward the light. 59 He was on the trail the whole night. 60 It had just dawned *when* 61 he arrived where the light was. 62 He saw a house standing there. 63 So he went right up to the door. 64 He began to called out *to anyone at home.* 65 Then a woman came out.

66 "Hello," he said.

67 "Hello," she said.

68 "Where do you come from? How did you get here? 69 Because we never have any visitors at this place. 70 Only I and my son live here."

71 He said,

53 Entonces dejó al viejo. 54 Y se fue. 55 Cuando llegó la noche, empezó a buscar la luz, como había dicho el viejo. 56 Entonces vio una lucecita. 57 Pero estaba muy lejos. 58 Y se fue derecho a donde brillaba la luz. 59 Toda la noche estuvo en camino. 60 Ya estaba amaneciendo 61 cuando llegó a donde estaba la luz. 62 Entonces vio una casa que allí había. 63 Entonces se acercó a la puerta. 64 Y empezó a llamar. 65 Salió una mujer.

66 —Buenos días —le dijo él.

67 —Buenos días —le contestó ella—.

68 ¿De dónde saliste cuando veniste para aquí? 69 Porque por aquí nunca hay nada de gente. 70 Sólo mi hijo y yo vivimos aquí —le dijo ella.

71 Entonces dijo él:

53 Orze' bla' losa'y yu bel ze'. 54 Orze' zay. 55 Na or becheñ, orze' brugyi' rgu' cuen yu ben ca rca gyi gal nu mnii yu bel ze'. 56 Orze' bzaac yu tub gyi mi'. 57 Par tona' la nu zet. 58 Orze' zay li laa par ze' nu rca gyi ze'. 59 Gua la rel zuy nez. 60 Bi rza' yu la. 61 Orze' bru'ñay ze' nu rca gyi ze'. 62 Orze' bzaac yu tub yu' zub ñi. 63 Orze' wecha'y gal ro' la. 64 Brugyi' rniiy. 65 Orze' bruu tub biñ mñaa.

66 Orze' «Shnur», nay.

67 «Shnur», nam.

68 Orze' nam:

«¿Ca bruur yad ru ii? 69 Gun ii lugaar nu rila sac mbecy. 70 Nomaas ya zi'l nu tub i'ña yu' de», nam.

71 Orze' nay:

"Something bad happened to me. 72 I am a man who deals in animals. 73 That is my business. 74 I went to a place to buy some animals. 75 As I passed the edge of a lagoon, 76 I thought I would like to drink some water. 77 But an alligator swallowed me on the shore of the lagoon. 78 Then it went down to the bottom of the water. 79 When it emerged on the other side *of the ocean* here, I killed it. 80 I got out from inside of it. 81 Now I have come to this house. 82 That is how I got here. 83 I am a poor lost soul. 84 Therefore, please tell me where I should go. 85 What trail would you suggest that I take?"

86 Then the woman said,

—Me pasó una desgracia. 72 Yo soy un hombre que compra animales. 73 Ese es mi negocio. 74 Fui a un lugar a comprar animales. 75 Entonces pasé por la orilla de una laguna. 76 Y me dio ganas de tomar agua. 77 A la orilla de la laguna me tragó un cocodrilo 78 que bajó al fondo de la laguna. 79 Cuando salió al otro lado, entonces lo maté, 80 y salí de su vientre. 81 Ahora vine a esta casa. 82 Así es como llegué hasta aquí. 83 Soy una persona que está perdida. 84 Por eso te pregunto por dónde debo ir. 85 ¿Qué camino me sugieres tomar? —le dijo.

86 Entonces le dijo la mujer:

«Ya bzaca tub desgras. 72 Ya naca tub yu nu rboo bañcyug. 73 Nde' daljez nu ricya. 74 Gua nu zi bañcyug tub lugaar. 75 Orze' bdeda ru' tub lagun. 76 Orze' mnii too nu do' nis. 77 Orze' ru' lagun ze' bdab be'n ya. 78 Na ma ze' bet ma iiñ nis. 79 Na ornu briib ma tub la' ga' ii, orze' ya bduta ma. 80 Orze' briba nañ ma. 81 Na bi yapa yu' ii. 82 Nde' nu bru'ña gal ii. 83 Ya naca mbecy bdune'. 84 Nde' nu na dugyi' lor ben ca par rusha. 85 ¿Ca par cuic ru nez nu cha?» nay.

86 Orze' na biñ mñaa ze':

"It is a very good thing that you came here. 87 But you can never again return to your home, because you will not be able to cross over the seven oceans. 88 Therefore forget your home, because there is no other place for you to go, except to me here, because there are no other people *here*. 89 So come on into the house," she said.

90 He entered the house. 91 She began to prepare *food* for him to eat. 92 Now when he finished eating, she began to discuss with him how he came from very far way, and would not be able to return to his home again, because he would not be able to cross over the seven oceans.

93 He began to feel very sad. 94 But he was already there. There was no other way. 95 So he took courage.

96 She said to him,

—¡Qué bueno que viniste aquí! 87 Pero ya no puedes regresar a tu pueblo, porque no puedes pasar por los siete mares. 88 Por lo tanto olvídate de tu pueblo, porque ya no hay otro lugar al que puedas ir, más que aquí conmigo, porque no hay nadie más *aquí* —dijo ella—. 89 Pasa adelante —dijo ella.

90 Entonces él entró la casa. 91 Ella empezó a preparar para que él comiera. 92 Cuando él terminó de comer las tortillas, ella empezó a platicar con él. Le decía que había muy lejos venido de, que ya no podía regresar a su pueblo, porque no iba a poder pasar por los siete mares —dijo ella.

93 Entonces él empezó a ponerse triste. 94 Pero como ya estaba allá, no había remedio. 95 Entonces él se animó.

96 Ella le dijo:

«Tona' la nap guc nu ii yad ru. 87 Tees ledz ru waca' cush cyar, gun wac ded ru lo gagy nisyudoo. 88 Nde' nu bloo la ic ru ledz ru, gun saca' zir lugaar nu char, nomaas lo zi'l ii, gun saca' zir mbecy», nam. 89 «Gyed nañ yu'», nam.

90 Orze' gu'y nañ yu'. 91 Orze' brugyi' nu rzu yem nu gow yu gyit. 92 Na ornu blazh bdoy gyit, orze' brugyi' rom riidz num yu nu dzi zet bruuy nunu waca' cush cyay par ledz yu, gun wac ded yu lo gagy nisyudoo, nam.

93 Orze' brugyi' ricy shniy. 94 Tees par nu bi zuy gal ze', saca' mod niñ. 95 Orze' briic yu baloor.

96 Orze' na ga'm rab miy:

"The hour has come for my son to arrive home. 97 Let's go into the other room, so that I can hide you, lest he mistreat you, because he doesn't know you."

98 She took him into the other room to hide him. 99 She put many pieces of cloth over him, so that he could not be seen. 100 She wrapped him in a mat so that her son could not see him.

101 Now after he had been there for a while, there was a sound like the coming of rain. 102 Then it sounded like a man landed outside of the house. 103 The man entered one of the rooms 104 and left off something that he had with him. 105 Then he went to his mother 106 and said to her,

"I just went to finish the rest of our work."

—Ya se acerca la hora de que llegue mi hijo. 97 Vamos al otro cuarto, porque te voy a esconder, para que él no te vaya a hacer ningún mal, porque no te conoce —le dijo ella.

98 Entonces ella lo llevó al otro cuarto para esconderlo. 99 Y puso muchos trapos sobre él, para que no se viera. 100 Lo enrolló en un petate para que no lo viera su hijo.

101 Después de un rato de estar allí, empezó un ruido como de lluvia que venía. 102 Entonces se oyó que él bajaba por afuera de la casa, 103 Y que entraba a uno de los cuartos. 104 Y que dejaba una cosa que traía. 105 Entonces fue a *donde estaba* su mamá. 106 Y le dijo a su mamá:

—Fui a terminar lo que nos faltaba —dijo.

«Yad nu bi yap or nu gri i'ña. 97 Yaa gyan nañ tuuba' cuart re, gun cacha ru, gun nis shiñ gyicy ñi nuñ ru, gun a' yu' loñ ru», nam rab miy.

98 Orze' ya num yu nañ tuuba' cuart nu cach miy. 99 Orze' pcuaam zañ negy tooy par nu cue' gabey. 100 Ptiish miy da' par nu cue' zac i'ñ mi yu.

101 Na ornu guchi ga' nu riy, orze' brugyi' nu rzigy nu yad gyey. 102 Orze' bzigy nu bet yu ich yu'. 103 Orze' gu'y nañ tub cuart ze'. 104 Bzeeñ yu tub coz nu nuuy. 105 Orze' yay lo ñaay. 106 Orze' nay rab yu ñaay:

«Na gua za' lo ze' nu bicy falt nin ze'», nay.

107 The man who was hidden was listening to the conversation that the young man was having with his mother, the woman who lived there. 108 Then she began to prepare something for him to eat. 109 While he was sitting there eating, he said,

"Where is that good smelling meat, mom?"

110 "*First* eat your tortillas. 111 After you have finished eating, I will tell you," she said.

112 "But I want you to at least give me a little piece to eat now, because I think it smells so good," he said.

113 "When you have finished eating, I will tell you where I got the meat," she said.

114 The young man was not at all pleased that his mother would not give him any meat to eat. 115 When he finished eating, he said,

"Show me the meat, mom."

107 Él que estaba escondido estaba escuchando las palabras que hablaba el joven, el hijo de la mujer de la casa.108 Entonces empezó ella a preparar las cosas para comer. 109 Mientras él estaba comiendo, le preguntó:

—¿Dónde está la carne que huele bien, mamá?

110 Su mamá le contestó:

—Come tortillas. 111 Cuando hayas terminado de comer, te lo diré —dijo ella.

112 —Pero quiero que me des aunque sea un poquito para comer, porque me parece que huele muy bien —dijo.

113 Entonces le dijo su mamá:

—Hasta que termines de comer las tortillas, te diré dónde conseguí la carne —dijo ella.

114 El joven no le gustó que su mamá no le diera esa carne para comer. 115 Cuando terminó de comer, le dijo:

—Enséñame la carne, mamá.

---

107 Orze' rzuub gyidag yu nu ri ngach ze' de riidz nu ro yu feñ, i'ñ biñ mñaa guyu' ze' nu ñaay. 108 Orze' brugyi' rzu yem de coz nu gow yu. 109 Na lat nu zub yu row yu gyit, orze' nay:

«¿Ca dzi nap ti' beel ze' ña'?» nay.

110 Orze' na ñaay rab mi yu:

«Bdow la gyit. 111 Lazh gow ru, gaze' nu nee lor», nam.

112 «Tees rlagya nu cuic lar mas ñuu miiñ daw, gun dzi nap ti' rzee», nay.

113 Orze' na ñaay:

«Gal laazh la gor gyit, gaze' nu nee lor ca guud beel», nam.

114 Orze' yu feñ ze' wagyu' lagy yu nu wacuic ñaay beel ze' gow yu. 115 Na ornu blazh bdow yu gyit na, orze' nay:

«Blyuu beel ze' lo ña'», nay.

116 His mother said,

"Let's not speak like that. 117 An unfortunate man has arrived here who had something bad happen to him. An alligator swallowed him on the shore of a lagoon. 118 The alligator didn't come out *from the water* until it was over here. 119 He killed it when it came out of the ocean. 120 He came out from inside of it over here. 121 Therefore, I thought that I should hide him, because you might suddenly arrive 122 and mistreat him."

123 Then the young man said,

"Where is he? 124 Show him to me."

125 She took her son to where the man was *hiding*. 126 She uncovered him. 127 He arose. 128 Then the woman's son said to the trail driver,

"Where do you come from? 129 And what happened *to cause* you to come here?"

116 Entonces le dijo su mamá:

—No lo digas. 117 Aquí llegó un pobre que le sucedió una desgracia porque se lo tragó un cocodrilo a la orilla de una laguna. 118 Y ese cocodrilo no salió del agua hasta que llegó aquí. 119 Entonces él mató a ese animal cuando salió del mar —dijo—. 120 Y él salió del vientre de ese animal aquí. 121 Por eso yo pensaba esconderlo, porque tú ibas a llegar pronto. 122 Y pensé que ibas a tratarlo mal —le dijo ella a su hijo.

123 Entonces le dijo el joven:

—¿Dónde está él? 124 Enséñamelo —dijo.

125 Entonces llevó a su hijo a donde estaba ese hombre. 126 Y lo destapó. 127 Entonces el hombre se levantó. 128 Le dijo el joven a esa persona:

—¿De dónde saliste? 129 Y ¿cómo fue que viniste hasta aquí? —dijo.

116 Orze' na ñaay:

«Cue' la niir. 117 Ii bru'ña tub pro mbecy nu bzac desgras nu bdab be'n mi ru' lagun. 118 Na be'n ze' gashtal ii la briib ma. 119 Orze' biit mi ma, ornu bruu ma lo nisyudoo», nam. 120 «Orze' bruum nañ ma gal ii. 121 Nde' nu ya mnii too nu cacham, gun ru lo pront la rir. 122 Orze' nis shiñ gyicy ru nur mi rnii too», nam rab mi i'ñ mi.

123 Orze' na yu feñ ze':

«¿Ca riy? 124 Blyuuy lo», nay.

125 Orze' ya num i'ñ mi ze' nu ri mbecy ze'. 126 Orze' pshaal mi tooy. 127 Orze' mbecy ze' weshtey. 128 Orze' na yu feñ ze' rab yu mbecy ze':

«¿Ca bruur? 129 Nunu ¿lac guc yad ru gashtal ii?» nay.

130 The trail driver told the young man, the son of the woman, all of the things that happened to him.

131 Then young man said, "You are very unfortunate if that is the case. 132 You are very unfortunate. 133 But don't worry about having come so far. If your business is that of a trail driver, that work is also very hard; because I know the whole world, and I know all the work that people do. 134 And I see people making a living as a trail driver. 135 I have even seen you, 136 although I don't know you. 137 Because I see the people who go about the business of buying animals. 138 At times they get rained on on the trail. 139 I see very well all the things that the people of the world do, because I know all of the places of the world.

140 "But don't worry now, because here you can get things to eat, and I will give you clothing *to wear*."

130 Ese hombre le contó todo lo que le había pasado a ese joven, el hijo de la mujer.

131 El joven dijo:

—Pobre de ti, si eso te pasó. 132 ¡Qué desafortunado eres! 133 No te preocupes que hasta aquí has llegado, porque si tu negocio es de arreador, también muy duro es ese trabajo; porque yo conozco todo el mundo, y conozco todo el trabajo que hace la gente. 134 Y he visto a personas que son arreadores. 135 Aún te he visto a ti. 136 Pero no te conozco. 137 Porque veo a la gente que anda comprando animales. 138 A veces les agarra la lluvia en el camino. 139 Yo bien veo todas las cosas que hace la gente en el mundo, porque yo conozco todo el mundo —dijo el joven—.

140 Pero ahora, no te preocupes, porque aquí puedes conseguir comida, y yo te voy a dar la ropa —le dijo él al hombre.

---

130 Orze' mbecy ze' mniiy loy dela coz nu bzac yu: lo yu feñ, i'ñ biñ mñaa ze'.

131 Orze' na yu feñ ze':

«Dzi ga cuaar beni. 132 Desgras bzac ru. 133 Beni cue' sug ic ru nu dzi zet yad ru, gun benu fis ni areadoor ricy ru, ni' dzi fers riiñ ze', gun ya yu' lo dutuub la gyishlombecy, nunu yu' lo dela riiñ nu ricy mbecy. 134 Nunu rzaca de mbecy nu ricy fis ni areadoor. 135 Mas rzaca ru.136 Tees a' yu' lo ru. 137 Gun rzaca mbecy nu rded daljez nu rzii bañcyug. 138 Yu' rash gyey dey nez. 139 Ya za naap la rzaca dela coz nu ricy de mbecy gyishlombecy, gun ya yu' lo dutuub la lugaar ni gyishlombecy», na yu feñ ze'.

140 «Tees na cue' la sug ic ru, gun ii gad coz nu gow ru, nunu ya rica shab ru», nay rab yu mbecy ze'.

141 The trail driver was very happy because he would get things to eat and clothing *to wear*.

142 Now when it dawned the next day, the young man said to the trail driver,

"Let's go, so that I can go show you around my garden. Then you will know where to work. But one of you men will not be enough to do my work."

143 "Okay," said the trail driver.

144 They went on their way. 145 Now when they arrived at the young man's garden, the trail driver was very surprised that it was so pretty, because he saw all of the kinds of cultivated plants that exist in the world. 146 He even saw trees that he hadn't ever seen before. 147 And all of them had fruit, 148 and all the plants had fruit on them all of the time.

141 Entonces ese hombre se puso contento, porque iba a tener cosas para comer y vestir.

142 Cuando amaneció el siguiente día, le dijo el joven al hombre:

—Vamos, porque te voy a enseñar mi huerta, para que sepas dónde vas a trabajar, porque uno solo no será suficiente para hacer mi trabajo —dijo.

143 —Está bien —dijo el hombre.

144 Entonces se fueron. 145 Cuando llegaron a la huerta del joven, el hombre se sorprendió por lo bonita qué estaba la huerta del joven, porque vio que tenía todas las clases de árboles frutales que hay en el mundo. 146 Hasta había árboles que él nunca había visto antes. 147 Y todos tenían frutas. 148 Todos los árboles frutales tenían frutas todo el tiempo.

141 Orze' mbecy ze' yet lagy yu par nu gad de coz goy nu shab yu.142 Na ornu bza' yu tuuba' dzi, orze' na yu feñ ze' rab yu mbecy ze':

«Yaa chan na, gun cha lyuu de lat naa lor, gun gad lagy ru ca gyicy ru riiñ, gun ni wal par tub ru ne ya par nu gyicy ru riiñ ne», nay.

143 Orze' «O», na mbecy ze'.

144 Orze' za dey. 145 Na ornu bru'ña dey lat naa yu feñ ze', orze' za nu la ic mbecy ze' nu tona' la cyit zu lat naa yu feñ ze' nu bzaac yu de lo la ya mni nu nash gyishlombecy. 146 Nunu gashtal yag nu a' zac lay bzaac yu. 147 Nunu delañ ta' uugy niñ. 148 Nunu dela ya mni ze' dub laa tiem ta' uugy niñ.

149 And there were young corn plants, mature corn plants, corn plants that had already tasseled, corn plants that already had corn silk, corn plants that already had ears of fresh corn, and corn plants that were already dry. 150 The trail driver was very surprised that it was so pretty in the garden of the young man. 151 The young man said,

"You will work here now."

152 Then the trail driver began to work *in the garden of the young man.*

153 Then the young man began to tell the trail driver how to work; how to work among those plants, and what to do whenever he should pick some of the fruit to eat. 154 Then he said to the trail driver,

"When you think of eating which ever of those fruit, don't pick many of them, because you will not be able to finish them all, because those fruit multiply. 155 Whenever we pick one, 156 it turns into about ten of them.

149 Había milpa chiquita, milpa grande, milpa ya en espiga, milpa en cabellito, milpa con elotes, y milpa ya seca. 150 Ese hombre estaba muy sorprendido de lo bonita que estaba la huerta del joven. 151 El joven le dijo:

—Aquí vas a trabajar ahora.

152 Entonces el hombre empezó a trabajar.

153 El joven comenzó a explicar al hombre cómo debía cultivar los árboles frutales y cómo debía recoger una fruta para comerla. 154 Y le dijo al hombre:

—Cuando quieras comer cualquier fruta, no recojas muchas, porque no se terminarán si las comes, porque esas frutas van a multiplicar. 155 Si recogemos una 156 salen como diez

149 Nunu nash gyel mi', gyel ily, gyel bi rado, gyel nu bi ralyuch, gyel nu bi yu' za', nu gyel bi guwach. 150 Orze' mbecy ze' tona' la za nu ic yu nu tona' la cyit zu lat naa yu feñ ze'. 151 Orze' na yu feñ ze':

«Ii gyicy ru riiñ na», nay.

152 Orze' mbecy ze' brugyi'y ricy yu riiñ.

153 Orze' brugyi' rgu' yu feñ ze' riiñ yaa mbecy ze' nu lac mod gyicy yu lat de ya mni ze', nunu lac mod gyicy yu ornu lag yu tub de uugy ze' par nu gow yu. 154 Orze' nay rab yu mbecy ze':

«Ornu nii toor nu gow ru ca na de uugy re, orze' cue' lag ru zañ ñii gun walaazh ñi gow ru, gun de uugy re ryañ ñii. 155 Tub ñi laag na. 156 Orze' yac tub tiiñ.

157 Or it will become about twelve of them. 158 Therefore, you should only pick one of them. 159 You will eat from it for many days. 160 If you pick one piece of corn to take home, now when you arrive home with it, it will multiply."

161 Now that is what the trail driver did. 162 He would cut a piece of fresh corn to take home. 163 Now when he would arrive home, it would multiply for him. 164 Or he would pick some of the fruit to eat. 165 He would take it home. 166 It would multiply. 167 The trail driver was very happy to live in that place.

168 Now when the trail driver had already been living there for a long time, the young man said to him,

"I am going to request now that you not enter that room over there."

169 "Why can't I go into it?" the trail driver asked.

157 o doce más. 158 Por eso, si cortas una, 159 lo comerás por varios días. 160 Si recoges un elote para llevar a la casa, cuando llegues a casa, se multiplicará —dijo.

161 Y eso es lo que hizo el hombre. 162 Cortaba un elote para llevar a casa. 163 Cuando llegaba a la casa, se multiplicaba para él. 164 Así que, cortaba cualquiera de las frutas para comer. 165 Entonces la llevaba a la casa. 166 Y se multiplicaba. 167 El hombre estaba muy contento viviendo en ese lugar.

168 Cuando ya hacía tiempo que vivía allí, le dijo el joven:

—Ahora te voy a pedir que no entres al cuarto que está allí.

169 Entonces el hombre le dijo:

—¿Por qué no puedo entrar?

157 O tub trocyup ñii yac ñi. 158 Nde' nu tub ñi lag ru. 159 Zañ dzi gow ru ñii», nay. 160 «Benu cyug ru tub za' gya nur yu', na ornu ri nur ñii yu', orze' gyañ ñii», nay.

161 Na mbecy ze' ni ricy yu. 162 Rshi'ñ yu tub za', rya nuy yu'. 163 Na ornu driy yu', ryañ ñii niy. 164 Na lag yu tub ca na de uugy nu goy. 165 Orze' ya nuy ñi yu. 166 Orze' ryañ ñii. 167 Orze' mbecy ze' tona' la yet lagy yu rcyiiñ yu lugaar ze'.

168 Na ornu bi gules rcyiiñ yu, orze' na yu feñ ze' rab yuy:

«Na nee lor nu cue' chu'r nañ cuart nu zub re», nay.

169 Orze' mbecy ze' nay:

«¿Lagu wac chu'?» nay.

170 "You can't *go in there*, because there is where I keep the things that I work with," the young man said.

171 "What things are those?" the trail driver asked.

172 "In that room are the cloaks that I take with me to cause it to rain. I put them on, because they are rain," the young man said.

173 "Even though I do not have permission to enter *the room* to take them, would you please just show them to me, so that I can see what they are like?" asked the trail driver to the young man.

174 The young man opened the door. 175 They entered the room. 176 The trail driver began to look at the raincloaks hanging *there*. There were seven of them, because there was one for each kind of rain that they cause to fall. 177 The first raincloak sent very fine rain.

170 El joven le dijo:

—No puedes, porque allí están las cosas con que yo trabajo —dijo.

171 —¿Qué cosas son? —pregunto el hombre.

172 —En ese cuarto están colgados los capotes que me pongo para hacer caer la lluvia; me los pongo, porque ellos son la lluvia —dijo.

173 Entonces dijo el hombre:

—Si no tengo permiso para entrar al cuarto y llevarlos, entonces ¿quisieras, por favor, mostrármelos para ver cómo son? —le dijo al joven.

174 El joven abrió la puerta, 175 y entraron a la casa. 176 El hombre se puso a mirar los capotes que estaban colgados. Había siete, porque cada uno de los siete capotes hacía caer una clase diferente de lluvia. 177 El primer capote, hacía caer llovizna muy tenue.

170 Orze' yu feñ ze' nay:

«Wac, gun re zaab de coz nu ricy du̱ riiñ», nay.

171 «¿La coz nu nde'?» na mbecy ze'.

172 Orze' yu feñ ze' nay:

«Nañ cuart re zaab de shees nu rza du̱ nu rsheta̱ gyey, gun nde' rcaa yeña̱, gun nde' nac ñii gyey», nay.

173 Orze' na mbecy ze':

«Benu wad rishbeey nu chu̱' nañ ñi nu cha̱ du̱ ñii, orze' mas ñuu nu lyuur ñii lo̱, gun zaca̱ la nañ», nay rab yu yu feñ ze'.

174 Orze' yu feñ ze' pshaal yu ro' ze'. 175 Orze' gu' dey nañ yu' ze'. 176 Orze' brugyi' rgüii mbecy ze' de shees zaab gyiñ. Gagy ñii nac ñii, gun lo gagy shees ze', tub gañ nu tub lo ga gyey nu rshet ñi. 177 Shees loga la, nde' rshet ñi gyey shely.

178 The second raincloak sent sprinkles. 179 The third raincloak sent drizzles. 180 The fourth raincloak sent mist. 181 The fifth raincloak sent light passing rain that sprays the ground. The sixth raincloak sent storms 182 The seventh raincloak was black. 183 It sent hail and thunderstorms.

184 Then the strong young man said to the trail driver,

"If you like, you can take *one of* these small raincloaks here to cause it to rain close by. 185 But don't touch the black one that is inside this box. I will close the top of it with this."[4]

186 Now when they were ready to leave, the young man said, "I have already told you not to touch *that which* is closed up there. 187 But you can take the third, and the fifth one."

---

[4]He secured the box, but it is not apparent what with.

178 El segundo capote hacía caer llovizna como rocío. 179 El tercer capote hacía caer una llovizna normal. 180 El cuarto capote, hacía caer lluvia ligera. 181 El quinto capote, ese hacía caer una llovizna pasajera. El sexto capote, hacía caer una tempestad. 182 El séptimo capote era el capote negro. 183 Ese hacía caer granizo y truenos.

184 Entonces el joven fuerte dijo al hombre:

—Si quieres, puedes tomar los capotes chiquitos para hacer caer lluvia en los alrededores. 185 Pero el negro que está en este cajón, no lo toques. Lo voy a tapar con esto —dijo.[4]

186 Cuando ya estaban por salir, el joven dijo:

—*Recuerda que* ya te dije que no toques lo que esta guardado allí. 187 Sólo puedes tomar el tercero y el quinto de los capotes —dijo.

---

[4]Él aseguró la caja, pero no es claro con qué.

178 Shees cyup, nde' rshet ñi gyey zee. 179 Shees chon, nde' rshet ñi gyey las. 180 Shees tap, nde' rshet ñi gyey nis shish be'y. 181 Shees gay, nde' rshet ñi gyey ni gyeez bizee. Shees shup, nde' rshet ñi gyey bi. 182 Shees gagy, nde' shees cas. 183 Nde' rshet ñi gyey gye nu guzii dañ.

184 Orze' na yu fert ze' rab yu mbecy ze':

«Benu yet lagy ru, orze' gac cha nur de shees mi' ii par nu shet ru gyey de gaab ga. 185 Tees nu cas nu ri nañ caj<u>oo</u> ii, cue' gan ru ñii, gun nu nii soow<u>a</u> ru'ñ», nay.

186 Na ornu bi zu dey nu gruuy, orze' na yu feñ:

«Tees bi mn<u>ee</u> lor nu cue' gan ru nu ri noow re. 187 Be shees chon nu nu gay gac cha nur», nay.

188 Now when a certain day came, the young man said to his mother,

"You go to one place. 189 I will go to another place."

190 They left. 191 The trail driver remained. 192 The trail driver thought,

"I will go and cause it to rain to see what it is like."

193 He took hold of a small raincloak to take with him.

Now when he arrived back, he saw that nothing happened to him on his trip.

194 He was happy. 195 Now another time when the young man and his mother went away, they went for about three days. 196 On the day on which the young man was to arrive, the trail driver thought he would go cause it to rain. 197 He said to himself,

"I will test *it*. 198 I will take the one he told me not to touch to see what it will do."

188 Ya cuando llegó un cierto día, ese joven dijo a su mamá:

—Vas a ir a un lugar. 189 Entonces yo iré al otro —dijo.

190 Y se fueron. 191 El hombre se quedó 192 y pensó:

"Voy a hacer llover a ver qué pasa."

193 Entonces tomó un capote chiquito para ponerse.

Cuando regresó, vio que no le había sucedido nada al salir *con el capote.*

194 Entonces se puso contento. 195 La siguiente vez que el joven y su mamá salieron, estuvieron fuera como tres días. 196 El hombre pensó que haría llover el día que el joven regresara. 197 Entonces le dijo:

—Voy a probar. 198 Voy a tomar el que me dijo que no debía tocar para ver lo que pasa —dijo.

188 Na ornu pshuub tub dzi, orze' na yu feñ ze' rab yu ñaay:

«Na ru char tub lugaar. 189 Orze' ya cha tub se' ga'», nay.

190 Orze' za dey. 191 Orze' byeeñ mbecy ze'. 192 Orze' mnii too mbecy ze':

«Par chan shet na gyey, ben lac ricy ñi», nay.

193 Orze' pshet yaay tub shees mi' za nuy.

Na ornu briy, rgüiiy nu se la la bzac yu ornu guay.

194 Orze' yet lagy yu. 195 Na tub tira', ornu gua yu feñ ze' nu ñaay, orze' gua dey tub chon dzi. 196 Orze' mbecy ze', dzi nu gri yu feñ ze', mnii tooy nu cha shet yu gyey. 197 Orze' nay:

«Par gyicy na preb. 198 Cha dun nu rniiy nu cue' dan na re ben la gyicy ñi"», nay.

199 He entered the room. 200 He opened the box. 201 He removed the black raincloak. 202 He put it on. 203 He went outside the house.

204 As soon as he left *the house*, lightening descended,[5] and he ascended into the air and flew away. 205 All along as he went, he sent a wind and thunder storm. 206 Now as he was passing a city, he destroyed it with that bad storm. 207 He saw that a very serious thing was happening. 208 He wanted to return, 209 but he could not return very fast, because the rain was so powerful.

---

[5]*guzii* is really a reference to a person, *doo guzii*. 'It thundered' in Zapotec is *mnii guzii* 'thunder spoke'. He is referred to with the third person masculine pronoun. Lightening is *gyi ni guzii* 'the light of thunder'.

199 Entonces, entró en el cuarto, 200 abrió el cajón, 201 y sacó el capote negro. 202 Se lo puso en los hombros. 203 Salió de la casa.

204 En cuanto salió, cayó un rayo,[5] y él voló, y se fue. 205 A lo largo de su camino, hacía caer granizos y truenos. 206 Cuando pasó por una ciudad, la destruyó con un diluvio. 207 Entonces se dio cuenta de que era algo grande lo que estaba haciendo, 208 y quiso regresar. 209 Pero no pudo regresar rápidamente, porque la lluvia era tan fuerte.

---

[5]La palabra *guzii* realmente se refiere a una persona. Para decir tronó en zapoteca, se dice *mnii guzii* 'el trueno habló'. También, se refiere el trueno con el pronombre de la trecera persona masculino. Relámpago literalmente *gyi ni guzii* 'la luz del trueno'.

199 Orze' gu'y nañ cuart ze'. 200 Pshaal yu ru' caj<u>oo</u> ze'. 201 Orze' blooy shees cas ze'. 202 Orze' pcaa la yeñ yu. 203 Bruuy ich yu'.

204 Cuanzir nu bruuy, bet la guzii, nunu wes nañ lay zay. 205 Dub gal nu zay, rshet yu gyey gye nu guzii dañ. 206 Na ornu bded yu tub siudaa, orze' mnit loy lugaar ze' nu gyey dañ ze'. 207 Orze' rgüiiy nu dzi coz ily ricy ñi. 208 Orze' rlagy yu cush cyay. 209 Tees wagac cush cyay dzach par nu dzi coz ily ricy gyey ze'.

210 Now he was already at the edge of another city, when the young man and his mother arrived at their house. 211 The young man saw that the black raincloak was gone. 212 He said to his mother, "Now he has really treated us badly. 213 Now I will go meet up with him. 214 He sure has acted badly, because I told him not to touch it. 215 Now I will go see where I might meet up with him."

216 He ascended *into the air* and flew away.

217 Now when he met the trail driver, he took the raincloak from *him*. 218 He put it around his own neck. 219 He took the trail driver home.

220 Now when they arrived at the house, The young man said to the trail driver,

210 Ya estaba entrando a los alrededores de otra ciudad, cuando el joven y su mamá llegaron a su casa. 211 El joven vio que no estaba el capote negro. 212 Y le dijo a su mamá:

—Ahora, sí que nos ha hecho daño. 213 Así que ahora voy a buscarlo. 214 Hizo muy mal, porque yo le dije que no lo tocara. 215 Ahora voy a ver dónde lo encuentro.

216 Entonces echó a volar, y se fue.

217 Cuando encontró al hombre, le quitó el capote. 218 Se lo puso en sus propios hombros, 219 y se llevó al hombre también.

220 Cuando llegaron a la casa, le dijo el joven al hombre:

210 Na bi rzu' ga'y ru' tuuba' siudaa ornu bri yu feñ ze' nu ñaay yu'y. 211 Orze' bzaac yu nu sac shees cas ze'. 212 Orze' nay rab yu ñaay:

«Na gaal shiñ bicy yu re nuy de ub na», nay. 213 «Par na cha cheela yu. 214 Shiñ ga bicy yu, gun ya mnee loy nu cue' gan yuñ. 215 Na cha güii ben ca gal dzeelay.»

216 Orze' wes nañ yu zay.

217 Na ornu bdzeel yu mbecy ze', orze' blooy shees ze'. 218 Pcaa yeñ ub yu. 219 Orze' ya nuy yu.

220 Na ornu bri dey yu', orze' na yu feñ ze' rab yu mbecy ze':

"You obeyed me so well at first. 221 But now you have not obeyed me. 222 Therefore, I will not give you a place to live here. 223 Now it will be best if I take you home, because just look at the great destruction you caused to someone's home. Now I know that you will not do good work, because *what you did* is not the work that God gave me to do. You have not acted right. 224 Now tell me what your house is like, and what kind of tree is in front of your house."

225 The trail driver told the young man what his house was like. 226 And he said,

"There is a large Indian laurel tree in my patio."

227 The young man took one of the raincloaks. 228 He put it on. 229 He took hold of the trail driver. 230 He ascended into the air. 231 He took him home. 232 Now when he arrived at the trail driver's home,

"Is that your house?" he said.

—Me obedeciste muy bien al principio. 221 Pero no me has escuchado. 222 Por eso ahora yo ya no te voy a permitir que sigas viviendo aquí. 223 Mejor te voy a llevar a tu pueblo, porque mira qué gran destrucción causaste en el pueblo de esas personas. Ahora sé que no vas a hacer bien el trabajo, porque no es éste el trabajo que me encomendó Dios que haga. Como tú no hiciste lo debido, 224 ahora dime cómo es tu casa, y qué clase de árbol tienes a tu puerta —dijo.

225 Entonces el hombre le dijo cómo era su casa. 226 Y dijo:

—Un árbol de laurel grande hay en mi patio.

227 Entonces el joven tomó un capote. 228 Se puso en los hombros. 229 Agarró al hombre. 230 Y voló en el aire. 231 Lo llevó a su pueblo. 232 Cuando llegó al pueblo de esa persona, dijo:

—¿Es ésa tu casa?

«Ru dzi nap rzuub gyidag ru ne nu loga. 221 Tees na wangyeñ ru ne. 222 Nde' nu na ya warica' lugaar nu cyiiñ ru ii. 223 Na nap zir gya seña ru ledz ru, gun güii ñuu la coz ily mnit lor ledz mbecy, gun na gud lagya nu wayicy ru riiñ nap, gun walab ni na riiñ nu bdu' Ñgyoozh yaa nu gyicya, gun ru walab se'ñ bicy ru na. 224 Na mnii la na yu' zub nir, nunu cyu yag zub ro' nir», nay.

225 Orze' mbecy ze' mniiy la na yu' zub niy. 226 Nunu mniiy nu

«Tub ya ca' ily zub lo li' ne», nay.

227 Orze' yu feñ ze' gush yu tub shees, 228 pcaa yeñ yu. 229 Nunu bdu' yaay mbecy ze'. 230 Orze' wes nañ yu lo bi. 231 Ya nuy yu par ledz yu. 232 Na ornu briy ledz mbecy ze',

«¿A nde' yu'r?» nay.

233 "It is," he said.

234 He cast the trail driver *to the ground* in a bolt of lightning. 235 The lightening descended on the Indian laurel tree, in order for there to be a way to cast the trail driver down onto his patio.

236 That is what happened to the man who took a trip inside an alligator. 237 That is why he knew that there were seven kinds of rain, and he knew that he had crossed seven oceans.

233 —Sí, ésa es —dijo.

234 Entonces por medio del rayo dejó caer *a la tierra* al hombre. 235 Pero el rayo cayó sobre el árbol de laurel, porque ésa era la única forma de dejar a ese hombre en su patio.

236 Éso es lo que le pasó al hombre que estuvo en el vientre del cocodrilo. 237 Por eso supo que hay siete clases de lluvia, y supo que había cruzado siete mares.

233 «Laab ñi», nay.

234 Orze' lat guzii pshet lag yu mbecy ze'. 235 Tees ya ca' ze', nde' bet guziiñ, par nu guud mod nu pshet lag yu mbecy ze' lo li' niy.

236 Nde' coz nu bzac yu nu gua nañ be'n. 237 Nde' nu yu ze' gud lagy yu nu yu' gagy lo gyey, nunu gud lagy yu nu bded yu gagy nisyudoo.

2

Matlaziwa, the Mountain Fairy

La Llorona is a folktale that is well known throughout much of México. It has been collected in three forms. The first form is the tale of *La Llorona* crying for her children. The second form is the tale of *La Llorona* as a seducer of men. The third form, a combination of the first two, is perhaps the most common. I never found anyone in San Lorenzo who had ever heard the name *La Llorona*, or who could recognize the story when related in the first or third forms. However, one of their folk characters, *Matlaziwa*, bears some resemblance to *La Llorona* of the second form of the tale, and elsewhere in Oaxaca she has been identified as *La Llorona* (Kearney 1972:110; MacLaury 1970:24). Thus, the study of *Matlaziwa* may shed some light on some of the questions folklorists have asked about *La Llorona*.

The folk tradition concerning *Matlaziwa* is wide spread throughout Oaxaca, although there are considerable differences from area to area in the details as to who she is. In Yalalag, de la Fuente (1949:268–69) describes her as a dangerous and deceptive spirit who is dual sexed. When she appears to a person, she takes on the form of one of his loved ones of the opposite sex. She lures him to a wild and unknown place in order to do him harm. She may cause mental confusion, craziness, or she may even cause death. Her true form is that of a skeleton. In Ixtepeji, *Matlaziwa* is more like *La Llorona* in the third version of the tale. A somewhat different folk tradition exists in San Lorenzo. I will present their folk tradition first. Then I will address several of the questions that have been asked about *La Llorona*.

In San Lorenzo, *Matlaziwa* is one of a number of supernatural beings who are designated by the classifier *doo*. The following chart lists of all members of that class. In the first column I give the Zapotec name. In the second column I give the Spanish name. In the third column I give an English translation of the Zapotec words.

	Spanish	English
doo gyi'	*Matlaziwa*	Mountain Fairy
doo guzii	*Cosijo*	Thunder Fairy
doo guyu'	*Chaneque*	Local Fairy
doo güidz	*El Sol*	the sun
doo be'y	*Teonanacatl*	Mushroom Fairy
do gyee ñaa	*Campana enredadera*	Morning Flower Fairy
(*doo lyuky*)		Vine Fairy
doo gyee yon	*Floripondio*	Holy Flower Fairy
doo gyech	*Toloache*	the Thorn Fairy

I translate the word *doo* as 'fairy'. Each one of the above is a person. They are like spirits in that they may be invisible. But they are not to be thought of as not having a body. Most people refer to *doo gyi', Matlaziwa,* as a woman. However a few people tell me that there are male *Matlaziwas. doo guzii* is a man. People say that he is a very short man. He is the causer of rain, and is called "the lord of the corn field." *doo guyu'* are a tall people who are called "the lord of the wild animals." They sometimes appear in dreams as bearded men, wearing white peasant garb, with large pointed black hats. The women wear traditional women's apparel. One must ask their permission in order to cut down virgin forest for planting. They are considered to be a primary cause of illness. *doo be'y, doo gyee ñaa, doo gyee yon,* and *doo gyech* are expressions that refer both to hallucinogenic plants, and to the people who appear when one is under the influence of the plant. In each case the person is a woman. *doo be'y* is commonly taken for purposes of divining. *doo gyech* is not widely known in San Lorenzo.

Modern-day folk tradition does not refer to the *doo's* as God, but as "the people who were not created by God." But it is not hard to see how the two words might have been equated even in the recent past. Once when I asked a man from Santa Maria Zaniza, where a related dialect is spoken, what the word *doo* means, he said "saint." Each person of San Lorenzo has an altar on which he keeps images of the saints. It is called *nuun ni doo* (lit. 'bed of *doo'*). People live in two houses. The kitchen is called *yu' gyech* (lit. 'house grinding stone'). The house which contains the altar is called *yu' ca doo* (lit. 'house exist *doo'*). The town cattle are called the *chigud ni doo* (lit. 'cattle of *doo'*), and income that comes from them is used to maintain the church. The ocean is called the water where the *doo* lives: *nis-yu-doo*, and in Zapotec cosmology, the god's lived on the other side of the seventh ocean. In addition, the pre-Columbian generic expressions for God reported in Alcina Franch (1972:12), *pitao, pitoo,* and *betao* are clear cognates with the modern Zapotec *doo*. Thus, it is not hard to see a close relationship between the folk concept of *doo* and God.

The *Matlaziwa* of San Lorenzo is somewhat different from the *Matlaziwa* of other areas. Unlike Yalalag, she is not thought to be dual sexed (de la Fuente 1949:268). Most people say that she is a woman. Like *La Llorona* she is usually described as being a very beautiful woman. She is very tall, with long unbraided hair, and light skin. Although she does not have the form of a skeleton, as in Yalalag, her beauty does have one flaw. People describe her as having the legs of a chicken, a goat, or a pig depending on who is talking about her. She is usually described as living in the mountains near a big rock. People meet her in uninhabited places. One of my good friends said that as a young man he saw her walking down a stream near town. He ran off, because he knew that she is a tormentor of men. As in Yalalag, she is known to cause mental confusion and sometimes death. Once during my stay in San Lorenzo a woman got lost in the mountains. When she was found a day later, she could not recall what happened to her. Everyone said that she had met *Matlaziwa*. However, since she had memorized some words from the catechism and kept saying them over and over, *Matlaziwa* was unable to harm her seriously.

The tale of *Matlaziwa* presented here does bear some strong resemblance to "*La Llorona* the seducer of men" despite the obvious differences. She is a beautiful woman. She lures men away to isolated and wild places. There she tries to seduce them. She is not described here as a killer, but rather she mistreats men by making them into women.

Folklorists have a number of questions about the identity of *La Llorona*. First, was she pre-Colombian? If *Matlaziwa* can be identified with "*La Llorona* the seducer of men," then I think that the answer is definitely "yes." She is one of a class of supernatural beings that are of native origin all of who are referred to by the Zapotec word *doo*. Horcasitas and Butterworth (1963) have noted that *La Llorona* has many of the attributes of an Aztec goddess. Was *La Llorona* a pre-Columbian goddess? Again the answer would appear to be "yes." A study of the word *doo* has shown a close relationship to the concept of God. Horcasitas and Butterworth also note that not many examples of *La Llorona* have been collected in native American languages. The "Story of *Matlaziwa*" presented here represents an example in Zapotec from an area that has had less Spanish influence than most.

Then in summary, the typical "*La Llorona*" tale seems to be a mixture of two tales: "*La Llorona* crying for her children," and "*La Llorona* the seducer of men." While "*La Llorona* crying for her children" is unknown in San

Lorenzo, "*La Llorona* the seducer of men" bears a resemblance to the folk tradition of *Matlaziwa*. If *La Llorona* can be identified as *Matlaziwa*, then the study of *Matlaziwa* may provide some understanding of the identity and origin of *La Llorona*.

I collected the tale of *Matlaziwa* while living in San Lorenzo in 1978. The tale came about during the discussion mentioned above of the woman who was lost in the mountains. The man who told it was in his thirties. It was recorded on a tape recorder. Claudio Martinez later transcribed it and edited it slightly.

Matlaziwa

La llorona es una leyenda muy conocida en todo México. Se ha coleccionado en tres formas. La primera dice que la Llorona está llorando por sus hijos. La segunda cuenta que la Llorona anda seduciendo a los hombres. La tercera, que es una combinación de las dos primeras, es tal vez la más común. Nunca he encontrado en San Lorenzo a alguien que haya oído el nombre de la Llorona, o que pudiera reconocer la historia cuando se relata en la primera o tercera forma. Sin embargo, uno de los personajes típicos del folklore, Matlaziwa, tiene alguna semejanza con la Llorona de la segunda versión de la leyenda, y en otras partes en Oaxaca la identifican con la Llorona (Kearney 1972:110). Por lo tanto, el estudio de Matlaziwa puede aclarar algunas de las preguntas que los estudiantes del folklore tienen acerca de la Llorona.

La tradición folklórica de Matlaziwa se extiende por todo el estado de Oaxaca, aunque hay diferencias considerables de una zona a otra, especialmente en los detalles de quién es ella. En Yalálag, de la Fuente (1949:268–9) la describe como un espíritu peligroso y engañador con sexo doble. Cuando se aparece a una persona, toma la forma de uno de sus seres queridos del sexo opuesto. La atrae a un lugar desconocido y desolado, para poder hacerle daño. Puede causarle confusión mental, locura o aun puede causarle la muerte. Su forma verdadera es la de un esqueleto. En Ixtepeji, Matlaziwa es más como la Llorona de la tercera versión de la leyenda. Una versión tradicional algo diferente existe en San Lorenzo. Presentaré su versión primero. Después me referiré a varias de las preguntas que se han hecho acerca de la Llorona.

En San Lorenzo, Matlaziwa es uno de los varios seres supernaturales designados por el clasificador *doo*. La siguiente es una lista de todos los miembros de esa clase.

	Español	Traducción
doo gyï'	Matlaziwa	Hada de la montaña
doo guzii	Cosijo	Hada del trueno
doo guyu'	Cheneque	Hada local
doo güïdz	El Sol	El Sol
doo be'y	Teonanacatl	Hada de los hongos
do gyee ñaa	Campana enredadera	Hada de la flor de la mañana
doo lyuky		Hada de la enredadera
doo gyee yon	Floripondio	Hada de la flor santa
doo gyech	Toloache	Hada del espino

En la primera columna doy el nombre zapoteca. En la segunda, el nombre en español. En la tercera, la traducción de las palabras zapotecas. Traduje la palabra *doo* como hada. Cada uno de los mencionados en la lista es una persona. Son como espíritus porque pueden ser invisibles. Pero no se debe pensar que no tienen cuerpo. La mayoría de la gente se refiere a *doo gyi'* como a una mujer. Sin embargo, algunos dicen que hay Matlaziwas hombres. *doo guzii* es un hombre. La gente dice que es un hombre bajito. Que es el que causa la lluvia, y le llaman "el señor de la milpa." *doo guyu'* son gente alta a quienes de les llama "señor de los animales salvajes." A veces se aparecen en sueños como hombres de barba, vestidos de calzones con grandes sombreros puntiagudos negros. Las mujeres llevan vestido femenino tradicional. Uno debe pedir su permiso para cortar selva virgen para poder sembrar. Se considera que son la causa principal de las enfermedades. *doo be'y, doo gyee ñaa, doo gyee yon,* y *doo gyech* son expresiones que se refieren a una planta alucinógena y a la persona que se aparece cuando se está bajo la influencia de la planta. En cada caso la persona es una mujer. *doo be'y* se usa generalmente para adivinar. *doo gyech* no es muy conocido en San Lorenzo.

La tradición folklórica moderna no se refiere a *doo* como a Dios, sino a "la gente que no fue creada por Dios." Pero no es difícil ver como las dos palabras se han hecho equivalentes aún en el pasado reciente. Cuando una vez le pregunté a un hombre de Santa María Zaniza, donde se habla un dialecto parecido, qué quiere decir la palabra *doo*, me contestó que significa "santo." Cada persona de San Lorenzo tiene un altar donde conserva las imágenes de los santos. Se llama *nuun ni doo* (lit. 'cama de *doo'*). La gente vive en dos casas: la *yu' gyech* (lit. 'casa metate') y la casa donde está el altar, que es *yu' ca doo* (lit. 'casa que existe *doo'*). El ganado del pueblo se llama *chigud ni doo* o ('ganado de *doo'*) y las ganancias que vienen de ese ganado se usan para mantener la iglesia. El océano se llama *nis-yu-doo* 'el agua donde el *doo* vive' y en la cosmología zapoteca, los dioses viven al otro lado del séptimo océano. Además, las expresiones pre-colombinas genéricas para Dios mencionadas en Alcina Franch (1972:12), *pitao, pitoo, betao*, parecen estar relacionadas con el zapoteca moderno *doo*. Por eso no es difícil ver una estrecha relación entre el concepto folklórico de *doo* y Dios.

La Matlaziwa de San Lorenzo es algo diferente a la Matlaziwa de las otras regiones. Al contrario de la de Yalálag, no se piensa que sea bisexual. La mayoría de la gente dice que es mujer. Como a la Llorona, la describen como una mujer hermosa. Es muy alta, con cabello largo y suelto y piel blanca. Aunque no tiene la forma de un esqueleto como la de Yalálag, su belleza tiene una falta. La gente dice que tiene piernas de gallina, de chivo o de puerco, dependiendo de quién está hablando de ella. Dicen que vive en las montañas cerca de una gran roca. Se le encuentra en lugares deshabitados. Un buen amigo mío dice que cuando él era joven la vio caminando por un arroyo cerca del pueblo. Dice que él se echó a correr porque sabía que ella atormenta a los hombres. Como en Yalálag, dicen que ella los hace perder la cabeza y a veces les causa la muerte. Una vez, cuando yo estaba en San Lorenzo, se perdió una mujer en las montañas. Cuando la encontraron, un día después, no pudo recordar nada de lo que le había sucedido; todos dijeron que había visto a Matlaziwa, pero como ella había memorizado algunas palabras del catecismo y las repitió una y otra vez, Matlaziwa no le pudo hacer mucho daño.

La leyenda de Matlaziwa que se acaba de presentar tiene gran semejanza con "la Llorona que seduce a los hombres" a pesar de las notorias diferencias. Es una mujer hermosa que atrae a los hombres a lugares apartados y desolados. Ahí trata de seducirlos. No la describen como una asesina, sino que castiga a los hombres convirtiéndolos en mujeres.

Los interesados en el folklore tienen varias preguntas acerca de la identidad de la Llorona. Primero, ¿era de la época pre-colombiana? Si Matlaziwa puede ser identificada como "la Llorona, seductora de hombres," entonces yo creo que definitivamente la respuesta es "sí." Es una de esas clases de seres sobrenaturales de origen nativo a los que los zapotecas se refieren con la palabra *doo*. Horcasitas y Butterworth (1963) han notado que la Llorona tiene muchos atributos de una diosa azteca. ¿Era la Llorona una diosa pre-colombina? Otra vez la respuesta parece ser afirmativa. Un estudio de la palabra *doo* ha mostrado una cercana relación con el concepto de Dios. Horcasitas y Butterworth notan también que no muchos ejemplos de la Llorona han sido coleccionados en las lenguas nativas americanas. La historia de "Matlaziwa" que se presenta aquí es un ejemplo zapoteca de una área que ha tenido menos influencia española.

En resumen, la "típica leyenda de la Llorona" parece ser una mezcla de dos "cuentos": La Llorona gimiendo por sus hijos y la Llorona seductora de hombres. Mientras que la Llorona que gime por sus hijos es desconocida en

San Lorenzo, la Llorona seductora de hombres tiene semejanza con la tradicional Matlaziwa. Si la Llorona puede ser identificada como Matlaziwa, entonces el estudio de Matlaziwa puede proveer de un mejor entendimiento de la identidad y origen de la Llorona.

Yo reuní los datos de Matlaziwa mientras viví en San Lorenzo, en 1978. La historia salió a relucir durante la discusión, mencionada antes, acerca de la mujer perdida en las montañas. La grabé en una cinta magnética. El hombre que la contó tenía como 30 años.

1 There once was a person 2 who had a wife, they say. 3 But when he slept with his wife, he didn't have his genitals[1], they say. 4 His wife said, "What did you do with them?"

5 "Who knows? 6 I only met a woman on top of the mountain there. 7 She looked very strange. 8 She had the feet of a hen," he said.

9 "But who could it be?" asked his wife.

10 "She only took hold of my hand." [2]

---

[1]Matlaziwa changes the sex of the person she meets. The man received the genitals of a woman.

[2]From here on the conversation is no longer between the man and his wife, but is between the man and Matlaziwa.

1 Había una vez una persona 2 que tenía una mujer, dicen. 3 Pero cuando durmió con su esposa, no tenía los genitales.[1] 4 Entonces le dijo su esposa:

—¿Qué hiciste con ellos? —dijo ella.

5 —¿Quién sabe? 6 Nada más me encontré con una mujer allá en el cerro. 7 Su aspecto era muy extraño. 8 Tenía patas de gallina —dijo él.

9 —Pero, ¿quién puede ser, pues? —dijo su esposa.

10 —Ella solamente así me agarró.

---

[1]Matlaziwa cambia el sexo de la persona que encuentra. El hombre había recibido los genitales de una mujer.

[2]De aquí en adelante, la conversación ya no es entre el hombre y su esposa, sino entre el hombre y Matlaziwa.

Doo Gyi'

1 Bzu tub mbecy. 2 Zu mñaay, nay. 3 Par or ptaas nuy mñaay na, saca' nguuy, nay. 4 Na, orze' na mñaay:

«¿Ze' ca bicy ru nde'?» nam.

5 «¿Cyu cuic rasoo? 6 Nomaas bdzeela tub biñ mñaa ru' bicy re. 7 Tona' la gareñ nam. 8 Gyi' gyid ricy cup mi», nay ze'.

9 «Par ze' ¿cyu beni?» na mñaay.

10 «Tees mi ze' zi'l i bdu' yaam yaa.»

11 "Where did you go?" the woman asked.

12 "I went to the other side *of the mountain* to look for my cattle, I told her," he said.

13 "Won't you go home with me?" the woman said.

14 "I won't go because it is so late," he said.

15 "Let's go even though you sleep there," she said. 16 "I have thought a lot about taking you home," *she said.*

17 "I won't go because it is so late. 18 My wife is expecting me to arrive, because she already said that she would make coffee for me to drink when I arrive home. 19 She might cry should I not arrive," he said.

20 "But let's go. 21 I was very happy because we were to take a trip to my house," said the woman.

11 —¿A dónde fuiste? —le pregunto.[2]

12 —Al otro lado, allí, fui a buscar mi ganado —le dijo.

13 —¿No vas a ir conmigo a mi casa? —me dijo esa mujer.

14 —No voy porque ya es muy tarde —dijo.

15 —Vamos aunque duermas allí —dijo ella—. 16 Tengo mucho deseo de llevarte a mi casa.

17 —Pero no voy, porque es muy tarde. 18 Ahora mi esposa está esperando que llegue yo, porque dijo ella que iba a hacer café para que yo beba cuando llegue. 19 Tal vez va a llorar si no llego —dijo.

20 —Pero vámonos. 21 Estaba muy contenta porque íbamos a pasear por mi casa —dijo la mujer.

11 Orze' «¿Ca guar?» nam.

12 «Par ich re gua gua yuba chigud ñe, mnee», nay.

13 Lac orze', «¿A wayar chan yu'?» na biñ mñaa ze'.

14 «Par waya gun dzi gudze», nay.

15 «Yaa chan mas re gas ru», nam. 16 «Tona' la mnii too nu tee ru cha du ru yu», na biñ mñaa ze'.

17 «Par waya, gun dzi gudze. 18 Yad nu cyish lo mñaa ya ri, gun bi mniiñ nu zaañ cafee do' or ri. 19 Dzi ga gun ñi nu wari», na'y.

20 «Par yaa la chan. 21 Tona' la bet lagya nu chan basyaar par yu'», na biñ mñaa ze'.

22 "We will go on a different day, if you will take me," he said. 23 "I will prepare accordingly. 24 I will come early 25 so that we can go to your house early, 26 because now it is very late. 27 I would not have enough time to return *home*," he said.

28 "If that is so, you should come on a different day. 29 You should start out early. 30 We will go to my house for the whole day," she said.

31 "Okay" he said.

32 "Okay" she said.

33 He went on his way. 34 But when he arrived home, he no longer had his genitals. 35 He no longer had his genitals. 36 But he set a day when he would go back. 37 He didn't go to her house right away. 38 He went on a different day. 39 He went another time early in the morning.

40 "Quickly take these *female genitals* back. 41 Why do you have these on you like this?" his wife said

22 —Entonces otro día vamos, si me llevas —dijo—. 23 Así me preparo. 24 Vendré temprano. 25 Entonces, temprano vamos a tu casa. 26 Porque ahora es muy tarde. 27 Ya no me da tiempo para regresar —dijo él.

28 —Si es así, otro día vienes, pues. 29 Debes ponerte en camino temprano, 30 para que estemos en mi casa todo el día —dijo.

31 —Bueno —dijo.

32 —Sí —dijo ella.

33 Se fue él. 34 Pero cuando llegó él a su casa, entonces ya no tenía sus genitales. 35 Ya no tenía sus genitales. 36 Pero fijó el día en que iba ir. 37 No fue a la casa de ella luego. 38 Fue después. 39 Entonces temprano salió.

40 —Rápidamente fue a entregar estos *genitales femeninos*. 41 ¿Por qué los tienes? —dijo su esposa.

---

22 «Orze' reña' dzi chan benu cha nur y<u>a</u>», nay 23 «Orze' dub ni zu lily l<u>aa</u>. 24 Napor yap<u>a</u>. 25 Orze' dub ni napor chan yu'r. 26 Gun na dzi gudze. 27 Wabica'ñ tiem par nu cush cy<u>a</u>», nay.

28 «Beni reña' dzi yad ru beni. 29 Orze' napor gash ru. 30 Orze' chan y<u>u</u>' dub dzii la», nam.

31 «O», nay.

32 «Si», dijo ella.

33 Yay. 34 Par or briy yu'y, orze' saca' nguuy. 35 Saca' nguuy. 36 Tees bzuy dzi gul chay. 37 Wanchay yu'm lueg la. 38 Orze' tuuba' dzi guay. 39 Tuuba' tir orze' napor la zay.

40 «Dzach ru gua señ nii. 41 ¿Lagu ni nuur nii?» na mñaay.

42 "I will give them back, since I don't intentionally have them on me, because I am ignorant *of what happened.*"

43 The situation was that the woman wanted to sleep with him. 44 She wanted them to sleep *together.* 45 But he didn't have anything *to do it with.*

46 So on Sunday he hurried. 47 He had breakfast while it was still dark. 48 He drank coffee. 49 Presumably he was in a hurry to go to the place where he met her.

50 When he arrived wherever she went about, she was sitting *there.* 51 She had a basket hanging from her arm. 52 It was full of bread. 53 There were tamales. 54 There were tortillas. 55 There were eggs. 56 There was meat. 57 In short, she really was rich.

58 "Come, let's eat now," she said to him.

59 "I will not eat," he said.

60 He acted unfriendly, because she caused him to become that way.

42 —Los voy a entregar, porque yo no los tengo intencionalmente, yo no lo sabía.

43 Lo que pasaba era que esa mujer quería dormir con él. 44 Quería dormir con él. 45 Pero él ya no tenía nada.

46 Entonces, el domingo estaba él muy apurado. 47 Todavía estaba oscuro cuando desayunó. 48 Tomó café. 49 Suponemos que estaba apurado por llegar al lugar donde lo había encontrado a ella.

50 Cuando llegó él donde ella salía, ella estaba sentada. 51 Y tenía una canasta en la mano. 52 Estaba llena de pan. 53 Tenía tamales. 54 Tenía tortillas. 55 Tenía huevos. 56 Tenía carne. 57 En fin, ella era rica.

58 —Vente, vamos a comer —le dijo.

59 —No comeré —dijo él.

60 Se mostraba disgustado, porque ella hizo que se había vuelto así.

42 «Cha seña, como walab nu du la ya nii, gun ya shtee ya», nay.

43 Yad como biñ mñaa ze' na rlagy mi nu gas num yu ze'. 44 Rlagy mi nu gas dem. 45 Par ze' yu ze' como se la' coz nuuy.

46 Na orze' noming rlal lay. 47 Cow ru' bicy yu siily. 48 Go'y cafee. 49 Rlal lay zay lugaar ze' nu bdzeel yu mi ze' gyicy peen.

50 Or bru'ñay ca cham, zub mi. 51 Bi zaab yaam tub chicyiw. 52 Dza laañ yu' gyishtily nañ ñi. 53 Yu' gyitco. 54 Yu' gyit. 55 Yu' nguu. 56 Yu' beel. 57 Por fii gaal guani'ñ mi.

58 «Gyeed don gyit na», nam rab miy.

59 «Wadaw» nay.

60 Ricy ñgyay par nu ni zuy bicy mi.

61 "Eat," she said.

62 "I will not eat because I do not like what you did to me. 63 Just look at how 64 ugly you made me! 65 My wife was very angry," he said.

66 "Why was she angry?" she asked.

67 "She was very angry because I didn't have anything when I went to her. 68 That is why she was angry. 69 She supposed that you took my things away," he said.

70 "True," she said. 71 "I will give them back later. 72 Come eat. 73 I will give them back later. 74 Let's go to my house," she said. 75 "Because I left them at home. 76 I left those things of yours at home. 77 I don't have them with me now," she said.

78 "But if you will give *them* back to me, I might eat. 79 Or let's go get mine first. 80 Then I will eat."

61 —Vas a comer, hombre —dijo.

62 —No comeré, porque no me gusta lo que has hecho conmigo. 63 ¡Mira que 64 hiciste que fuera muy feo! 65 Se enojó mucho mi esposa —dijo.

66 —¿Por qué se enojó ella? —pregunto ella.

67 —Se enojó mucho porque no tenía yo ninguna cosa cuando llegué ante ella. 68 Por eso ella estaba enojada. 69 Se imaginó que tú me quitaste mis cosas —dijo él.

70 —Así es —dijo ella—. 71 Al rato te las entrego. 72 Ven a comer. 73 Al rato te las entregaré. 74 Vamos a mi casa. 75 Porque en la casa lo dejé. 76 En la casa dejé esas cosas tuyas. 77 Ahora no las tengo aquí —dijo ella.

78 —Pero si me las entregues, entonces puedo comer tortillas. 79 O vamos a traer mis cosas primero. 80 Después voy a comer —dijo él.

61 «Gow laa ru», nam orze'.

62 «Wadaw gun wayet lagya coz nu bicy ru nur ya. 63 ¿A mbecy ru? 64 Shiñ na ya bicy ru. 65 Ze' tona' guzi lagy mñaa», nay.

66 «¿Lagu guzi lagy ñi?» nam ze'.

67 «Guzi lagy tona' lañ como se la' coz du or bri looñ. 68 Nde' nu rzi lagy ñi. 69 Ru byash ru ne rsa' lagy ñi», nay.

70 «Laab», nam orze'. 71 «Niga zi gyabica. 72 Da gor gyit. 73 Niga zi gyabica. 74 Gyan yu'», nam orze'. 75 «Gun gal yu' bzeeña», nam. 76 «Gal yu' bzeeña nde' nir. 77 Na a' du ñii», nam.

78 «Par be gyabic ru ne, orze' mas daw gyit. 79 O yaa gyan gya gyir ne loga la. 80 Gaze' nu daw gyit», nay.

81 "Come eat, so that we can eat. 82 I sure like you," she said.

83 "Enough of that even though you like me. 84 What *do I have*? 85 I don't have anything."

86 "I can give them back to you right away, if you will eat so that we can eat. 87 Because I am very hungry. 88 I have been sitting here waiting for you for a long time," she said. 89 "I was hungry much earlier. But I wanted you to arrive first. 90 I said *to myself*, we won't eat until you arrive," she said.

91 "If that is the case, let us eat then," he said.

92 They sat down to eat.

93 "Only I will be wanting some water to drink, because I get very thirsty when I eat," he said.

94 "In that case I will go get some water for you to drink. 95 But be careful not to go," she said to him.

81 —Ven a comer, porque vamos a comer tortillas. 82 Mucho me gustas —dijo ella.

83 —¡Basta!, aunque te guste. 84 ¿Qué cosas tengo? 85 No tengo ninguna cosa —dijo.

86 —Puedo entregártelas luego, si comes tortillas conmigo, 87 porque yo tengo mucha hambre. 88 Ya hace mucho rato que estaba sentada esperándote —dijo ella—. 89 Ya hace mucho rato que tengo hambre, pero solamente quería que tú vinieras. 90 Entonces hasta que llegues no comeremos tortillas, decía yo —dijo ella.

91 —Si es así, comeremos pues —dijo él.

92 Y se sentaron a comer.

93 —Nada más que yo quiero tomar agua, porque a mí me da mucha sed cuando como —dijo él.

94 —Si es así, entonces voy a traer agua para que bebas, pues. 95 Ten cuidado de no irte — le dijo ella a él.

81 «Da la gor, gun dow na gyitʉ», nam orze'. 82 «Tona' la bet lagya ruʉ», nam orze'.

83 «Par na bded nde' mas yet lagy ru ya. 84 ¿La coz? 85 A' du la coz», nay orze'

86 «Gac gyabica nir lueg la» nam orze', benu gor don gyit. 87 Gun ya dzi rana. 88 Seba tona' la zuba rleza ru», nam. 89 «Tona' la seba rana, tees par nu rlagy zi'la ru'ña ru. 90 Orze' tal ru'ña lar don gyit mee», nam.

91 «Beni dow lan beni», nay.

92 Gucua dey roy gyit.

93 «Nomaas ya galagya do' nis, gun ya dzi rbigya nis or rdaw gyit», nay.

94 «Par beni orze' cha gyii nis go'r beni» nam. 95 «Cuidad dzi nu gyarʉ» nam rab miy.

96 "How should I go when you haven't given them back to me?" he said.

97 The basket remained in front of him.

98 "Eat, because I will go get water," she said. 99 "There is water close by here," she said.

100 How could she have gone to where there is water? 101 There wasn't any water at all. 102 She dipped the water out *of a water hole* right close by. 103 She brought *it* back at a run, because she was afraid that he would go home.

104 When she arrived, he had begun to hiccup. 105 His throat was sore, because a *piece of* tortilla got stuck *in it*. It wouldn't go down his throat, because he was so angry.

106 "Eat. 107 Don't be concerned. 108 I will give them back to you later. 109 Then let's go to my house," she said.

110 So he continued eating in the same way. 111 Actually, they both sat down to eat. 112 Now when they finished eating,

96 —¿Cómo me voy a ir si falta que me las entregues? —dijo él.

97 Se quedó la canasta en frente de él.

98 —Come, porque voy a traer agua. 99 Hay agua aquí cerca —dijo ella.

100 ¿Cómo se fue ella al lugar donde hay agua? 101 Allí no había nada de agua. 102 Sacó ella agua de un hoyo de agua que estaba allí cerca. 103 La llevó corriendo porque tenía miedo que se fuera él.

104 Cuando llegó ella, entonces le dio hipo a él. 105 Le dolía mucho la garganta, porque se le había pegado la tortilla, no bajaba, porque estaba enojado.

106 —Come. 107 No te preocupes. 108 Al rato te las entrego. 109 Y vamos a la casa —dijo ella.

110 Así siguió comiendo. 111 En realidad que se sentaron los dos comiendo. 112 Cuando terminaron de comer,

96 «¿Lac gya ze' ricy falt nu gyabic ru nde' ne?» nay.

97 Byeeñ la chicyiw, byeeñ la loy.

98 «Bdow la gyit, gun orze' ya cha gyii nis», nañ. 99 «Ii ga ca nis», nam.

100 ¿Lac zam lugaar ze' nu ca nis? 101 Ze' sac la nis. 102 Ze' ga la bda'm nis. 103 Yeed num carer, par nu rdzib mi nu gyay.

104 Or bru'ñam, orze' bi gusub bisreg yu. 105 Shiñ rac yeñ yu par nu guca gyit nu wayet gyit yeñ yu par nu rzi lagy yu.

106 «Bdow gyit. 107 Cue' gyicy ru cuen. 108 Orze' niga zi gyabica ñii nir. 109 Nunu cha lan gal yu'», nam.

110 Lac ni zi'l zub yu roy gyit. 111 Gusub yu roy rup laay por cuen. 112 Na orze' ornu blazh bdoy gyit na,

"Give them to me now, because I am ready to go," he said.

113 "They are at the house." But it was only because she wanted him to go to the house. 114 However, when he finished eating, they set out for the woman's house. 115 *When* they arrived at the house, *he saw that* it was a very big house. 116 There were all kinds of things *in it*. 117 There were all the things that are in a store. 118 It was a tile *roofed* house. 119 There were cattle. 120 There was noise everywhere. 121 The animals were making noise.

122 "These animals are mine," she said.

123 "You are very rich," he said.

124 "I am rich. 125 If you all will speak with me[3], I will give you a little something," she said.

126 "Well if you will give *them*, that is what I want," he said.

—Ahora entrégamelas, porque ya me voy —dijo él.

113 —Están en la casa —dijo ella.

El caso era que ella quería que él fuera a la casa. 114 Pero, cuando él terminó de comer, entonces se fueron a la casa de esa mujer. 115 Cuando llegaron a la casa, era una casa muy grande. 116 Había toda clase de cosas. 117 Había todas las cosas que hay en una tienda. 118 Era una casa de tejas. 119 Había ganado. 120 Había mucho ruido. 121 Gritaban los animales.

122 —Éstos son mis animales —dijo ella.

123 —¡Qué rica eres tú! —dijo él.

124 —Soy rica. 125 Si Uds. me hablaran, le daría algo —le dijo a él.

126 —Pero si me los das, eso es lo que quiero —dijo él.

---

[3]"Speak with" is a euphemism for sexual relatiions.

«Gyabic ru nde' n̲e, na» nay, «gun y̲a bi gy̲a̲», nay.

113 «Tal yu' byeeñ ñi», nam orze' par tal nu rlagy zi'l mi nu chay gal yu'.

114 Lac or blazh bdoy gyit na, orze' za dey gal yu' biñ mñaa ze'. 115 Orze' bru'ñay yu' na, orze' na tub yu' ily zub. 116 Nguaa cuanzir coz nguaa. 117 Dela coz nu yu' tien nguaa. 118 Yu' tej. 119 Ta' chigud ta'. 120 Se zu redz zi'l rac. 121 Rbish ti bañcyug rbish ti.

122 «De bañ ii bañcyug n̲e y̲a̲», nam.

123 «Dzi ga guani'ñ ru», nay.

124 «Guani'ñ̲a̲. 125 Benu de ru nu nii nur y̲a̲, y̲a̲ ric̲a̲ ñuu algo nir», nam rab miy.

126 «Par benu cuic ru, nde' rlagy̲a̲», nay.

127 "Come let us talk a little," she said to him.

128 She sat down on the bed. 129 She sat down on the bed. 130 Then he said, "But what will I talk to you *with*? 131 I don't have anything on me," he said.

132 "Lower your pants for me to see if it is true," she said.

133 When he lowered his pants, he already had them on him. 134 He actually had his genitals back. 135 She had already given *them* back.

136 Now the situation was that he did not know what to do. because he had not taken holy flowers[4] to hang around her neck.

137 "But now I will not give you *your due*," he said to her.

138 "Give *it* to me. 139 Then you can come another time. 140 I will give *them* to you," she said.

---

[4]Holy flowers are those that are put out before the statues in the Catholic church.

127 —Ven para que platiquemos un poco —le dijo a él.

128 Entonces se sentó en la cama. 129 Se sentó ella en la cama. 130 Entonces él dijo:

—Pero ¿con qué voy a platicar contigo? 131 No traigo ninguna cosa —dijo él.

132 —Bájate el calzón para que yo vea si es verdad

133 —Entonces cuando se bajó el calzón, ya tenía ésos. 134 En realidad, él ya tenía sus genitales. 135 Ella se los había de vuelto.

136 Ahora él no sabía qué hacer porque no había llevado la flor bendita para ponerle a ella en el cuello.[3]

137 —Pero ahora yo no te lo doy lo que quieres —le dijo él a ella.

138 —Dámelo. 139 Entonces podrás venir otra vez. 140 Yo te los doy —dijo ella.

---

[3]Flores santas son las que se ponen delante de las imágenes de la iglesia católica.

127 Orze' «Da gun do ñuun riidz», nam rab miy.

128 Orze' gusub mi lo nuun. 129 Gusub mi lo nuun orze'. 130 Na orze' nay,

«Par ¿la coz do du̠ ru riidz? 131 A̠' du̠ la coz», nay. 132 Orze' «Pshet te carsuñ ru güi̠i̠ ben», nam.

133 Orze' ornu blet tey carsuñ yu, bi nuu lay nde'. 134 Bi nuu lay nguuy por cuen. 135 Bi byabic lam orze'.

136 Na orze' yad nu wagad lagy yu lac gyicy yu como wancha nuy gyee guta nu cui yeñ mi ze'.

137 «Tees na wayabica̠' nir na», nay rab yum orze'.

138 «Gyabic ru ne̠. 139 Orze' gac cyida'r tub byaja'. 140 Gyabica̠, nir» nam orze'.

141 "I will not give *it*," he said.

142 Right after he found them, he ran away. 143 He ran for home. 144 He was continually feeling *them*. 145 He was continually feeling them, he was afraid that she might take possession *of them* again, they say. 146 He was feeling his genitals as he went home. 147 He only walked a little ways and they were not *there* anymore. 148 They were not *there* anymore. 149 She had taken possession *of them* again.

150 "But what can I do?" he said.

151 He went back again.

152 "Well, I told you to wait all day and then go. 153 Then you can take your things home no matter what," she said.

154 But he didn't want to wait, because he was afraid that she would take *them* back again. 155 So he sat there as before. 156 He sat there.

141 —Yo no te lo doy —dijo él.

142 Tan pronto como los encontró, se fue corriendo. 143 Se fue corriendo a su casa. 144 A cada rato se los tocaba. 145 A cada rato los tentaba, porque él tenía miedo de que ella se los quitara otra vez. 146 Tocando sus genitales se fue. 147 Un poco caminó, y ya no estaban. 148 Ya no estaban. 149 Ya los había cogido ella otra vez.

150 —Pero ¿que hago? —dijo él.

151 Regresó otra vez.

152 —Conque yo te dije que esperaras todo el día, y después te fueras. 153 De todos modos, puedes llevar esas cosas tuyas —dijo ella.

154 Pero él no quiso esperar, tenía miedo que ella volviera a quitárselos. 155 Entonces se sentó como antes. 156 Estaba sentado.

141 «Wayabic<u>a</u>», nay.

142 Byad zi'l nde' niy, gush lay carer. 143 Gush lay carer yay. 144 Zaab cya' la ran yu. 145 Zaab cya' la ran yu, gun rdzib yu dzi ga gyasha'm nay. 146 Ran yu, ran yu nguuy yay. 147 Ñumiiñ zi'l bzay saca'ñ. 148 Saca'ñ. 149 Bi byaasha'm.

150 «Par ¿lac gyicy na?» nay orze'.

151 Gua'y.

152 «Gunca y<u>a</u> mn<u>ee</u> cuez ru dub dzii la, gaze' gyar. 153 Ca ni gaal gya nu ru nde' nir», nam.

154 Ze' yu ze' walagy yu nu cuez yu par nu rdzib yu nu gyasha'm. 155 Orze' ni zi'l zub yu. 156 Zub yu.

157 "What little bit will you eat?" she said to him. 158 "Here they are. 159 Take eat. 160 Take it to keep. 161 Take," she said.

162 "I won't take anything for myself, " he said.

163 "You can have it, man. 164 From all of this you can have whichever you enjoy. 165 Take hold of whatever you like to take with you. 166 You may have it for yourself. 167 If *you want* anything to eat, there are many things for you to eat. 168 Take eat," she said.

169 "I will not eat," he said, because he was afraid.

170 "If that is so, go home. 171 You should come again in eight days. 172 You will find them then," she said.

173 He went home. 174 They were not found.

157 —Entonces ¿qué vas a comer? —le dijo a él—. 158 Aquí están. 159 Toma, lo que comas. 160 Tómalo para ti. 161 Tómalo —dijo ella.

162 —No me quedo con nada —dijo él.

163—Que lo tengas, hombre. 164 De todo esto, toma lo que te guste. 165 Agarra lo que te gusta para llevártelo. 166 Se te quedará —dijo ella—. 167 Si quieres cosas para comer, hay muchas cosas. 168 Toma, come —dijo ella.

169 —No como —decía él, porque tenía miedo.

170 —Si es así, entonces vete. 171 Regresa dentro de ocho días. 172 Entonces lo encontrarás —dijo ella.

173 Se fue él. 174 No se encontró eso.

157 «Orze' ¿la ñuu coz gor?» nam rab miy. 158 «Ii nguaañ. 159 Gush gow ru. 160 Gush ganir. 161 Gush», nam orze'.

162 «Ni tub la wane», nay.

163 «Guni hombre. 164 Dela de nii guni ca na nu gusht nir. 165 Bdu' yaa ca na nu gusht nir gya nur. 166 Gani lar», nam. 167 «Benu coz gow ru, nguaa tona' coz gow ru. 168 Gush gow ru», nam.

169 «Wadaw», rniiy, par nu rdzib yu.

170 «Tees be ni orze' gyar. 171 Gal shuñ dzi yada'r. 172 Gal ze' gyada'ñ nir», nam.

173 Yaa ga'y. 174 Wangyad ñi.

175 Then an old man came forth. 176 He said to the old man, "This is what happened to me. 177 Once I went into the mountains. 178 It happened that I met a woman. 179 She treated me very badly. 180 It happened that she removed my testicles," he said.

181 "How unfortunate if she did that to you," the old man said.

182 "That is what she did to me. 183 But what should I do for her to give *them* back to me. 184 She gave *them* back to me when I went *to her*. 185 I only walked a little way when she took them from me again. 186 When I looked, they were not *there* anymore."

187 Then the old man said, "I will find a way for you to deal with her, if you are man enough to take her *for your wife*," he said.

188 "I will take her. 189 Only as for taking her to my house, I will not take her, because I have a wife," he said.

175 Entonces se presentó un viejito. 176 Y le dijo al anciano:

—Esto es lo que me pasó. 177 Fui al cerro una vez. 178 Me encontré con una mujer. 179 Me dio muy mal trato. 180 Me quitó los testículos.

181 —¡Qué lástima que te hizo eso! —dijo el viejo.

182 —Así hizo ella conmigo. 183 Pero, ¿qué debo hacer para que me los entregue? 184 Me los entregó ella cuando fui allá. 185 Caminé un poquito, y me los quitó otra vez. 186 Cuando miré, ya no había nada —dijo.

187 Entonces dijo el viejo:

—Yo buscaré algo que hagas con ella, si de veras eres hombre para tomarla *por esposa* —dijo.

188 —La tomaré. 189 En cuanto a llevarla a la casa, no lo haré, porque tengo esposa.

175 Orze' brusu tub yu bel. 176 Orze' mniiy loy nay:

«I bzaca. 177 Gua logyi' tub tir. 178 Lac bdzeela tub biñ mñaa. 179 Tona' la shiñ bicy num ya. 180 Lac bloom urnguu», nay.

181 «Par maa be ni bicy num ru», na yu bel.

182 «Ni bicy num ya. 183 Par ¿lac mod gyicya nu gyabic mi ne? 184 Byabic mi ne ornu gua. 185 Ñumiiñ zi'l bza, byasha'm ñii ne. 186 Or bgüii, saca'ñ», nay.

187 Orze' na yu bel nay:

«Ya yuba mod nu gyicy nur mi par gun tees benu lyar gyeey ru nu gash lar mi», nay.

188 «Rush lam. 189 Nomaas nu gya dum yu', waya dum, gun zu mñaa», nay.

190 "But what is there to do? 191 You should take her home. 192 Doesn't your wife live in poverty?" he asked.

193 "She gets a little money. 194 But it's not that *she* gets a lot," he said.

195 "You will be able to take her to your house. 196 But put her house apart," he said. 197 "Set the house of your wife apart *from hers*. 198 She should live in the house of your real wife, because she is rich. 199 If so, I will give her a cure. 200 This is what you do," he said to him. 201 "You should take holy flowers. 202 As soon as you arrive, as soon as she has given back your testicles, put them around her neck. 203 'Please put this shawl around your neck', say," he said.

190 —Pero, ¿qué puedes hacer? 191 Tienes que llevarla a tu casa. 192 ¿No es pobre tu esposa? —dijo.

193 —Pero también gana un poco de dinero. 194 Pero no gana mucho —dijo.

195 —Puedes llevarla a tu casa. 196 Entonces pones aparte la casa de ella. 197 Le pones casa aparte de la casa de tu esposa. 198 La casa de tu mera esposa, ella puede quedar en esa casa, porque ella es rica. 199 Si es así, yo le doy un remedio a ella. 200 Así vas a hacer —le dijo—. 201 Vas a llevar una flor bendita. 202 Entonces en cuanto llegues, cuando se te entrega ella tus genitales, lo pones ésa en el cuello de ella entonces. 203 "Ponte un poco de este pañuelo en el cuello," le dices a ella —dijo él.

190 «Par ¿lac gyicy ru? 191 Tees gya nur mi. 192 ¿A walab gyel zi zu mñaar?» nay.

193 «Par ni' rad ñuu tiñ niñ. 194 Par tees walab nu dzi rad la» nay orze'.

195 «Gac gya nur mi yu'r. 196 Par tees orze' zuub reñ ru yu'm», nay. 197 «Zuub reñ ru yu' mñaar», nay. 198 «Yu' mñaa gaal ru, mi ze' cyiiñ lam yu' la, gun mi ze' guani'ñ mi», nay orze'. 199 «Beni ya rica tub guñaa ni mi ze'. 200 Orze' i gyicy ru», nay rab yu yu ze'. 201 «Cha nur tub gyee guta. 202 Orze' laab ru'ña lar, orze' benu byabic zi'l mi nguur, rii lar nde' yeñ mi orze'. 203 Bri ñuu bay ii yeñ ru, niir gab rum», nay.

204 Slowly he put it *around her neck*[5]. 205 She became a person. 206 Her feet were no longer the feet of a hen. 207 Her feet were like our feet. 208 She supposedly never changed him again.

209 "Great! Let's go then. 210 I will marry you," she said to him.

211 "But I have a wife," he said.

212 "That is nothing. 213 I will determine what you should do. 214 You will make a house for her. 215 I will provide the money," said the Mountain Fairy. 216 "Cause her to live separately *from us*. 217 We will go to your house," she said. 218 "And I will feed her," the Mountain Fairy said. 219 "Will she be very angry with me? 220 I will feed her well. That's nothing.

---

[5]Location changes here from where the old man is, to where the main character is with Matlaziwa again.

204 Suave lo puso eso.[4] 205 Entonces ella convirtió en gente. 206 Entonces ya no era patas de gallina que tenía. 207 Así como nuestras pies, así son las pies de ella entonces. 208 Entonces supongamos que ya no cambió a él más.

209 —Nos vamos, pues. 210 Me caso contigo —le dijo ella a él.

211 —Pero yo tengo esposa —dijo él.

212 —No importa. 213 Yo veré qué harías. 214 Haga una casa para ella. 215 Yo te doy el dinero —dijo Matlaziwa[5]—. 216 Entonces aparte ponla. 217 Entonces a tu mera casa vamos nosotros —dijo ella—. 218 Y yo mismo doy lo que coma ella —dijo Matlaziwa—. 219 ¿Me odiará mucho ella? 220 Pero yo le doy cosas buenas que coma ella. Es nada.

---

[4]Aquí hay cambio de lugar de donde el viejo está a donde el personaje principal está con Matlaziwa otra vez.

[5]Yo he tomado la alfabetización de matlaziwa de De la Fuente.

---

204 Dze la riy nde'. 205 Orze' byac lam mbecy. 206 Orze' walaba' gyi' gyid gyi'm orze'. 207 Gal na la gyi'n na gyi'm orze'. 208 Orze' por cuen wanchaa ga'm yu orze'.

209 «Maa zir beni gyan. 210 Chelaa ru beni», nam rab miy.

211 «Par nomaas ya zu mñaa», nay.

212 «Se la la gyicy. 213 Orze' ya güii lac gyicy ru. 214 Zaar tub yu'm. 215 Ya rica tiñ», na doo gyi'. 216 «Orze' caa reñ ru mi ze'. 217 Orze' yu' lar gya de ub na», nam. 218 «Nunu laab ya goowa ñii», na doo gyi'. 219 «¿A dzi gazi lagy mi lo? 220 Tees ya goow napam. Se la la.

221 And she will not work. 222 You will only *have to* change her residence," said the woman.

223 "It is not possible, because it would be a big sin, because we were married. 224 She is my real wife before God," he said.

225 "You can. 226 I too will be your wife before God," she said.

227 He brought her home. 228 However, when he arrived at the house, he had many dogs. The woman, his wife, sicked her dogs on her, because she was angry with her for coming to her house. 229 She sicked her dogs on her. 230 They bit all over here. 231 They bit all over here. 232 She took to the trail and went home. 233 He didn't get anything. 234 Nothing was acquired. 235 Only she supposedly gave back his genitals. 236 She only gave them back. 237 If only it hadn't *happened* that way she would be living at his house now.

221 Y ella no va a trabajar nada. 222 Nada más cambia el lugar donde vive ella —dice la mujer.

223 —No se puede porque es un pecado grande, porque ya nos casamos —dijo él—. 224 Ella es mi mera esposa ante Dios —dijo él.

225 —Se puede —dijo ella—. 226 Yo también soy tu esposa ante Dios —dijo ella.

227 La trajo a su casa. 228 Pero, cuando llegó a casa, había muchos perros. Su mera esposa azuzó a los perros contra ella, porque estaba enojada porque venía a su casa. 229 Le azuzó los perros. 230 Los perros la mordían por todas partes. 231 Aquí mordían los perros. 232 Entonces se puso en camino, y se fue. 233 Él no consiguió nada. 234 No consiguió ninguna cosa.235 Nada más le entregó ella sus genitales. 236 Sólo se los entregó. 237 Si no hubiera pasado así, entonces viviría ella en la casa de él ahora.

221 Nunu wayicy lam riiñ. 222 Nomaas chaa zi'l ru se'm», na biñ ze'.

223 «Par wac gun dzi cyi na, gun de ya pchelaa», nay. 224 «Ze' nde' gaal mñaa par lo fañgyoozh», nay orze'.

225 «Gac», nam orze'. 226 «Mas ya ni' mñaar par lo fañgyoozh», nam orze'.

227 Yeed nuy mi raj. 228 Lac or briy yu' na, dzi yu' che' niy, blyuu biñ mñaa, mñaay ze', blyuum che' mi ze', par nu guzi lagy mi nu yeed mi yu'm. 229 Blyuum che'm. 230 Se ze' i zi'l la rucua' ma, dela de nii. 231 Dela nii rucua' ma. 232 Orze' gush nez mi yam. 233 Wangad la algo niy. 234 Se la la coz guud. 235 Nomaas nu byabic zi'l mi nguuy por cuen. 236 Byabic zi'l mi nde'. 237 Bicy na nu cue' ni, orze' rcyiiñ lam yu'y na.

238 The dogs treated her very badly. 239 They pulled at the cloth of her clothing tearing it all over her legs and all over her back. 240 She went home. 241 If this hadn't happened, if only she hadn't sicked the dog on her, she would be here now, we assume. 242 She would be at his house now, if only she hadn't sicked the dogs on her.

238 La trataron bastante mal los perros. 239 Todas sus piernas, toda su espalda, y aquí abajo los perros le rompieron la ropa. 240 Se fue a su casa. 241 Si no hubiera sucedido este, si no le hubiera azuzado los perros, estaría ella aquí ahora. 242 Estaría ella en la casa de él, si ella no le hubiera azuzado los perros.

238 Tanta' bicy nu che̱'m. 239 Dela gyi' mi, dela ya ich mi ii pshet te che' nu pshaa ma shab mi. 240 Yam orze'. 241 Ti cue' ni, bicy na nu cue' nlyuum che'm, zum na gyicy peen. 242 Zum yu'y ze' na, bicy na nu cue' nlyuum che̱'.

3

The Poisonous Tuber and a Young Man

Many Zapotec folktales reveal striking European influences. Some of the easiest tales to collect, for example, are fables involving talking animals, because they are so numerous. Stories of poor men winning king's daughters are also numerous. I have chosen to not include many folktales of strictly European types in my collection because they give the wrong impression: that European influence dominates Zapotec folk tradition. Instead, I have sought out folktales that have something distinctly Zapotec about them.

Once, after I had been discussing European influence in Zapotec folklore with Claudio Martinez, he brought me the tale of "The Poisonous Tuber." This, he thought, was a tale of purely Zapotec origin. But what is it that makes this tale Zapotec? Claudio could not be specific. To him it merely had a Zapotec flavor to it. Perhaps, it is because it presents a Zapotec perspective on human relationships.

Zapotecs are very individualistic. They feel that they stand alone against the aggression of a hostile world (Kearney 1972:44). Often times they do not even find trusting relationships within the family. The characters in this folktale reveal some of the conflict in human relationships. The story begins with an old man who wants to eat a young man and his brother. The relationship between the old man and the two young men is not specified. Thus, the conflict is between one generation and another. In

47

the real world conflict between father and son, uncle and nephew are common. There seems to be a constant struggle between a man and his sons to see who is in control. If a man's children are disobedient, he might sell his property to keep them from inheriting it. If a man threatens his children with selling his property, the children might respond by secretly selling it themselves. When a man living at home earns money, he is expected to give it to his father. But if his father does not know how much he makes, he might try to hang on to as much as he can. Thus, conflict between father and son is common.

Feuds between uncle and nephew are also common. When a man dies, it is not uncommon for his brothers to take his land away from his children, especially if they are daughters. I heard one man justify taking his brother's land from his nephew by saying, "He (his nephew) is not the son of my father (from whom the land originally came)." In the story, the old man wants to eat the two young men, but the hostility and aggression between generations is bilateral, for in fact the young man eats the old man.

The relationship between the brothers in this tale also reflects Zapotec individualism. The older brother looks to the younger brother for help. In the end he betrays him by not leaving him anything to eat. He then flaunts his successful betrayal offering him the meat stuck between his teeth. The close relationship that might exist among brothers is deceptive, because to the Zapotec each man primarily seeks his own interest. Among Zapotecs, sibling rivalry often turns into open feuds in adulthood, because of conflicting interest in inheritance. Thus, the story of "The Poisonous Tuber" presents a distinctly Zapotec view of human relationships.

The one relationship which is presented in a positive manner, is the one between man and his mother. The young man does not save anything for his brother to eat, but he does save something for his mother to eat.

The story of "The Poisonous Tuber" was given to me by Claudio Martinez in 1976. He tape recorded it, transcribed it in practical orthography, and edited it.

El chichicamole y el joven

Muchos cuentos del folklore zapoteca revelan sorprendentes influencias europeas. Por ejemplo, uno de los más fáciles de coleccionar son los cuentos en que toman parte animales que hablan, porque son numerosos. Cuentos de hombres pobres que ganan la mano de la hija del rey son también muchos. Decidí no incluir muchos con esa influencia europea en mi colección porque esas dan la impresión equivocada: que la influencia europea domina la tradición folklórica zapoteca. En lugar de eso, he tomado los que tienen algo típicamente zapoteca en ellas.

Una vez, después de haber discutido con Claudio Martínez acerca de la influencia europea en el folklore zapoteca, él me trajo el cuento de El chichicamole y el joven. Él pensó que éste era un cuento de origen puramente zapoteca. Pero, Claudio no pudo explicar qué es lo que hace este cuento puramente zapoteca. Él sólo sabe que tiene el "sabor" zapoteca. Posiblemente, porque presenta una perspectiva zapoteca en cuanto a relaciones humanas.

Los zapotecas son muy individualistas. Sienten que están solos en contra de la agresión de un mundo hostil. Frecuentemente no pueden tener relaciones de confianza aun dentro de la propia familia. Los personajes de este cuento revelan algo del conflicto en las relaciones humanas. La historia comienza con un viejo que quiere comerse a un joven y su hermano. La relación entre el viejo y los dos jóvenes no está especificada. Así es el conflicto entre una generación y otra.

En la vida real, conflictos entre padres e hijos, tíos y sobrinos son comunes. Parece haber una constante lucha entre el hombre y sus hijos para ver quién es el que manda. Si los hijos de un hombre son desobedientes, puede que él venda sus propiedades para que no las hereden los hijos. Si un padre amenaza a sus hijos con vender sus propiedades, los hijos pueden vengarse vendiéndolas en secreto ellos mismos. Cuando un joven vive en la casa trabaja, se espera que dé a su padre el dinero que gana. Pero si el padre no sabe cuánto gana, el hijo tratará de quedarse con lo más que pueda. Este conflicto entre padre e hijo es muy común.

Pleitos entre tíos y sobrinos también son comunes. Cuando un hombre muere, no es raro que sus hermanos les quiten su terreno a los hijos, especialmente si son mujeres. Yo oí a un hombre justificarse al quitarle a su sobrino sus tierras diciendo: "Él (su sobrino) no es hijo de mi padre (de quien era originalmente la tierra)." En el cuento el viejo se quiere comer a los dos jóvenes, pero la hostilidad y agresividad entre generaciones es igual por los dos lados, porque al final el joven se come al viejo.

La relación entre los hermanos en este cuento refleja también el individualismo zapoteca. El hermano mayor busca al hermano menor para que le ayude. Al final lo traiciona y no le deja comida. Luego hace alarde de su victoriosa traición diciéndole que puede comer la carne que le queda entre los dientes.

Las relaciones estrechas que parecen existir entre hermanos pueden ser solamente en apariencia, porque para el zapoteca cada hombre busca su propio interés. Entre zapotecas la rivalidad entre hermanos con frecuencia se vuelve en pleitos cuando ya son hombres por los intereses problemáticos de la herencia. Así que la historia de la raíz venenosa presenta un punto de vista realmente zapoteca de las relaciones humanas.

La única relación que se presenta de manera positiva es la que hay entre madre e hijo. El hermano no guarda nada de comida para su hermano, pero sí guarda para que coma su madre.

Esta historia me la dio Claudio Martínez en 1976. Después se puso en la forma escrita.

1 There once was a young man. 2 It came about that an old man wanted to eat him. 3 So *the young man* lived in constant danger. 4 He decided that it would be better if he killed himself, because it would be worse if the old man ate him. 5 But he didn't have the courage to kill himself. 6 So he decided that he would go look for a *chichicamole* tuber to eat in order to die. 7 Because he didn't have the courage to kill himself in any other way. 8 So he took to the trail and went *to look for it*.

9 When he arrived where the *chichicamole* tuber grows, he began digging it up right away. 10 While he was there digging, it began to speak. 11 It asked him, "Why are you digging me up?"

1 Había una vez un joven 2 y también un viejo que quería comérselo. 3 Por tanto, andaba siempre en peligro. 4 Por eso pensaba que sería mejor si se matara, porque sería peor si se lo comiera el viejo. 5 Pero no se arriesgaba a matarse a sí mismo. 6 Después pensó ir a buscar el chichicamole para comer, para que así se muriera. 7 Porque no se arriesgaba a matarse en otra forma. 8 Entonces tomó su camino, y se fue.

9 Cuando llegó donde había el chichicamole, luego se puso a sacarlo. 10 Mientras lo estaba sacando, empezó a hablar. 11 Y le dijo:

—¿Por qué me estás sacando?

Gu doo nu tub yu feñ

1 Bzu tub yu feñ. 2 Lac orze' brusu tub yu bel. Rlagy yu gow yuy. 3 Tanta' nu laab rishdzidz rded yu. 4 Gaze' nu mnii tooy nu nap zir benu ub lay cut yu ub yu, gun cuaa zir yu benu gow yu bel yu. 5 Tees wagash lagy yu cut yu ub yu. 6 Gaze' nu mnii tooy nu cha yub yu gu doo gow yu par nu gat yu. 7 Gun wagash lagy yu cut yu ub yu nu reña' mod. 8 Gaze' nu gush nez yu zay.

9 Ornu bru'ñay ze' nu nash gu doo, syaas la gutiy rguuñ yuñ. 10 Lat nu riy rguuñ yuñ, orze' brugyi' la rniiñ. 11 Gaze' nu nañ rab ñiy:

«¿Lagu rguuñ ru ya?» naañ.

12 He replied,

"I am only digging you up to eat you, so that I will die, because an old man wants to eat me."

13 Then the *chichicamole* tuber said, "Don't eat me, because I would be so unfortunate. 14 There is no *reason* for you to be afraid. 15 What can he do? 16 You will eat him. 17 He will not eat you. 18 Go home. 19 When he comes wanting to eat you, *then say,* 'What is difficult? What is the work of an old man called? 20 The spines of a stinging caterpillar'.[1] 21 When you say that, he will be embarrassed. 22 He will start to run away. 23 While he is running, swing a stick at his legs. 24 Kill him. 25 Put him in a pit oven and eat him."

---

[1]The words that the young man is to say are important more for their effect than for their meaning. The meaning is unclear even to the native Zapotec speaker.

12 Entonces él contestó:

—Sólo te estoy sacando para comerte, para que así me muera, porque el viejito quiere comerme.

13 Entonces el chichicamole dijo:

—¡Pobre de mí!, no me comas. 14 No tengas miedo. 15 ¿Qué va a hacer? 16 Tu lo comerás a él. 17 No es él el que te va a comer. 18 Anda, vete. 19 Cuando llegue él, queriendo comerte, entonces le dices, '¿Qué es difícil? ¿Cómo se llama el trabajo del viejo? 20 Las espinas de la oruga que pica', le dices.[1] 21 Cuando le digas eso, se avergonzará 22 Se echará a correr, huirá. 23 Mientras él corre, hazle dar un traspié con un palo. 24 Entonces lo matas. 25 Lo horneas y te lo comes.

---

[1]Las palabras que el joven va a decir son importantes más por el efecto que por el significado. El significado no está claro, aun para el hablante zapoteco.

12 Orze' nay rab yuñ:

«Ni zi'l rduña ru nu daw ru, gun gata, gun yu bel rlagy yu gow yu ya», nay.

13 Orze' na gu doo:

«Cue' gow ru ya, gun cuaa. 14 Wagad nu dzib ru. 15 ¿La gyicy yu ze'? 16 Ru gow ruy. 17 Walab yu ze' gow yu ru. 18 Yaa la. 19 Orze' ornu ru'ñay nu galagy yu gow yu ru, orze' '¿la biigy? ¿La la riñ ni yu bel? 20 Shely gula zuub', gab ruy. 21 Ornu niir nde', orze' gat loy. 22 Gash lay carer chay. 23 Lat nu zay carer ze', tel laar yag gyi'y. 24 Orze' cut ruy. 25 Cu'r yu yo gow ruy», na gu doo.

26 "But surely he won't be afraid if that is all I say. 27 If he is not afraid of that, he will surely eat me," he said.

28 Then the *chichicamole* tuber said, "Go on home. 29 Just agree to what I say."

30 Then the young man went home. 31 But when he arrived, he had forgotten what the *chichicamole* tuber had told him to say to the old man who wanted to eat him. 32 Then he went back to the *chichicamole* tuber again. 33 But *this time* he took his younger brother with him. 34 When he arrived at where the *chichicamole* tuber was, he said, "What did you tell me to say to the old man? 35 Because I forgot what you said."

26 —¿Pero a poco se va a asustar él si eso nada más digo? 27 Si con eso no se asusta, entonces seguro que me va a comer —dijo.

28 Entonces dijo el chichicamole:

—Anda, vete. 29 Sólo esté de acuerdo con lo que dije.

30 Después tomó el joven su camino, y se fue. 31 Pero cuando llegó, se le olvidó lo que dijo el chichicamole que tenía que decir al viejito que se lo quería comer. 32 Entonces se fue otra vez a donde estaba el chichicamole. 33 Pero entonces llevó a su hermano menor. 34 Cuando llegó a donde estaba el chichicamole, dijo:

—¿Cómo dijiste que le dijera al viejo? 35 Porque se me olvidó lo que dijiste.

26 «¿Tees walab gaal dzib yu nu ni zi'l nee? 27 Benu nde' wanchib yu, orze' waded la gow yu ya», nay.

28 Orze' na gu doo:

«Yaa la. 29 O zi'l mnii coz nu rnee» naañ.

30 Gaze' nu gush nez yu feñ yay. 31 Tees ornu briy, mnit lagy yu lac mnii gu doo nu niiy lo yu bel nu rlagy gow yu ze'. 32 Gaze' nu gush neza'y zay lo gu doo. 33 Tees orze' za nuy bicy miiñ yu. 34 Ornu bru'ñay lo gu doo na, orze' nay:

«¿Lac mniir nu nee lo yu bel? 35 Gun mnit lagya lac mniir», nay.

36 The *chichicamole* tuber said, "Could you really have forgotten that? 37 How difficult is it? 38 I told you to say, 'What is difficult? 39 What is the work of an old man called? 40 The spines of a stinging caterpillar'."

41 "Okay," he said.

42 Then he went home. 43 He said to his brother, "Remember, lest you forget what we should say when the old man arrives."

44 However, when the hour for the old man to arrive came, he appeared coming. 45 The young man had already forgotten what to say. 46 Then he said to his brother, "What did the *chichicamole* tuber say?"

47 His brother said, "*He said, 'What is difficult? 48 What is the work of an old man called? 49 The spines of a stinging caterpillar.*'"

36 Entonces dijo el chichicamole:

—¿De veras a poco nada más se te olvidó? 37 ¿Tan difícil es? 38 Yo dije que dijeras, '¿Qué es difícil? 39 ¿Cómo se llama el trabajo del viejo? 40 Las espinas de la oruga que pica', es lo que vas a decir.

41 —Está bien —dijo.

42 Entonces tomó su camino, y se fue. 43 Entonces le dijo a su hermano:

—Acuérdate. No se te vaya a olvidar lo que debemos de decir cuando llegue el viejo.

44 Cuando llegó la hora de que llegara el viejo, apareció cuando venía. 45 Pero al joven se le olvidó lo que debía de decir. 46 Entonces le dijo a su hermano:

—¿Qué dijo el chichicamole que debo de decir?

47 Entonces le dijo su hermano:

—¿Qué es difícil? 48 ¿Cómo se llama el trabajo del viejo? 49 Las espinas de la oruga que pica.

36 Orze' na gu doo:

«¿Walab gaal nde' mnit lagy ru? 37 ¿Ca biigya'? 38 Mnee ya nu nii ru' ¿La biigy? 39 ¿La la riñ ni yu bel? 40 Shely gula zuub, niir», na gu doo.

41 Orze' «O», nay.

42 Gaze' nu gush nez yu yay. 43 Orze' nay rab yu bicy yu:

«Zu lagy ru, gun nis nit lagy ru lac niin ornu ru'ña yu bel», nay.

44 Lac ornu byap or nu ru'ña yu bel, bruu za lay yad yu. 45 Ze' yu feñ ze' bi mniita' lagy yu lac niiy. 46 Orze' nay rab yu bicy yu:

«¿Lac mnii gu doo nu nee?» nay.

47 Gaze' nu na bicy yu:

«¿La biigy? 48 ¿La la riñ ni yu bel? 49 Shely gula zuub, niir», nay.

50 "Okay," said the older brother.

51 When the old man arrived, "What is difficult? 52 What is the work of an old man called? 53 The spines of a stinging caterpillar," he said.

54 The old man started to run away. 55 While he was running, the young man swung a stick right at his legs. 56 He killed him. 57 He was delighted that he had succeeded in killing the old man. 58 Then he began to dig a pit oven to cook him in so that he could eat him. 59 After digging the pit oven, he immediately put fire in it. 60 When the coals turned hot, he immediately put the old man in the oven. 61 *The young man and his brother* sat there way into the night. 62 The old man wouldn't cook. 63 They were there late into the night. 64 The *younger brother* went to sleep. 65 While he was sleeping, the old man finished cooking. 66 The older *brother* was delighted that his young brother was asleep.

50 —Está bien —dijo su hermano mayor.

51 Cuando llegó el viejo:
—¿Qué es difícil? 52 ¿Cómo se llama el trabajo del viejo? 53 Las espinas de la oruga que pica —le dijo.

54 Entonces el viejo se fue corriendo. 55 Mientras se iba, el joven hizo que diera un traspié con el palo en allí nada más. 56 Lo mató. 57 Estaba contento que había logrado de matar al abuelo. 58 Después empezó a excavar el horno para cocerlo y comerlo. 59 Terminó de excavar el horno, y luego prendió el fuego. 60 Cuando las brasas se pusieron calientes, luego puso al viejo en el horno. 61 Estuvieron allá hasta bien avanzada la noche. 62 El viejo no se cocería. 63 Estuvieron allá muy de noche. 64 El joven se durmió. 65 Mientras él dormía, se coció el viejo. 66 Contento estaba el mayor porque estaba durmiendo su hermano menor.

50 «O», na bicy gush yu orze'.
51 Ornu bru'ña la yu bel, orze'
«¿La biigy? 52 ¿La la riñ ni yu bel? 53 Shely gula zuub», nay.
54 Orze' gush la yu bel carer zay. 55 Lat nu zay ze' ptel laa yu feñ yag gyi'y ze' ga la. 56 Biit yuy. 57 Cyit niy nu bicy yu gan biit yu yu bel na. 58 Gaze' nu brugyi' la rguuñ yu yo nu cyi'y yu gow yu. 59 Blazh bduuñ yu yo, nigaal briy gyi. 60 Bet boo na, nigaal syaas la bri lay yu bel yo. 61 Bi rel nguaa dey. 62 Wagay yu bel. 63 Tanta' bi rel nguaa dey. 64 Orze' gush pcaal yu mi' ze'. 65 Lat nu nas yu, guuy yu bel. 66 Cyit ni yu gush ze' nu nas bicy miiñ yu.

67 He finished off the entire old man. 68 He only left one thigh.

69 Now when the younger brother woke up, he said, "Is the old man ready to eat?"

70 Then the older *brother* said, "What old man? 71 I already finished eating the old man. 72 I only saved one of his thighs for mom to eat."

73 The younger brother said to him,

"You sure are bad. 74 Why didn't you save a little bit for me to eat? 75 If I hadn't remembered *what to say*, what would you have said to him? 76 If not for that, he would have eaten you a long time ago."

77 Then the older *brother* said, "Tut, tut, don't bother me. 78 If you want to eat some meat, go get a toothpick so that I can remove some from between my teeth for you to eat."

67 Entonces se comió al viejo, él solito. 68 Sólo un lado del muslo dejó.

69 Entonces cuando despertó el menor, le dijo:

—¿Ya se coció el viejo para que lo comamos?

70 Entonces dijo el mayor:

—¿Qué viejo? 71 Ya terminé de comer al viejo. 72 Sólo dejé un pedazo de muslo para que lo coma mamá.

73 Entonces le dijo el menor a él:

—¡Qué malo eres! 74 ¿Cómo no dejaste un poquito para que yo comiera? 75 Si no fuera por mí, que me acordé, ¿qué le hubieras dicho a él? 76 Si no fuera por eso, desde hace tiempo que ya te hubiera comido.

77 Entonces dijo el mayor:

—Quítate, quítate. No me estés molestando. 78 Si quieres comer carne, ve a traer un palillo para sacar la carne de entre mis dientes para que comas.

---

67 Orze' blaazh lay dutuub la yu bel bdow yu. 68 Stub la' zi'l cuiigy yu bzeeñ yu.

69 Na ornu briish yu mi' ze' yaa na, orze' nay:

«¿A bi guuy yu bel don?» nay.

70 Orze' na yu gush ze':

«¿La yu bel? 71 Yu bel bi blazh bdaw. 72 Stub la' zi'l cuiigy yu bzeeña gow ña'», nay.

73 Orze' na yu mi' rab yuy:

«Dzi ga a' nap ru. 74 ¿Lac wanseeñ ru sñumiiñ yu daw? 75 Ti cue' ya byeza' lagya, ¿lac mniir loy? 76 Ti cue' ni, gulas bi bdow yu ru», nay.

77 Orze' na yu gush:

«Cha' cha' cue' gyicy zeed ru ya. 78 Benu rlagy ru gor beel, gua gyii ya nguzh loo beel gyi' laya gor», nay.

4

The Skunk Takes a Compadre

Zapotec folk tradition includes numerous tales involving animal characters. Most of these tales are either fables, like "The Skunk Takes a Compadre," or trickster tales. "The Skunk Takes a Compadre" is interesting, because in spite of the European influence displayed in this tale, the setting and the moral of this tale are distinctly Mesoamerican.

"The Skunk Takes a Compadre" is set in the events surrounding the baptism of the skunk's child. During certain times in the life of a Zapotec child, like baptism, major illness, first communion, and marriage, the father of the child will ask someone to be the child's sponsor, or godparent. This person becomes the compadre of the child's parents. In this way alliances are formed between families. People form alliances of this type for a number of reasons. Sometimes a person will chose a man to be his compadre because he is a hard worker. Compadres are expected to cooperate in their work. Sometimes a man will choose a person to be his compadre because he is afraid of him. Compadres are expected to treat each other with respect, and to never cheat or deceive one another. Sometimes a man will chose a person to be his compadre because of the potential for financial gain. Ideally, people think that wealthy men should be willing to lend money without expectation of being paid back. One man told me, "That is what wealthy people are for." The only wealthy people I know of, who are widely respected, are those who are generous in lending money without asking for it back. A man can expect his compadre to be more generous to him than to others.

The skunk in the story chooses a mountain lion to be his compadre, hardly an equal alliance. The mountain lion places a large chunk of meat in the skunk's doorway. The skunk suffocates. The story teaches that unequal alliances are not good and that ambition does not pay. The idea that ambition is a vice is very Zapotec.

Polycarpo Martinez told this story to Claudio Martinez and me in 1973 as we worked in his house. Polycarp was twenty-four years old at the time. It was recorded on the tape recorder, and Claudio transcribed it.

El zorrillo

Los cuentos zapotecos tradicionales incluyen un gran número de historias de animales. La mayoría de estos cuentos son fábulas, como el cuento del zorrillo o cuentos de embusteros. El cuento del zorrillo es interesante porque a pesar de la influencia europea que se nota en él, el escenario y la moraleja son claramente mesoamericanos.

El cuento del zorrillo está basado en los eventos que se desarrollan alrededor del bautismo del hijo del zorrillo. En ciertas ocasiones en la vida de un niño zapoteco, como el bautismo, enfermedades serias, primera comunión y casamiento, el padre del niño le pide a alguien ser el responsable del acto o el padrino. Esta persona se convierte en el compadre de los padres del niño. De esta manera se crean alianzas entre las familias. La gente forma esta clase de alianzas por varias razones. Algunas veces una persona escoge a un hombre para que sea su compadre porque es un buen trabajador. Se espera que los compadres cooperen en el trabajo. Algunos escogen a una persona porque le tienen miedo. Los compadres deben tratarse uno al otro con respeto y nunca hacer trampas o engañarse mutuamente. Otras veces escogen a una persona por su posición económica, que se supone es una ganancia. Idealmente, la gente cree que un compadre rico puede prestarle dinero sin esperar que se le devuelva. Un hombre me dijo que para eso era la gente rica. La única gente rica que conozco que es ampliamente respetada, es la que ha sido generosa en prestar dinero sin esperar que se les devuelva. Un hombre espera que su compadre sea más generoso con él que con los demás.

El zorrillo en este cuento escoge a un león de la montaña para que sea su compadre, una alianza no muy equitativa. El león de la montaña pone un gran pedazo de carne en la puerta de la casa del zorrillo y el zorrillo se asfixia. La historia enseña que las alianzas desiguales no son buenas y que la ambición no da buen resultado. La idea de que la ambición es un vicio es muy zapoteca.

Policarpio Martínez contó esta historia a Claudio Martínez y a mí en 1973 cuando trabajábamos en su casa. Policarpio tenía entonces 24 años. Fue grabada en una cinta magnética y Claudio la transcribió.

1 A skunk spoke to his wife when she gave birth to their baby. 2 He asked her, "Would it be very shameful if I ask the mountain lion to be our compadre?"

3 She said, "But why should it be *shameful* if the mountain lion agrees. 4 If only Uncle Lion should agree," said his wife.

5 Then *the skunk* took to the trail and went to *see* the mountain lion. 6 When he arrived at where the lion was, "Will you sponsor my baby at his baptism?" he asked.

7 "Is that the errand you come on?" said the mountain lion.

8 "That is the errand I come on," *answered the skunk.*

9 "I can *sponsor him* then," said the mountain lion.

1 Un zorrillo le dijo a su mujer cuando dio a luz. 2 Le dijo a su mujer:

—¿Sería muy vergonzoso si fuera a hablar con ese león para que fuera nuestro compadre?

3 Entonces contestó su mujer:

—Pero ¿por qué? si tan sólo el león aceptara. 4 Si dijera que sí.

5 Entonces el zorrillo se fue a donde estaba el león. 6 Cuando llegó a donde estaba el león, le dijo:

—¿No vas a llevar mi nene al bautismo?

7 —¿Para eso viniste? —le dijo el león.

8 —Para eso vine.

9 —Entonces, sí puedo —dijo el león.

Rishtoo ni Bit

1 Bit mnii ma gugy ma mñaa ma ornu bgaal mñaa ma mdoo. 2 Orze' na ma rab ma mñaa ma:

«¿A dzi to' lo cha nee du biidz re gac mbaly na?» na ma rab ma mñaa ma.

3 Orze' na bañ mñaa ze':

«Par, ¿lagu benu shet ic zi'l biidz? 4 Benu shet ic zi'l shi biidz» na mñaa ma.

5 Orze' gush nez ma za ma lo biidz. 6 Bru'ña ma lo biidz na,

«¿A waya nu ñuur mdoo ne zu nis yu?» na ma.

7 «¿A nde' riiñ yad ru?» na biidz.

8 «Nde' riiñ yapa.»

9 «Gac beni», na biidz.

10 So in that way his baby was baptized.

11 "Only be patient. 12 On such a day I will bring food to you to eat," said the skunk to his compadre the mountain lion.

13 "That is nothing. 14 You don't have to be concerned about that. 15 Let things continue just the way they are. 16 Why should you exert yourself if you do not have the energy?" said the mountain lion to his compadre the skunk.

17 Now the day arrived when *the skunk* took a meal to his compadre to eat. 18 He arrived with a bowl of cricket gravey. 19 He arrived with grubs.

20 "Compadre, you sure eat a sad meal. 21 This is not the *kind of* meal I eat. 22 Come on such a day, and 23 we will go to a plain that is in that mountain. 24 We will get meat to eat there. 25 There you will know a little about what it is like to eat meat."

26 "Okay," said the skunk.

10 Así se bautizaron al nene.

11 —Nada más tengas paciencia. 12 Tal día vengo a dejar una tortilla para que comas —dijo el zorrillo a su compadre el león.

13 —No es nada. 14 No tienes que preocuparte por eso. 15 Dejemos que se vaya así. 16 ¿Por qué te vas a preocupar si no tienes fuerza? —dijo el león a su compadre el zorrillo.

17 Entonces llegó el día en que se llevó la comida a su compadre. 18 Llegó con un cajete de mole de grillo. 19 Lo llevó con bichanos.

20 —¡Qué sencilla es la comida que comes, compadre! 21 No es ésta la comida que yo como. 22 Ven este día. 23 Y vamos a un llano que está allá arriba. 24 Allá hay carne para comer. 25 Allá te darás cuenta de lo que es comer carne.

26 —Está bien —dijo el zorrillo.

10 Orze' ni zi'l bzu nis mdoo ni ma orze'.

11 «Nomaas gyicy ru pasez. 12 Gal i dzi yap du tub gyit gor», na bit rab ma mbaly ma biidz.

13 «Se la la nde'. 14 Wagad nu gyicy ru cuen nde'. 15 I zi'l cha ni nde'. 16 ¿Lagu gyicy ru fers benu sac fers?» na biidz rab ma mbaly ma bit.

17 Orze' pshuub dzi nu za nu ma comid gow mbaly ma na. 18 Bru'ña nu ma tub teg la niscub byuy bru'ña nu ma. 19 Bañ za, bañ bru'ña nu ma. 20 Orze'

«Dzi ga shni na comid ror mpaadre. 21 Walab nii comid rdaw ya. 22 Ca dzi yad ru. 23 Chan tub lacy riib ru' bicy re. 24 Re gad beel don. 25 Re gad lagy ñuur gor beel».

26 «O», na bit ze'.

27 When the day arrived he went to the mountain. 28 He accompanied his compadre, the mountain lion, to the mountain. 29 There was a large steer *there*. 30 The mountain lion jumped, and 31 took hold of the back of the steer's neck. 32 He killed it.

33 "Eat a little, compadre, because *its time* to eat *now*. 34 This is what I, a husky fellow, eat. 35 I take only young bulls to eat. 36 I don't eat humble meals. 37 Eat a little," he said.

38 "Okay," said the skunk.

39 He bit at *the meat* little by little. 40 But he was unable to bite any off. 41 He was flopping back and forth *on the ground* beside *the meat*.

42 "You sure are not of much use, compadre. 43 You should tear some off like this."

44 He took hold of what is called the thigh meat of the young bull and tore it off. 45 Rip, he tore it off.

27 Cuando llegó ese día, se fue al cerro. 28 Fue con su compadre, el león, al cerro. 29 Había allí un buey grande. 30 El león brincó. 31 Agarró al buey del pescuezo. 32 Mató al buey.

33 —Come un poco compadre, porque vamos a comer. 34 Este es lo que yo como, de cuerpo fornido, como. 35 Yo agarro sólo bueyes para comer. 36 Yo no como comida sencilla. 37 Come un poco —dijo.

38 —Bueno —dijo el zorrillo. 39 Lo mordió poco a poco. 40 Pero el zorrillo no podía quitar ni un pedazo. 41 Estaba revolcándose el zorrillo.

42 —Tú no sirves para nada, compadre. 43 Debes cortarlo así.

44 Agarró a una pierna del buey. Y cortó un pedazo. 45 Zaz, la cortó.

27 Pshuub dzi ze' za ma logyi'. 28 Za nu ma mbaly ma biidz logyi'. 29 Riib tub nobi ily. 30 Bzab la biidz. 31 Pshet la yaa ma gyib yeñ nobi. 32 Biit ma nobi ze'.

33 «Bdow ñuu mpaadre, gun don. 34 Nii rdaw ya̱, feñ nap. 35 Ya̱ rshet ya̱a̱ ga ub nobi la rdaw ya̱. 36 A̱' daw ya̱ comid gyidz. 37 Bdow ñuu», na ma.

38 «O», na' bit.

39 Rucua' ma ñuu ga, ñuu ga. 40 Ni wagyes la ni bit ca ma. 41 Rdudub laa bit ri ma orze'.

42 «Dzi ga wacyiiñ ru mpaadre. 43 I shes ru.»

44 Pshes la ma, pshet la yaa ma tub la' laa nu rnii beel cuiigy nobi ze'. 45 Cheeng la pshes ma.

46 "Take this to eat with my godchild, and my comadre. 47 The humble meal that you eat is disgusting. 48 You will rest easy after eating this," he said.

49 "But I can't lift it, compadre," the skunk said to the mountain lion.

50 "How can it not be lifted? 51 If *you* can't lift it, I will take you home. 52 So eat," said the mountain lion to his compadre the skunk.

53 The mountain lion put *the meat* on his shoulders and took it home, "Go into the house, compadre, so that I can put this in your doorway so that you can eat it. 54 I will put it in your doorway so that you can eat it," the mountain lion said to his compadre.

55 "Okay," he said.

46 —Lleva esto para que coma mi ahijado, y para que comas con la comadre. 47 No está buena la comida sencilla que comen Uds. 48 Les haría más provecho comer este —dijo.

49 —Pero no lo puedo levantar compadre —le dijo el zorrillo a su compadre, el león.

50 —¿Cómo que no puedes? 51 Si no puedes cargar, entonces yo voy a dejarte a tu puerta. 52 Así que, ¡come! —le dijo el león a su compadre.

53 Entonces el león puso la pierna en su lomo y la llevó,

—Pasa adentro, compadre, porque yo lo voy a poner en tu puerta para que lo comas. 54 Lo pondré en la puerta para que lo comas —le dijo el león a su compadre.

55 —Está bien —dijo.

46 Orze', «nii gya nur gow i'ñ wedz<u>a</u>, gow mbaly, gow nur mbaly. 47 Shiñ na comid gyidz row der. 48 Nii zu lagy der gor», na ma.

49 «Par nu wayes mpaadre», na' bit raba' ma mbaly ma biidz.

50 «Niir wayes. 51 Benu wayes, orze' y<u>a</u> gya señ<u>a</u> ru ro'r. 52 Orze' gow ru», na biidz rab ma mbaly ma bit.

53 Na ornu briib la yeñ biidz nde' ya nu ma,

«Gu' par nañ yu' mpaadre, gun y<u>a</u> g<u>u</u>' nii gyero' nir gow ru. 54 Rish<u>a</u>ñ gyero' nir gow ru», na biidz rab ma mbaly ma.

55 «O la», na ma.

56 His compadre the skunk entered the house. 57 He plugged the doorway of the skunk with the meat. 58 Now on the third day, he went to see his compadre. 59 He went to meet with him 60 to see if he had already finished the meat, so he could take more to him to eat. 61 Now when he arrived, his compadre was already dead, because he could not get out. 62 Air could not get in for him to breathe. 63 He had already died. 64 It was over. 65 The end.

56 Entró su compadre, el zorrillo, a la casa. 57 Atoró la carne en la puerta de la casa del zorrillo. 58 A los tres días, fue a ver a su compadre. 59 Fue a encontrarse con su compadre. 60 Fue a ver si ya había terminado la carne, para que llevara más para que comiera. 61 Cuando llegó, su compadre ya había muerto, porque no había podido salir. 62 No podía entrar el aire para que respirara. 63 Se había muerto. 64 Ya había terminado todo. 65 Se acabó el cuento.

56 Gu' la mbaly ma bit nañ yu'. 57 Bdu' chu' laa ma beel ro' bit. 58 Na or bza' gawidz, za güii ma lo mbaly ma. 59 Za ma za cheel ma mbaly ma. 60 Za güii ma ben a bi blaazh ma beel, gun cha nu zir ma gow mbaly ma. 61 Ornu bru'ña ma na, bi gut la mbaly ma nu wangac nruu ma. 62 Wanchu' ga' bi ñgyash ma. 63 Bi gut ma. 64 Bded. 65 Bya' lo nde'.

5

Peter Deceives the King

Tales of the trickster Pedro de Urdemalas are wide-spread throughout Mesoamerica. I have heard four of them in San Lorenzo: "Peter Deceives the King," "Peter Deceives the Priest," "Peter Deceives the Gringo," and "Peter Deceives the Muleteer." These tales are typical of the trickster type. Peter, a commoner, pits his wit against the wealthy, the educated, the pillars of society, and proves that he is superior to them. I include this tale as a representative of this type.

"Peter Deceives the King" was told to me by Alvaro Marcial in 1974 when he was twenty-seven years old. The occasion was during a visit with his sister at the house of Fausto Martinez where Claudio and I were studying Zapotec. It was recorded on the tape recorder and transcribed by Claudio Martinez.

Pedro engaña al rey

Cuentos como el de Pedro de Urdemalas son ampliamente conocidos en todo Mesoamérica. Yo he oído cuatro en San Lorenzo: Pedro engaña al rey, Pedro engaña al sacerdote, Pedro engaña al gringo, y Pedro engaña al arriero. Estos cuentos son típicos del tipo de cuentos de embusteros. Pedro, un hombre vulgar, prueba su ingenio contra los ricos, los bien educados, los pilares de la sociedad, y prueba que es superior a ellos. Incluyo este cuento como ejemplo de este tipo.

"Pedro engaña al rey" me lo contó Álvaro Marcial en 1974 cuando él tenía 27 años. Fue en casa de Fausto Martínez, cuando él y su hermana vinieron a visitar mientras Claudio y yo estábamos estudiando el zapoteca. La grabé en una cinta magnética y la transcribió Claudio Martínez.

1 What Peter, the liar who went about along time ago, did was to go to work at the house of a king, they say. 2 When he arrived at the house of the king, "Do *you* have any work for me to do" he asked.

3 "*I* have some if you have the patience to watch over my pigs. 4 The pigs are the only ones who don't have anyone to watch over them," said the king.

5 "I will watch over them," Peter said.

6 When it dawned, *Peter* opened the pig pen. 7 He took them out onto the trail. 8 Now the king had said, "There is a marsh at such a place. 9 Take them there at noon, so that they can bathe.

1 Lo que hizo Pedro, el engañador que anduvo aquel tiempo, dicen, fue trabajando en la casa del rey. 2 Cuando llegó a la casa del rey, le preguntó:

—¿Hay trabajo para que yo haga? —dijo.

3 —Sí hay, si tienes paciencia para cuidar mis cuches. 4 Solamente los cuches no tienen quien los cuide —dijo el rey.

5 —Los cuidaré yo —dijo.

6 Cuando amaneció, se abrió la puerta del chiquero de los cuches. 7 Él se fue el a cuidarlos. 8 El rey le dijo:

—Hay una ciénaga en tal lugar, entonces al medio día, 9 los llevas allí, porque allí se van a bañar al medio día.

Bed rguu rey

1 Bicya' Bed, yu rguu nu gusa gulas ze', na dey, zay gyicy yu riiñ yu' rey. 2 Lac ornu bru'ñay yu' rey na,

«¿A gad riiñ gyicya̠?» nay.

3 «Gad ñi benu ricy cup ru pase̠z nu ñar cuch ne̠. 4 Se cuch zi'l, ma re wagad cyu ña ma», na rey.

5 «Ña̠ ma», nay.

6 Na or bza' yu, nigaal byaal ru' chicyer ni cuch. 7 Gush nez yu za nuy ma. 8 Orze' na rey nay nu:

«Or wi doo, orze' ri tub gudz i lugaar. 9 Ze' cha nur ma, gun laagy ma or wi doo», nay.

10 In the morning and in the afternoon you are to take them to the other side of the wilderness. 11 This is all you have to do with them."

12 "Okay," Peter said.

13 He went on his way. 14 On the first day that he took *them* out, he took them to where the king said. 15 When noon came, he took them to the marsh. 16 That was what he did on the first day. 17 The second day was the same. 18 But in the afternoon of the third day, he began to think about what to do to *be able* to sell them to get some money. 19 At dawn, on the fourth day, a trail driver came down *from the mountains*. 20 He said to Peter, "Sell me all of the pigs you are watching over here."

21 "I will sell them *to you*. 22 I will sell them to you. 23 But I will only sell their bodies. 24 I will cut off all of their tails. 25 They remain here with me," said Peter to the trail driver.

10 En la mañana y en la tarde, entonces vienes al otro lado de la selva. 11 Así nada más vas a andar con ellos —dijo el rey.

12 —Bueno, pues —dijo Pedro.

13 Y se fue. 14 El primer día que estuvo allí, fue a donde le dijo el rey. 15 Cuando llegó el medio día, llevó los cuches a la ciénega. 16 Entonces así anduvo el primer día. 17 El segundo día fue igual. 18 Pero el tercer día, en la tarde, empezó a pensar de qué manera le haría para vender los cuches para tener dinero. 19 Pero cuando amaneció el cuarto día, ya llegó un arreador. 20 Y dijo a Pedro,

—Véndeme todos los cuches que estás cuidando aquí.

21 —Te los venderé —dijo Pedro—. 22 Los venderé. 23 Pero eso sí, vendo nada más los cuerpos. 24 Les cortaré las colas a todos. 25 Y entonces me quedaré con las colas —dijo Pedro.

10 «Or napor nu or gudze, orze' cyid ru tub la' ga' ich ngush ze' nur ma. 11 Ni zi'l chesar nur ma», na rey.

12 «O beni», nay.

13 Gush nez yu zay. 14 Dzi loga la nu zay na, ni zi'l za nuy ma ze' nu mnii rey ze'. 15 Byap or wi doo na, za nuy ma lo gudz ze'. 16 Orze' ni zi'l rded yu dzi loga. 17 Dzi cyup ni' zi'l. 18 Par dzi chon, or gudze, gaze' nu brugyi' rnii tooy nu lac mod gyicy yu par nu cut yu de ma ze', gun gad tiñ niy. 19 Par or bza' yu dzi tap na, gaze' nu bi bet lag la areadoor. 20 Gaze' nu nay rab yu Bed:

«Cut ru dela cuch nu rñar ii ne», nay.

21 «Duta ma» na Bed orze'. 22 «Duta ma. 23 Par esii cuerp zi'l ni ma duta. 24 Ne dela ma, shi'ña ñii. 25 Orze' gyiyeeñ ne ma ne» nay rab yu areadoor.

26 "Okay," said the trail driver.

27 Then *Peter* cut off the tails of all of the pigs, 28 and the trail driver took them all away with him. 29 So Peter got some money. 30 As for the pig tails that *Peter* kept, he planted them in the mud at the place where they had bathed. 31 He went to the place where he had taken them in the afternoon, and planted their tails *there*. 32 He planted all of *the tails there*.

33 Then when the sun began to set, *Peter* ran home to the king, his boss. 34 When he arrived he said, "Unfortunately, when all of the pigs that I watch descended into the mud to bathe, they all sunk *into it*. 35 Only a little bit of their tails can be seen. 36 Let's go look *at them* to see if we can still see their tails, or if they are already gone. 37 They might already be covered over by the mud."

26 —Está bien —dijo el arreador.

27 Después, cortó todas las colas de los cuches. 28 Y se fue el arreador con todos los cuches. 29 Entonces Pedro tuvo dinero. 30 Pero las colas que se le quedaron, fue a sembrarlas en la ciénaga donde los llevaba a bañar. 31 Allá donde los llevaba al medio día, allí fue a sembrar las colas. 32 Las sembró todas.

33 Después cuando ya estaba bajando el sol, fue corriendo al rey, su patrón. 34 Cuando llegó, dijo:

—¡Qué desgracia! Cuando bajaron a la ciénaga para bañarse, todos los cuches que cuido se hundieron todos. 35 Nada más un poco de las colas se pueden ver. 36 Por eso vamos a ver, porque puede ser que todavía logremos ver las colas, o puede ser que ya desaparecieron. 37 Puede ser que los animales que están en la ciénaga ya estén todos cubiertos.

26 «O beni», na areadoor.

27 Gaze' nu pcyug yu ne dela cuch. 28 Gaze' nu gush nez la areadoor ya nuy dela cuch. 29 Gaze' nu guud tiñ ni Pedro. 30 Ze' ne ma nu byeeñ ze', orze' la guay gua nuuz yuñ lo biñ ze' nu rlaagy ma ze'. 31 Ze' nu rza nuy ma or wi doo ze', ze' guay mnuuz yu ne ma. 32 De lañ mnuuz yu.

33 Gaze' nu ornu byap bish cya doo na, gaze' nu gush nez yu yay carer lo rey, lo patr<u>oo</u> niy. 34 Na ornu briy, orze' nay:

«Maa zir dela cuch, bañ nu rñ<u>a</u>, ornu bet ma lo biñ ze' nu rlaagy ma ze', dela ma weez t<u>i</u> ma. 35 Se ñuu ga zi'l ne ma rabee. 36 Nde' nu chan cha güiin, gun ben a gabee gzac ru'n ne ma, o ti bi blazh ma. 37 Byoow bañcyug nu ri lo biñ ze'», nay rab yu rey.

38 "Okay," said the king.

39 Then the king went to look over *the situation*. 40 When he arrived at the marsh, only the very tips of their tails could be seen. 41 When he began to up-root them, pluck, pluck, they came out because *Peter* had only planted the tips of them in the mud. 42 Then Peter said, "How unfortunate! 43 But if we dig, we ought to find them. 44 Their tails broke off because they have sunk so deep. 45 But *we can* dig them out."

46 Then the king said: "In that case go get a shovel, a hoe, and a crowbar 47 so that we can do some digging to see if *we* can't get even half of them out."

48 "Okay," said Peter.

49 Peter began to run to the *king's* house. 50 When he arrived at the house, he said *to the king's wife,* "I have come because the king sent me to fetch three different things.

38 —Bueno, pues —dijo el rey.

39 Entonces se fue el rey a ver. 40 Cuando llegó a la ciénega, solamente las puntas de las colas de los cuches se veían. 41 Cuando empezó el rey a jalar las colas, zaz, zaz, salían, porque sólo estaban sembradas en la ciénega. 42 Entonces dijo Pedro:

—¡Qué desgracia! 43 Si excavamos, dudo que los encontremos. 44 Ellos se sumieron más hondo; por eso se cortaron las colas. 45 Pero saldrán si las excavamos.

46 Entonces dijo el rey:

—Si es así, ve a traer una pala, con una coa, y la barreta. 47 Porque vamos a excavar a ver si sacamos aunque sea la mitad *de todos.*

48 —Está bien —dijo Pedro.

49 Entonces se fue Pedro corriendo. 50 Cuando llegó a la casa, dijo:

—Me mandó el rey que viniera, a traer tres clases de cosas.

38 «O benɨ», na rey.

39 Gaze' nu gush nez rey zay za güiiy. 40 Ornu bru'ñay lo gudz ze', la se ñuu ga lo ne cuch rabee zuñ. 41 Ornu brugyi' la rboo lyu rey nde', cheeng, cheeng la druu zañ, como nde' lo zi'l mnuuz yuñ lo biñ ze'. 42 Orze' na Bed nay:

«Maa zir. 43 Ze' benu duñ na, ti ti wayap na ma. 44 Yagyi ma ze', nde' nu bdurug ne ma. 45 Par gruu ma benu duñ na ma», na Bed rab yu rey.

46 Orze' na rey:

«Be ni gaze' nu char cha gyir yapal, gal nu gyichcyiib, gal nu baret», nay. 47 «Gun duñ na gun ben a waruu mas se ñuu se cyaal ma», na rey.

48 «O benɨ», na Bed.

49 Gaze' nu gush nez Pedro yay carer. 50 Ornu briy yu' na, orze' nay:

«Ya̲ bzuu nez rey ya̲ yapa̲, gun yap gyɨ chon lo coz.

51 And he said a day is coming, a time is coming when I will have all three of you. 52 That is what he said."

53 "You are lying," the king's wife said.

54 "Really. 55 Therefore, give me your word, because whatever happens I will have all three of you. 56 That is what he said. 57 Because then *we* will get his pigs out *of the mud*. 58 That is what he said," said Peter.

59 "Okay then," she said.

60 Then she gave Peter her word that he would have her and her children, the three of them. 61 Then she asked the king *a question*. 62 She stood there calling out to him: "*Do you* really *mean* all three of us?"

63 "All three," yelled the king *from where* he was standing.

64 Then the king's wife replied, "It will be as you wish."

51 Y dijo que ustedes tres iban a ser mías algún día, algún tiempo. 52 Así me dijo.

53 —Estás mintiendo —dijo la mujer del rey.

54 —Es verdad. 55 Así que, dame tu palabra, porque de todos modos voy a tenerles a ustedes tres. 56 Eso me dijo. 57 Porque así saldrán sus cuches. 58 Eso me dijo.

59 —Está bien —dijo ella.

60 Después, ella dio su palabra que las tres, ella y sus hijas serían de Pedro. 61 Entonces ella le preguntó al rey, 62 llamándole a gritos:

—¿Es cierto que las tres?

63 —Las tres —dijo el rey desde donde estaba.

64 Entonces dijo la mujer del rey:

—Se podrá como tú quieres —le dijo ella.

51 Nunu mniiy nu gyon laa de ru gane ru yad dzi, yad tiem. 52 I nay», na Bed.

53 «Par nu rguur», na mñaa rey.

54 «Ni gaal. 55 Nde' nu cuic lar rishnii nir, gun ca ni gaal gane der gyon laar. 56 I nay. 57 Gun orze' gruu cuch niy. 58 I nay», na Bed.

59 «O beni», na mi ze'.

60 Gaze' nu briic mi rishnii nu gyon laam nu i'ñ mi gani Bed. 61 Gaze' nu bdugyi'm lo rey. 62 Rbish tim zum:

«¿A ni gaal gyon laa de?» nam rab mi rey.

63 «Gyon laa», na rey zuy.

64 Orze' na mñaa rey:

«Gac gal nu rlagy ru», nam.

65 The situation was that the king had commanded Peter to go get three different things. 66 But *Peter* had changed the errand on which he went. 67 He did not bring back a shovel to get the pigs out of the mud, 68 but took to the trail and went away, since *the king's wife* had already given him her word that he would possess her in the future. 69 Now *when* Peter did not show up where the king was, 70 the king ran home to see *what had happened* at the house.

71 "But why? 72 What is Peter doing? 73 Why hasn't he shown up?" he asked.

74 "You ordered him to come here. 75 We gave him our word that he will possess all three of us, 76 because then *you* would get the pigs out *of the mud.* 77 That is what he said," said the king's wife.

65 Pero lo que el rey le había mandado a Pedro era que trajera tres cosas. 66 Y él había cambiado lo que el rey le había mandado. 67 Y ya no llevó la pala para sacar los cuches del lodo. 68 Después tomó Pedro su camino, y se fue, porque ella ya había dado su palabra que sería de Pedro en el futuro. 69 Como Pedro no llegaba a donde estaba el rey, 70 el rey fue corriendo a la casa a ver qué había pasado.

71 —¿Pero por qué? 72 ¿Qué tanto hace Pedro? 73 ¿Por qué no ha regresado? —dijo.

74 —Tú le mandaste que viniera. 75 Le dimos nuestra palabra que las tres seríamos de él. 76 Porque sólo así saldrían los cuches. 77 Eso dijo —dijo la mujer del rey.

65 Ze' como rey chon lo coz bicy yu mandaar nu za gyi Bed. 66 Ii yu ze' pchaay riiñ nu yay. 67 Nunu wancha nu'y yapal ze' nu mboo zay cuch lo biñ. 68 Gaze' nu gush nez la Bed za laay orze', como bi briic mi ze' rishnii nu ganiy mi par lo. 69 Gaze' nu wacabee Pedro nu ru'ñay lo rey na. 70 Gush nez rey yay carer ya güiiy yu'.

71 «¿Ze' lagu? 72 ¿La coz ricy Bed? 73 ¿Lagu wacabeey?» nay.

74 «Ru bicy ru mandaar loñ nu gyed ñi. 75 Bric d̲e̲ rishnii nu gyon laa d̲e̲ ganiñ d̲e̲. 76 Gun orze' gruu cuch. 77 I nañ», na mñaa rey.

78 "Now Peter will see *what will happen to him* if that is the case. 79 Why does he go about lying so much? 80 Why did he lie? 81 The pigs sunk in the mud, did they! 82 I sent him to get a shovel, a pick, and a crowbar. 83 Now I will follow him and kill him. 84 Why did he kill my pigs?[1] 85 He killed them," he said.

86 Then the king started out following *Peter*. 87 He went a long way. 88 When he met a woman, he said, "Where are you going? 89 Have you met a gentleman around here?"

90 "On the other side of that wilderness I met the man who they call Peter. 91 He was traveling. 92 He is the only one I met. 93 I didn't meet anyone else," said the woman.

94 "Okay then," said the king.

95 He walked and walked.

---

[1]These sentences are ambiguous. The words for "kill" and "sell" are homophonous. They could alternately read, "Why did he sell my pigs? He sold them."

78 —Ahora va a ver Pedro si dijo eso. 79 ¿Por qué anda engañando tanto? 80 ¿Por qué mintió? 81 Los cuches se hundieron en el lodo. 82 Lo mandé a traer la pala, el pico y la barreta. 83 Pero ahora voy a perseguirlo para matarlo. 84 ¿Por qué mató mis cuches?[1] 85 Él los mató —dijo.

86 Entonces se fue el rey a seguirlo. 87 El rey caminó mucho. 88 Cuando encontró a una mujer, le preguntó:

—¿A dónde vas? 89 ¿No te encontraste con un señor por aquí? —dijo el rey.

90 —Detrás de la loma encontré a uno que le llaman Pedro. 91 Estaba viajando. 92 A él nada más encontré. 93 No encontré a nigúna otra persona —dijo la mujer.

94 —Está bien —dijo el rey.

95 Siguió su camino.

---

[1]Estas oraciones son ambiguas. Las palabras para "matar" y "vender" son homófonos. Las oraciones se pueden interpretar, ya sea "¿Por qué vendió mis cuches?", "Él los vendió."

78 «Par na gzac Bed beni. 79 ¿Lagu dzi rguuy rded yu? 80 ¿Lagu bguuy? 81 Gunca cuch weez ti ma lo biñ. 82 Ze' yapal, gal nu pic, gal nu baret, nde' bzuu neza yu yeed gyiy. 83 Par na cha cha ca ich yu beni, gun duta yu. 84 ¿Lagu nu biit yu cuch ne? 85 Yu re biit yu ma», nay.

86 Gaze' nu za rey zay za cay ich yu. 87 Za rey, za rey. 88 Ornu bdzeel yu tub biñ mñaa, bdugyi'y:

«¿Ca char? 89 ¿A wancheel ru tub señoor par ii?» na rey.

90 «Ich ngush re ga zi'l bdzeela tub biñ nu rnii dem Bed. 91 Zam. 92 Mi ze' zi bdzeela. 93 Wancheela' zir mbecy», na biñ mñaa ze'.

94 «O beni», na rey.

95 Zay, zay, zay.

96 Now when Peter passed a man who was a butcher of goats, he said, "Sell me what they call the stomach of a goat. 97 And put all of the intestines and all of the blood from two goats in it."

98 "Okay," said the man who kills goats.

99 He gave Peter one of their stomachs. 100 He put the intestines inside it. 101 He put the amount of blood that they say is in two goats inside it. 102 Peter tied the neck closed and put it in front of his abdomen. 103 Then he put his shirttail over it. 104 Then he went on his way.

105 "If the king arrives and asks about me, tell him I will wait for him above a rock that is on the other side of this wilderness. 106 That is what you are to say." This is what Peter said to the man whom he bought the stomach of the goat from.

96 Cuando pasó Pedro donde estaba uno que tenía negocio de carnicero de chivos, le dijo:

—Véndeme todo el menudo del chivo, 97 todas las tripas, y la sangre, de dos chivos me pones con ello —dijo Pedro.

98 —Está bien —dijo el que mata chivos.

99 Le dio un menudo. 100 Puso las tripas adentro. 101 Puso la sangre de dos chivos adentro. 102 Después le amarró la boca de ese, y se puso sobre el estómago. 103 Lo tapó con su camisa. 104 Y se fue.

105 —Si llega el rey y te pregunta por mí, le dices que lo espero sobre la piedra que está detrás de la loma. 106 Así le dices —le dijo Pedro al señor a quien le había comprado el menudo de chivo.

96 La ornu bded Bed lo tub yu nu ricy fis carniser ni chiib, orze' la na Pedro:

«Biit nu rnii la she tub chiib ne. 97 Nunu dela duu ñgye' ma, gal nu reñ nu yu' nañ cyup ma cu'r nañ ñi ne», na Pedro.

98 «O beni», na yu nu rut chiib.

99 Ze' briic yu tub she ma niy. 100 Bdu'y duu ñgye' ma bdu'y nañ ñi. 101 Bdu'y reñ nu rnii la nu yu' nañ cyup chiib bdu'y nañ ñi. 102 Gaze' nu pcyiig yu yeñ ñi pcaay lo shish yu. 103 Gaze' nu briib yu gyi' yaag yu ich ñi. 104 Gaze' nu gush nez yu zay.

105 «Ze' benu ru'ña rey cugyi'y ya, orze' niir nu too gyita' nu zub ich ngush ii glezay. 106 I niir», na Bed rab yu yu nu wiiy she chiib lo ze'.

107 Then Peter went on his way. 108 When he arrived above the rock, he sat down there to wait. 109 When the king arrived where the man who kills goats was, "What word can you give me about a gentlemen *who is around* here?"

110 "A man by the name of Peter came by here earlier. 111 He said that he would wait on the other side of this wilderness," said the man who kills goats.

112 "Okay," said the king.

113 He went on his way. 114 When he arrived on the other side of the wilderness, Peter was already there sitting above the rock waiting for him. 115 The king drew his knife right there intending to kill Peter. 116 But Peter said, "Wait. 117 I will kill myself first. 118 I, myself, will kill myself. 119 Then I will recover again. 120 Then you kill yourself, too. 121 And you will recover again. 122 Then I will return your money to you."

107 Después, Pedro siguió su camino. 108 Cuando llegó a la piedra, se sentó allí a esperar. 109 Cuando llegó el rey donde estaba él que mata chivos le preguntó:

—¿Qué razón me das de un señor por aquí? —dijo el rey.

110 —Hace un ratito pasó uno que se llama Pedro. 111 Y dijo que va a esperar detrás de esa loma —dijo él que mata chivos.

112 —Bueno —dijo el rey.

113 Y se fue. 114 Cuando llegó detrás de la loma, allí ya estaba esperando Pedro sobre esa piedra. 115 Allí sacó el rey su cuchillo, tratando de matar a Pedro. 116 Entonces Pedro le dijo:

—Espera. 117 Me mataré yo mismo primero. 118 Yo mismo me mataré. 119 Después volveré a sanar. 120 Y entonces, después te matas tú. 121 Y vuelves a sanar. 122 Luego te entregaré el dinero.

---

107 Gaze' nu za Bed. 108 Ornu bru'ñay too gyita' ze', ze' la gusub yu rbez yu. 109 Gaze' nu, ornu bru'ña rey lo yu rut chiib na:

«¿La rasoo cuic ru tub señoor ii?» nay.

110 «Saa la za tub yu nu la Bed. 111 Nunu ich ngush ii ga mniiy nu cuez yu», na yu nu rut chiib ze'.

112 «O beni», na rey.

113 Zay. 114 Ornu bru'ñay ich ngush ze' na, ze' bi zub Bed too gyita' rbez yu. 115 Ze' la gaze' nu bloo za laa rey gyiscyiib nu ricy peey nu za tut yu Bed. 116 Orze' Bed nay:

«Blez. 117 Duta uba loga. 118 Ub la ya duta uba. 119 Nunu gaze' nu gyaca'. 120 Nunu orze' gaze' nu cuta' ru ub ru. 121 Nunu gyaca'r. 122 Gaze' nu gyabica tiñ nir», na Bed.

123 "But how will you do it?" asked the king.

124 "Lend me your knife so that I can stab myself in the stomach. 125 I will remove all of my intestines. 126 All of the blood that is inside me will pour out. 127 *My abdomen* will *bleed* dry. 128 Then I will recover again. 129 Then you do the same. 130 Then you will recover again. 131 Then I will give back all of the money from *the sale of* your pigs."

132 "Okay," said the king.

133 Having been taken in, he put the knife in Peter's hand. 134 Peter slit the knife across the skin of his abdomen. 135 Since he already had the goat stomach on him, he slit right along the stomach of the goat. 136 All of the its intestines came out. 137 The blood came out.

138 "Did you see? 139 Look at what I did now," he said to the king.

140 "Are you really a man?" the king said to Peter.

123 —Pero ¿cómo lo vas a hacer? —dijo el rey.

124 —Préstame tu cuchillo para que me meta en el estómago, 125 y sacaré todas mis tripas. 126 Y saldrá toda la sangre que tengo en el estómago. 127 Se secará. 128 Y entonces volveré a sanar. 129 Entonces haces tú lo mismo. 130 Y vas a sanar otra vez. 131 Entonces te entregaré todo el dinero de tus cuches —dijo Pedro.

132 —Está bien —dijo el rey.

133 Habiéndose engañado, le pasó el cuchillo a Pedro. 134 Entonces le pasó Pedro el cuchillo por el cuero de su estómago. 135 Como tenía el menudo de chivo, lo cortó al pasarle el cuchillo. 136 Entonces salieron todas las tripas de los chivos. 137 Salió la sangre.

138 —¿Viste? 139 Mira lo que acabo de hacer —le dijo al rey.

140 —¿Eres de veras un hombre? —le dijo el rey a Pedro.

123 «Par ze' ¿lac gyicy ru?» na rey.

124 «Doo gyiscyiib nir diña nu gne' naña. 125 Nunu loo za dela duu ñgye'. 126 Nunu grib dela reñ nu yu' naña. 127 Nunu cuigya'ñ. 128 Orze' gyaca'. 129 Gaze' nu ni' gyicy ru. 130 Gaze' nu gyaca'r. 131 Gaze' nu gyabica dela tiñ ni cuch nir», na Bed orze'.

132 «O la beni», na rey.

133 Guton yu bzuu lay gyiscyiib yaa Bed. 134 Orze' briily la Bed gyiscyiib gyid nañ yu. 135 Como yu ze' bi nuuy she chiib na, ze' la ich she chiib ze' briily yu. 136 Orze' bruu za dela duu ñgye' chiib ze'. 137 Bruu za reñ ze' bruu za.

138 «¿A bzaac ru? 139 Güii la bicya na», nay rab yu rey.

140 «¿A ru gaal yu gyeey ru beni?», na rey rab yu Bed.

141 "Give me *the knife*. I will do *it*, to see if I will recover too," said the king.

142 "Okay," said Peter.

143 He put the knife in the king's hand. 144 *The king* stuck *the knife* into his abdomen. 145 What king was there then? 146 He died. 147 Since he didn't have anything on his abdomen, he died. 148 Peter remained *alive*. 149 He gained all of the money from the *sale of the* pigs. 150 The end.

141 —Pásamelo ahora para que yo lo haga, a ver si vuelvo a sanar —dijo el rey.

142 —Bueno, pues —dijo Pedro.

143 Le pasó el cuchillo al rey. 144 El rey se metió el cuchillo en su estómago. 145 ¿Qué quedó del rey entonces? 146 Se murió. 147 Como él no tenía nada para proteger el estómago, se murió. 148 Entonces Pedro se quedó vivo. 149 Se quedó con todo el dinero de los cuches. 150 Y se acabó el cuento.

141 «Doo ben gyicya' ya na, gun ben a ni' gyaca», na rey.

142 «O la beni», na Bed.

143 Bzuu ga' lay gyiscyiib yaa rey. 144 Bzeed la rey nañ yu. 145 ¿La rey orze'? 146 Yu ze' gut lay. 147 Como yu ze' sac la la coz ca nañ yu, gut yu ze'. 148 Orze' byeeñ gaal Pedro. 149 Bicy yu gan dela tiñ ni cuch. 150 Bya' loñ.

6

The Foolish Man

The story of "The Foolish Man" is not only a popular folktale among the Texmelucan Zapotecs, but people I talk to tell me it is also very popular in other areas of Oaxaca, as well. I think its appeal comes from the egalitarian nature of indigenous society, and the way in which it clashes with national society. In order to understand this appeal, I discuss the words translated "clever" and "foolish" and what they mean to a Zapotec.

The word that I translated "clever" is sometimes applied to people of high social rank, like wealthy Spanish speakers, the bishop, or former town presidents whom are well thought of. It is also sometimes applied to people who have special skills, like a carpenter who does very nice work, or a doctor. In its root meaning it refers to people who command respect. The "clever" brother in the story does things right. He knows how to work in the corn field. He knows how to take care of his mother. On the negative side, he takes advantage of his brother's foolishness by making him do the heavy work.

It is important to understand that Texmelucan Zapotecs do not identify with the "clever" brother. They are very contemptuous of people who act like they are better than others. They never openly refer to themselves as "clever." They frequently refer to themselves as being poor, humble people. Part of the marriage ritual goes like this: "We are humble people who do not have any wealth to leave our children, but this one thing we can give them, a wife." The father of the bride refers to his daughter as

77

"worthless, puny, incapable, foolish." It is important to a Zapotec to never portray himself as anything other than ordinary.

The word I translate 'foolish' can be either an adjective or an adverb. When it is an adverb, it indicates foolish behavior. A person who "speaks foolishly," for example, says something that is out of place or absurd. When it is an adjective it refers to people who are socially inept, or who do not have ordinary skills, or who lack normal intelligence or ability. The foolish man in the story acts exactly according to expectation. He cuts down the corn plants with the weeds. He bathes his mother in boiling water. And he thinks she is content when in fact she is dead. Interesting enough, however, his foolishness appears to be only an illusion, he turns out to be more clever than the "clever" brother.

The appeal of the story does not lie in the character of the "foolish" brother, but rather in the clash between him and his "clever" brother. It is symbolic of clashes Zapotecs experience in every day life: the clash between Indian and non-Indian, between wealthy and poor, between powerful and weak. Zapotecs may be poor, weak, and Indian, but in their minds they are in no way inferior to educated, wealthy people of the national culture.

This story was given to me by Polycarpo Martinez in 1973 when he was twenty-four years old. At that time I was living in San Lorenzo. Polycarpo's parents, Faustino and Lucía, lent me their house to work in during the day. As Claudio Martinez and I worked, Polycarpo would often come in to talk. It was during one of these talks that he told us this story. It was recorded on the tape recorder. Claudio Martinez transcribed the story at a later date.

El hombre tonto

Esta historia es un cuento popular no sólo entre los zapotecas de Texmelucan, sino, según las personas con quienes hablé, también en otras regiones de Oaxaca. Yo creo que su atracción viene de la naturaleza igualitaria de la sociedad indigenista y en la forma conque choca con la sociedad nacional. Para poder entender esta atracción averigüé entre los zapotecas el significado que para ellos tienen las palabras "listo" y "tonto."

La palabra que yo traduje como "listo" a veces se atribuye a personas de un nivel social elevado, como personas adineradas que hablan el español, el obispo, o expresidentes municipales a los que se tiene en buena estima. También se atribuye algunas veces a gente con habilidades especiales, como el carpintero que hace un buen trabajo o el doctor. En su significado original se refiere a personas que merecen respeto. El hermano listo de la historia hace las cosas bien. Sabe trabajar en el campo. Sabe cuidar a su

The Foolish Man   79

mamá. En el lado negativo de la historia, se aprovecha de la simpleza de su hermano y le da para hacer todo el trabajo pesado.

Es importante entender que los zapotecas de Texmelucan no se identifican con el hermano listo. Ellos desprecian a las personas que se creen mejor que otras. Nunca se refieren abiertamente a ellos mismos como "listos." Frecuentemente se consideran gente pobre y humilde. Parte del rito del matrimonio dice así: "Somos gente humilde que no tiene ninguna riqueza para dejar a sus hijos, pero una cosa podemos darles, una esposa." El padre de la novia se refiere a su hija como sin valor, insignificante, incapaz, tonta. Para los zapotecas es importante no dar la impresión de ser nada más que una persona ordinaria.

La palabra que traduje como "tonto" puede ser un adjetivo o un adverbio. Cuando es un adverbio indica conducta tonta. Una persona que habla tontamente, por ejemplo, es la que dice algo fuera de lugar o absurdo. Cuando es un adjetivo se refiere a gente socialmente incapaz o que no tiene las aptitudes ordinarias o que carece de inteligencia o habilidades normales. El hombre tonto de la historia actúa exactamente como se espera de él: corta la milpa junto con las hierbas, baña a su mamá con agua hirviendo y piensa que ella está feliz cuando en realidad ya está muerta. Sin embargo, es interesante notar que su "tontera" parece ser sólo imaginaria, pues resulta ser más listo que el hermano "listo."

El sabor de la historia no se basa en el carácter del hermano "tonto" sino en el contraste entre él y su hermano "listo." Es un simbolismo del choque de experiencias en la vida diaria de los zapotecas: el choque entre indígenas y los que no lo son, entre ricos y pobres, entre los poderosos y los débiles. Los zapotecas podrán ser pobres, débiles e indígenas, pero su mente no es de ninguna manera inferior a la de los ricos y educados de la cultura nacional.

Esta historia me la dio Policarpio Martínez en 1973, cuando él tenía 24 años. En ese tiempo yo vivía en San Lorenzo. Los padres de Policarpio, Fausto y Luciana, me permitieron trabajar en su casa durante el día. Mientras Claudio Martínez y yo trabajábamos, Policarpio pasaba varias veces a platicar. Fue durante una de esas visitas que me contó esta historia que se grabó en una cinta magnética. Claudio Martínez la escribió más adelante.

1 There once was a foolish man. 2 He had a brother, a clever man. 3 The clever man said to the foolish man, "Go put the machete to *the weeds in* our corn field, so that I can stay and give mother a warm bath, because she is sick, and may not get well again."

4 "Okay," said the foolish man.

5 He went to put the machete to the *weeds in* the corn field. 6 When he arrived at the corn field, he went at everything evenly, the weeds and the corn plants. 7 After one day he had just a little bit of the corn field left *to do*. 8 He arrived home when the sun was still high. 9 When he arrived at the place where his brother was, "I am finished *for today*. 10 There is only a little left *to do*. 11 I need to go back for only a little bit more. 12 I will finish tomorrow," said the foolish man to the clever man.

13 At dawn of *the next day,*

1 Había una vez un tonto 2 que tenía un hermano listo. 3 Entonces le dijo el listo al tonto:

—Ve a echar machete a nuestra milpa, porque yo me voy a quedar a bañar a nuestra mamá con agua tibia, porque está enferma, porque ya no va a sanar.

4 —Está bien —dijo el tonto.

5 Se fue a echar machete a la milpa. 6 En cuanto llegó a la milpa, fue cortando parejo las hierbas y la milpa. 7 Después de un día, sólo había dejado un poquito de milpa. 8 Cuando el sol estaba todavía alto, llegó el tonto a la casa. 9 Cuando llegó el tonto a donde estaba su hermano:

—Ya acabé. 10 Sólo queda un poquito. 11 Sólo tengo que ir otro ratito nada más. 12 Mañana ya se termina —le dijo el tonto al listo.

13 Amaneció y el listo dijo:

Rishtoo ni tub yu ton

1 Gulas bzu tub yu ton. 2 Ze' zu tub bicy yu, yu lily. 3 Orze' na yu lily ze' rab yu yu ton ze':

«Char cu'r mandzicy gyel nin, gun ya gyiyeeña laagya ñaan nu nis bdza', gun rat mi, gun wayaca'm», na yu lily rab yu yu ton.

4 «O», na yu ton.

5 Zay cu'y mandzicy gyel. 6 Laab bru'ñay lat gyel, se tub ru' la zay nu gyish, nu gyel. 7 Na sñumiiñ zi'l gyel bzeeñ yu tub dzi. 8 Na or gya ru' doo, bi bri yu ton. 9 Orze' ornu bri yu ton lo bicy yu na,

«Blazh. 10 Sñumiiñ zi'l zu. 11 Stub miiñ zi'l cha. 12 Ina bi laazha» na yu ton rab yu yu lily.

13 Bza' yu nde'.

14 "You could not *possibly* finish today. 15 I am going to see if you are *telling* the truth. 16 Because if I can only accomplish a little bit *in a day*, how much less could you *accomplish*? 17 How could you finish *today*? 18 You are a fool. 19 Now you stay *home*. 20 Put a tub of warm water on for our mother to bathe in. 21 Then take hold of her. 22 Put her in the tub. 23 Bathe her," said the *clever man*.

24 "Okay," said the foolish man.

25 *The clever man's* brother went to get two buckets of water. 26 The buckets were this big. 27 He put a large tub over the coals. 28 He put fire under it. 29 He put a big fire under it. 30 *The water* was boiling. 31 As it was boiling, he took hold of his mother.

14 —Ahora ya no vas a acabar tú. 15 Yo voy a ver si has dicho la verdad. 16 Porque si yo avancé un poquito nada más, 17 ¿cómo puede ser que hayas terminado? 18 Tú eres tonto. 19 Ahora, tú te quedas. 20 Pon una olla de agua tibia para que se bañe nuestra mamá. 21 Entonces agarras a mamá. 22 La pones en una canoa. 23 Y la bañas.

24 —Está bien —dijo el tonto.

25 En cuanto se fue su hermano, fue a traer dos cubetas de agua. 26 Las cubetas eran muy grandes. 27 Puso una olla grande en el fuego. 28 Puso fuego debajo. 29 Puso el fuego fuerte debajo. 30 Estaba hirviendo. 31 Mientras hervía, agarró él a su mamá.

14 «Par waya' ru na. 15 Y̲a ch̲a na ben a lyar. 16 Gunca y̲a ñumiiñ tona' la by̲a' yer ru. 17 ¿La gya' ga' ru? 18 Ton nar», na yu lily rab yu yu ton. 19 Orze' «Ru na gyiyeeñ ru. 20 Zuub ru tub gyis la nis bdza' laagy ñaan. 21 Orze' cu' yaar ñaan. 22 Rir mi nañ cano. 23 Laagy rum», nay.

24 «O», na yu ton.

25 Laab za laa bicy yu za gyiiy cyup cubet nis. 26 I ga la na cyup cubet nis. 27 Na gyis ily bzuub yu lo boo. 28 Briy gyi iiñ ñi. 29 Fert briy gyi iiñ ñi. 30 Rlaab lañ. 31 Rlaab lañ, bdu' la yaay ñaay.

32 She was on the bed. 33 He took hold of her. 34 He put her in the tub. 35 He put her in the boiling water. 36 *Later* he removed her *from the water*. 37 He dunked her whole head in the boiling water. 38 Then he removed her *from the water*. 39 He put her on the bed.

40 "When you finish bathing our mother with warm water, find a good chicken, 41 and kill it so that mother can eat it," the clever man had said.

42 "Okay," he had said.

43 Then he killed a chicken. 44 He cooked *it*.

45 "Soak some tortillas for her to eat, because she is so unfortunate. 46 She does not have any teeth. 47 Perhaps she will eat just a little," the clever man had said.

48 "Okay," he had said.

32 Su mamá estaba en la cama. 33 Agarró a su mamá. 34 La metió en la olla. 35 En el agua hirviendo la puso. 36 Entonces la sacó. 37 Le mojó a la cabeza en esa agua hirviendo. 38 Entonces la sacó. 39 La puso en la cama.

40 —Cuando termines de bañar a mamá en agua tibia, entonces buscas una gallina buena, 41 y la matas para que coma mamá —dijo el listo.

42 —Bueno —dijo el tonto.

43 Después, mató la gallina. 44 Y la cocinó.

45 —Pones luego un poco de sopa para que coma mamá, ¡pobrecita!, 46 ya no tiene dientes. 47 A ver si come aunque sea un poquito —había dicho el listo.

48 —Bueno —había dicho el tonto.

32 Orze' riib ñaay lo nuun. 33 Bdu' la yaay ñaay. 34 Bri lay mi nañ gyis. 35 Lo nis rlaab la ze' briy mi. 36 Orze' blooy mi. 37 Psal yu dutuub la toom psal yu lo nis rlaab ze'. 38 Orze' blooy mi. 39 Briib yum lo nuun. 40 Orze'

«Lazh laagy ru ñaan nis bdza', orze' yub ru tub gyid nap. 41 Gyid nap la cut ru gow ñaan», na yu lily.

42 «O», nay.

43 Gaze' nu biit yu tub gyid. 44 Gaze' nu guuy ma ze'. 45 Gaze' nu orze'

«Cu' chal ñuur gow ñaan, gun cuaam. 46 Saca' lay mi. 47 Ben a wow mi mas ñumiiñ, ben a wow mi», na yu lily.

48 «O», nay.

49 After he had bathed his mother, he immediately put the chicken on *to cook*. 50 It cooked furiously. 51 He dipped out a bowel of soup. 52 He soaked *some tortillas* in the soup. 53 Then he opened her mouth. 54 He took hold of the soaked tortillas and stuffed them into her mouth. 55 Then he sat her down, 56 and leaned her over, 57 as if she were asleep. 58 But she was really sitting there dead. 59 There were soaked tortillas in her mouth. 60 That was all. 61 He assumed that she had eaten. 62 He wiped her mouth. 63 He cleaned it with water. 64 He leaned her over. 65 Then the clever man arrived.

66 "How is mother doing?" the clever man said to his brother.

49 Cuando terminó de bañar a su mamá, luego puso a cocer la gallina. 50 Rápidamente se coció. 51 Entonces puso caldo en un plato. 52 Mojó las tortillas en el caldo. 53 Y le abrió la boca a su mamá. 54 Tomó las tortillas mojadas, y la metió en la boca de su mamá. 55 Entonces la sentó 56 recargada. 57 Como si estuviera durmiendo. 58 Pero ella estaba muerta. 59 Tenía tortillas en la boca. 60 Y se acabó. 61 Él pensó que ella había comido. 62 Le lavó la boca. 63 Le lavó con agua. 64 Despues la recargó. 65 Entonces llegó el hermano listo.

66 —¿Qué hace mamá? —le preguntó el listo.

49 Laab blazh la blaagy yu ñaay, ni gaal bzuub yu gyid. 50 Loc, loc la guuy ma ze'. 51 Orze' bda'y tub gya'n nispit. 52 Bdu' chal yu. 53 Gaze' nu pshaay ru'm. 54 Ze' bdu' yaay gyit chal rgu' chu' laay, rgu' chu' laay ru'm orze'. 55 Orze' na gusub mi. 56 I pca teeñ yum. 57 Nas lam. 58 Gut la mi ze' zub mi. 59 Orze' yu' gyit chal ru'm na. 60 Orze' blazh ze'. 61 Por cuen niy ze', bdow mi ze'. 62 Orze' bdiib yu ru'm. 63 Nu nis bdiib yu ru'm. 64 Gaze' nu pca teeñ yum. 65 Orze' bri yu lily ze'.

66 «¿La ricy ñaan?» na yu lily rab yu yu ze'.

67 "She has a smiling expression *on her face* now. 68 She has eaten a little. 69 She ate quite a few soaked tortillas. 70 She drank some soup. 71 She should get better because she drank some soup. 72 Therefore, she should get well now," said the foolish man.

73 Now when the clever man entered *the house* to look at his mother, *he said,* "What *kind of a person* are you anyway? 74 You sure are a fool! 75 You killed mother. 76 Now see what you can do about burying her. 77 Because just look *at what you have done*! 78 You killed her."

79 "Okay," said the foolish man.

67 —Parece que ella está riendo ahora —dijo el tonto—. 68 Ya comió un poco. 69 Comió bastante sopa de tortillas. 70 Ya tomó caldo. 71 Se va a sentir mejor, porque tomó caldo. 72 Por eso ahora va a sanar.

73 Cuando entró el listo a mirar a su mamá:

—¿Cómo eres tú?, 74 ¡Qué tonto eres! 75 Mataste a mamá. 76 Ahora tú verás qué vas a hacer para enterrar a mamá. 77 ¡Porque mira lo que hiciste! 78 La mataste —dijo el listo.

79 —Está bien —dijo el tonto.

67 «Mod nu bi rigy ñuum na», na yu ton. 68 «Bi bdoow la ñuum. 69 Bdow la ñuum gyit chal na ingaab. 70 Bi go'm nispit. 71 Nu gan la go'm nispit. 72 Nde' nu gyac mi na», nay.

73 Na ornu gu' yu lily bgüiiy lo ñaay,

«¿La bee ru la? 74 Dzi ga ton nar. 75 Biit ru ñaan», nay. 76 Orze' «Par na güiir lac gyicy ru cach ru ñaan. 77 Gun güii la! 78 Biit rum», na yu lily.

79 «O la», na yu ton.

80 He went to fetch his donkey. 81 He saddled it. 82 Then he put his mother on it. 83 Then he went to get a forked stick. 84 He supported her under her jaw *with it*. 85 He wrapped a shawl around her head. 86 He traveled for quite a while. 87 He walked a long ways. 88 *He came to* a corn field that belonged to someone. 89 He went right through it because the trail took a turn, and he was too lazy to take the turn. 90 So he went right through it.

91 "Man, where are you going?" said the owner of the corn field he was in.

92 He took hold of a rock. 93 He threw it at the donkey that the man's mother was on. 94 He hit her right here on the back of the neck. 95 Plop! she fell to the ground.

80 Entonces fue a traer su burro. 81 Lo ensilló. 82 Después puso a su mamá en el burro. 83 Entonces fue a traer una horqueta. 84 La puso debajo de su quijada. 85 Le cubrió la cabeza con el rebozo. 86 Y se fue, se fue, se fue. 87 Caminó muy lejos. 88 Entonces había una milpa de otra persona. 89 Bajó derecho en la milpa, porque el camino daba vuelta, y él tenía flojera de dar vuelta. 90 Entonces bajó en la milpa.

91 —¿A dónde vas, hombre? —dijo el dueño de la milpa que estaba allí.

92 Tomó una piedra. 93 Se la tiró al burro en que iba su mamá. 94 Le dio en la nuca a su mamá. 95 ¡Paf!, se cayó su mamá al suelo.

80 Orze' gua te lay bur niy. 81 Bdu' lay shab ma. 82 Gaze' nu briib lay ñaay. 83 Gaze' nu gua gyiiy tub ya ru' biiz. 84 Blaagy yu nañ ya ru'm ii. 85 Ptiish lay bay toom. 86 Zay, zay, zay, za yu. 87 Tuñ bzay. 88 Orze' ri tub gyel ni mbecy. 89 Li gaal la lat gyel bet yu nu par nu ryach nez ze', par nu razeed yu gyach yu. 90 Orze' bet lay lat gyel ze'.

91 «Epa mbecy, ¿ca cha ru?» na shuaan gyel riy.

92 Bdu' la yaay tub gyita'. 93 Bzaan lay too bur nu riib ñaay. 94 Pshet lay gyib yeñ ñaay par ii. 95 ¡Poong! bet lag ñaay lo yu. 96 Orze'

96 "Wickedness! 97 The bitch that gave you birth! 98 Why did you kill my mother?" said the foolish man. 99 "Now look here. 100 If you don't bury my mother, and if you don't pay for *damages against* her, I will press charges against you. 101 Then you will go to prison," said the foolish man.

102 "Oh how unfortunate I am! 103 I killed your mother. 104 I will pay you whatever you say for her," said *the owner of the corn field.*

105 "She costs one million pieces of money," said the foolish man.

106 "Okay. 107 She is already dead. 108 So I will pay *you* the money," he said.

109 He went home to get the money. 110 He gave him the money and attended to the burying his mother.

96 ¡Mal haya! 97 ¡Sinvergüenza! 98 ¿Por qué mataste a mi mamá? —dijo el tonto—. 99 Ahora verás. 100 Si no entierras a mi mamá, y si no pagas por mi mamá, entonces yo te voy a denunciar. 101 Irás a la cárcel.

102 —¡Ay! ¡Pobre de mí! 103 Maté a tu mamá. 104 Entonces te voy a pagar. A ver cuánto quieres por tu mamá —dijo.

105 —Mi mamá vale un millón de dinero —dijo el tonto.

106 —Está bien —dijo—. 107 Ya se murió. 108 Te voy a dar el dinero —dijo.

109 Entonces fue por el dinero a su casa. 110 Le dio el dinero, y enterró a la mamá del tonto.

«¡Malay! 97 ¡Put nu bgaal ru! 98 ¿Lagu biit ru ñaa?» na yu ton. 99 «Par na güii lar. 100 Benu wacach ru ñaa, nunu benu wayish ru ñaa, orze' ya cha tu' cyir. 101 Char pres», na yu ton.

102 Orze' «¡Ay! lashta ya beni. 103 Bduta ñaar. 104 Orze' rica tiñ nir ben labe niir ñaar», nay.

105 «Ñaa sac mi tub miyoo tiñ» na yu ton.

106 Orze' «O la beni», nay. 107 «Bi gut mi. 108 Ric la tiñ», nay.

109 Orze' bya gyiy tiñ yu'y. 110 Briic yu tiñ nunu bgüiiy pcach yu ñaay pcach yu.

111 Now when *the foolish man* received the money, he ran off 112 to meet his brother. 113 He went *to the place* where his brother was, because his brother had gone in the other direction. 114 They say that the foolish man had gone in the opposite direction. 115 *The foolish man* walked a long way. 116 He met up with his brother *who said,*

117 "What did you do with mother? 118 Did you bury her?"

119 "They gave her a party and a lot of gifts. 120 They gave mother a very good funeral. 121 Her funeral was very nice. 122 And she got quite a bit of money. 123 Her *funeral* expenses did not use up all of the money. 124 Look! 125 Mother got a lot of money," he said.

126 He was traveling with a whole load of money on his back. 127 The clever man was very angry that the foolish man killed his mother.

111 Cuando él tuvo el dinero, se fue corriendo. 112 Se fue a encontrar con su hermano. 113 Fue a donde estaba su hermano, porque su hermano agarró otro camino cuando estaba yendo. 114 Pero el tonto se fue por otro lado. 115 Caminó mucho. 116 Alcanzó a su hermano.

117 —¿Qué hiciste con mamá? 118 ¿La enterraste? —le dijo.

119 —Dieron muchas limosnas para mamá y una fiesta. 120 Manejaron muy bien el entierro de mamá. 121 Ella tuvo un buen entierro. 122 Y recibió un poco de dinero. 123 Los gastos no acabaron el dinero de ella. 124 ¡Mira! 125 Nuestra mamá recibió mucho dinero —dijo.

126 Estaba viajando con una carga de dinero en su espalda. 127 El listo tenía mucha muina, porque el tonto había matado a su mamá.

111 Na laab guud tiñ la, gush yu carer zay. 112 Yay ya cheel yu bicy yu. 113 Yay lo bicy yu, gun bicy yu gush yu tub la' ga' nez zay. 114 Ze' yu ton ze' zay tub la' ga', nay. 115 Orze' tanta' nu rzay, rzay. 116 Bdzeel loy bicy yu.

117 «¿La bicy nur ñaan? 118 ¿A pcach rum?» nay.

119 «Tona' la bicy dey gun lo ñaan, nu gyel cyit, nu. 120 Tona' la nap pcach dey ñaan na. 121 Nap bgach mi na. 122 Nunu guud ñuu tiñ nim. 123 Wanlazha' tiñ gac gasht lo ñaan. 124 Güii. 125 Ñaan ingaab tiñ guud nim», nay.

126 Tub yuu la tiñ zub ich yu zay. 127 Orze' tanta' nu rzi lagy yu lily ze' nu biit yu ton ñaay.

128 "This is what is to happen now: give me the money to carry. 129 Then go get mother's bed and the trough in which she bathed."

130 "I cannot lift the trough. 131 I will only bring the bed," said the foolish man.

132 He ran home. 133 He carried the trough *in his arms*. 134 and the bed on his back as he returned. 135 He traveled for quite a while. 136 He walked a long ways. 137 There was a large green tree. 138 It was dusk.

139 "We should climb up this green tree," they said.

140 They could see the foot of the tree, because its leaves had become a little thin. 141 That night people seemed to arrive at that place. 142 So they climbed to the very top of the tree. 143 They settled in. 144 When it was well into the night, people began to gather there.

128 —Lo que se va a hacer ahora es que tú me vas a dar el dinero para que yo lo cargue. 129 Entonces vas a traer la cama de mamá y la canoa en que ella se bañaba —dijo.

130 —No aguanto la canoa. 131 La cama nada más voy a cargar —dijo el tonto.

132 Y se fue corriendo. 133 Trajo la canoa en sus manos, 134 y la cama en su espalda cuando fue. 135 Se fue, se fue. 136 Caminó lejos. 137 Entonces había un árbol verde grande. 138 Ya era de noche.

139 —Subamos a este árbol verde —dijeron.

140 Se veía el pie de ese árbol verde, porque estaba un poco pelón. 141 Parecía que llegaba gente allí de noche. 142 Se subieron hasta la punta del árbol. 143 Y se sentaron allí. 144 Cuando ya era bien de noche, se empezó a juntar la gente allí.

128 «Par na nu gac na, doo tiñ ze' nir du̱. 129 Orze' cha gyir nuun ni ñaan, nu cano nu blaagy mi», nay.

130 Orze' «Wayes cano. 131 Nuun zi'l du̱», na yu ton.

132 Yay carer. 133 Na byuun yu cano. 134 Zub ich yu nuun zay. 135 Orze' zay, zay. 136 Tanta' bzay. 137 Orze' na zub tub yag ca' ily zub. 138 Orze' becheñ. 139 Orze'

«Chup na lo yag ca' ii», na dey.

140 Rabee la gyi' yag ca' ze' byayagy ñuu. 141 Bri mbecy ze' rel ze' rlyu. 142 Orze' gup dey gashtal lo la yag ze'. 143 Gucuay. 144 Orze' becheñ nap zi'l, brugyi' rde' mbecy ze'.

145 Some thieves gathered there. 146 *They* began to cook supper. 147 There was a fire. 148 There was a lot of noise among them. 149 They were all sitting around.

150 "I am so unfortunate brother. 151 I have the urge to urinate," said the foolish man as he sat there. 152 "I have the urge to urinate."

153 "Don't urinate, because if you urinate, they will see us. 154 They might shoot us," said the clever man.

155 "Okay," he said.

156 He sat down again. 157 A little while later,

158 "I must urinate now brother. 159 I cannot endure *waiting*. 160 I cannot endure *waiting*. 161 I must urinate," said *the foolish man*.

162 He unfastened his pants. 163 Trickle! He was there urinating. 164 Then the men who were sitting down below said,

145 Unos ladrones se juntaron allí. 146 Empezaron a hacer la comida. 147 Había fuego. 148 Hacían mucho ruido entre ellos. 149 Estaban allí.

150 —¡Qué lástima!, mi hermano. 151 Quiero orinar —dijo el tonto—. 152 Quiero orinar.

153 —No orines, porque si orinas, nos van a ver. 154 Nos matarán a balazos —dijo el listo.

155 —Está bien —dijo.

156 Se sentó otra vez. 157 Entonces pasó otro ratito.

158 —Ahora voy a orinar, hermano —dijo el tonto—. 159 Ya no aguanto. 160 No aguanto. 161 Me orino —dijo.

162 Desató sus pantalones. 163 ¡Psss!, estaba regando su orina. 164 Entonces dijeron los que estaban allí:

145 De gubaan rde'y ze'. 146 Brugyi' ray comid. 147 Rgua gyi. 148 Rgua zu redz yu' dey. 149 Orze' nguaay.

150 «Lashta ya̱ bicy na. 151 Rlagya̱ nisa̱», na' yu ton zuba'y. 152 «Rlagya̱ nisa̱.»

153 «Cue' nis ru, gun benu nis ru, orze' zac dey de ub na. 154 Cooy de ub na», na' yu lily ze'.

155 Orze' «O beni», na' yu ze'.

156 Gusuba'y. 157 Orze' tub miiñ rac.

158 «Nisa̱ na bicy na» na' yu ton bi zuba'y. 159 «Wagye̱e. 160 Wagye̱e. 161 Nisa̱», nay.

162 Pshaagy lay nañ yu. 163 Ushshsh riy rnis yu. 164 Orze' na de yu nguaa ze':

"The poor tree of God! 165 Look! 166 Water is coming from it."

167 Some men held out gourds, some men opened their mouths, some men held out their hands. 168 They had been without water to drink. 169 That is all, it was over. 170 It was very quiet. 171 Nothing appeared *to be happening*. 172 After a little while passed, "I must defecate, brother. 173 I cannot endure *waiting*. 174 I must defecate now," said *the foolish brother*.

175 "Don't defecate, because if you defecate, they will surely know *we are here*. 176 They will kill us," said the clever man to the foolish man.

177 "Okay," he said.

178 He sat down for a little bit. 179 After that,

180 "I might possibly have to defecate now, because I cannot endure *waiting* any more," said the foolish man to the clever man.

181 "Don't defecate I say," said *the clever man*.

—¡Pobre del árbol de Dios! 165 ¡Miren! 166 Sale agua de él—.

167 Algunos ponían sus jícaras, algunos ponían sus bocas, algunos ponían sus manos. 168 Habían estado sin agua para beber. 169 Entonces, así nada mas pasó. 170 Había mucho silencio. 171 No parecía que pasaba nada. 172 Entonces, después de otro ratito,

—Voy a cagar, hermano. 173 Ya, no aguanto. 174 Voy a cagar —dijo.

175 —¡No lo hagas! porque si hagas, entonces, seguro que se van a dar cuenta. 176 Nos van a matar —le dijo el listo al tonto.

177 —Está bien pues —dijo.

178 Se sentó un ratito. 179 En otro ratito:

180 —Ahora sí voy a cagar, porque yo no aguanto más —dijo el tonto al listo.

181 —Te estoy diciendo que no lo hagas —dijo.

«Dzi ga cuaa yag ni Ñgyoozh. 165 ¡Güii la! 166 Druu nis loñ.»
167 Yu rzaab ig ni, yu rzaab ru', yu rzaab loryaa. 168 Wagad nis go' dey yu'y. 169 Orze' ni zi'l guc. 170 Ri zu la. 171 Nde' wacabee la. 172 Orze' tub miiñ zi'l rac orze',
«Zu'na bicy na. 173 Wagyee. 174 Zu'na na», na'y.
175 «Cue' zu'n ru, gun benu zu'n ru, orze' segur la gad lagy yu. 176 Cut yu de ub na», na yu lily rab yu yu ton. 177 Orze'
«O beni», na'y.
178 Gusub yu tub miiñ. 179 Ba rac nde',
180 «Par labee na la zu'na, gun wagyee ga' na», na yu ton rab yu yu lily.
181 Orze'
«Cue' rzu'n ru rnee», nay.

182 He unfastened his pants once more. 183 He squatted down. 184 He defecated. 185 His excrement went plop, plop as it fell in the tree. 186 His excrement fell *to the ground.*

187 "It is the excrement of an opossum," said the men who sat there.

188 Some time passed. 189 That was over. 190 He didn't speak. 191 Some time passed.

192 "Mother's bed, I cannot endure holding it. 193 The back of my neck is very tired from all this. 194 My chest is tired. 195 I cannot endure any more now," said the foolish man.

196 "Don't, because if you do, they will surely kill us," said the clever man.

197 Then his brother said, "I cannot endure any more. 198 I cannot endure any more now," said the foolish man.

199 He let go of the bed. 200 It went bang, bang, bang, bang down the tree. 201 The bed fell *down the tree.*

182 Pero él se desató el cinturón otra vez. 183 Se sentó. 184 Cagó. 185 ¡Chas, chas! caía entre las ramas. 186 Estaba cayendo su caca.

187 —Caca de tlacuache es esta —dijeron los que estaban allí.

188 Pasó otro rato, 189 Pasó eso. 190 No dijo nada. 191 Al otro rato:

192 —Ya no aguanto cargar la cama de mamá. 193 Se me cansó el lomo para cargarla. 194 Se me cansó el pecho. 195 Ya no aguanto más —dijo el tonto.

196 —No, porque si así seguro nos van a matar —dijo el listo.

197 Entonces dijo su hermano:

—Yo no aguanto. 198 Yo no aguanto más —dijo el tonto.

199 Soltó la cama. 200 ¡Prass, prass, prass, prass! sonaba en el árbol. 201 Cayó la cama.

---

182 Pshaagya'y nañ yu tub tira'. 183 Gusub yu. 184 Rzu'n yu. 185 To', to' rac rlag ñgye'y lat yag. 186 Yet lag ñgye'y.

187 «Ñgye' lez nii», na de yu nu nguaa ze'.

188 Ba rac nde'. 189 Bded nde'. 190 Wanniiy. 191 Orze' ba rac nde'. 192 Orze'

«Nuun ni ñaan, wagyee ga' du na. 193 Tona' la bda gyib yeña nu de nii. 194 Lyusha nu bda. 195 Wagyee ga' na», na yu ton orze'. 196 Orze'

«Cue', gun be ni, segur la cut yu de ub na», na yu lily.

197 Orze' na bicy yu nay:

«Wagyee ga'. 198 Wagyee ga' na», na yu ton.

199 Bzaan la yaay nuun niy. 200 Paang, paang, paang, paang rac lo yag. 201 Bet lag nuun.

202 The thieves scattered, and went away. 203 They scattered and went away. 204 The *brothers* descended quickly. 205 The foolish man descended quickly. 206 But the clever man descended slowly. 207 When the foolish man descended, supper was ready: meat in chile sauce and bread. 208 He ate the bread. 209 He drank the meat sauce. 210 He ate the meat. 211 There were bags of money this big. 212 He took hold of a bag of money to take with him. 213 But the clever man was afraid. 214 He ran away. 215 He didn't get anything to eat.

216 Some time passed. 217 Then another thief arrived. 218 Another arrived. 219 "Give me a little to eat, friend," said the thief because he was afraid.

220 "Open your mouth. 221 Then I will give you something to eat," said the foolish man.

222 "Okay," said the thief.

202 Se dispersaron los ladrones; se fueron. 203 Se dispersaron. 204 Los hermanos bajaron corriendo. 205 El tonto se bajó rápido. 206 El listo se bajó despacio. 207 Cuando se bajó el tonto, ya estaba la comida: caldo de res y pan. 208 Comió el pan. 209 Tomó el caldo de la carne. 210 Comió la carne. 211 Había costales grandes de dinero. 212 Entonces tomó un costal de dinero para llevar. 213 Pero el listo tuvo miedo. 214 Y se fue corriendo. 215 No comió nada.

216 Pasó otro ratito, 217 entonces llegó otro ladrón. 218 Llegó otro.

219 —Dános un poquito de comer, amigo —dijo el ladrón que se asustó.

220 —Abre tu boca. 221 Entonces te daré de comer —dijo.

222 —Está bien —dijo el ladrón.

202 Orze' brush las la de gubaan zay. 203 Zay brush las la dey. 204 Bet dey carer. 205 Yu ton ze' dzach bet yu carer. 206 Ze' yu lily ze' guly bet yu. 207 Ornu bet yu ton ze', bi nguaa comid, niscyiiñ beel, gyishtily. 208 Bdow yu gyishtily. 209 Go'y niscyiiñ beel. 210 Bdoy beel bdoy orze'. 211 I ga la na mangoch tiñ nguaa. 212 Orze' bdu' la yaay tub mangoch tiñ za nuy. 213 Orze' yu lily ze' gudzib yu. 214 Za laay ze' carer. 215 Wangad la ñgyoy ze'.

216 Ba la rac nde'. 217 Orze' bru'ña stub gubaan. 218 Orze' bru'ña stub yu.

219 «Doo sñumiiñ don amigo», na gubaan nu gudzib yu.

220 Orze' «Pshaa ru'r. 221 Gaze' nu rica gor», nay.

222 «O», na gubaan.

223 He opened his mouth. 224 Then *the foolish man* grabbed his tongue. 225 Swish, he slid his knife across the tongue.

226 "Ah!" said *the thief.*

227 His tongue came out *of his mouth.*

228 *The foolish man* went on his way.

229 "You sure are foolish, brother.[1] 230 Are you a man? 231 You did not grab a bag *of money.* 232 Look at all that is here. 233 This is the only one *I brought.* 234 If I were to take hold of it all, I could not lift it. 235 I would have taken hold of two *bags,* but I could not lift them. 236 I only have this one *bag* with me," he said.

---

[1]It is not clear who is talking here. The clever brother seems to fade from the picture starting at this point.

223 Abrió la boca. 224 Le agarró el tonto la lengua. ¡Cas!, se la cortó con el cuchillo.

226 —¡Ay! —dijo.

227 Su lengua salió.

228 Y se fue.

229 —¡Cómo eres de tonto, hermano![1] 230 ¿Eres hombre? 231 No agarraste el costal. 232 Mira qué tanto hay. 233 Este es el único. 234 No aguantó mi mano. 235 Pensé agarrar dos, pero no aguanté. 236 Sólo éste cargué —dijo.

---

[1]No está claro quién está hablando aquí. El hermano inteligente parece empezar a desaparecer del mapa en este punto.

223 Pshaa la ru'y. 224 Bdu' la yaay lyudz yu. 225 Cheeñ la briily yu gyiscyiib. 226 Orze'

«¡Ah!», na' yu ze'.

227 Bruu lyudz yu.

228 Zay. 229 Orze'

«Labee ru ton nar bicy na. 230 ¿A mbecy ru? 231 Wancu' yaar mangoch. 232 Güii ñuu la nguaañ. 233 Tub zi nii. 234 Wangyes du' y<u>aa</u>. 235 Bicy p<u>ee</u> ndu' y<u>aa</u> cyup, par wangyes. 236 Tub zi nii d<u>u</u>», nay.

237 Then he went away.
238 He was going along in this
way. 239 There was a tree in a
town. 240 People were gathered
there. 241 People passed by on
the road. 242 It was a green tree.
243 He stuck all of the money he
had gotten on the tree with sap.

244 "I have a money tree," he
said.

245 Spanish speakers passed
by. 246 Spanish speakers passed
by that place.

247 "I have a money tree to
sell in case you might be interested in buying it."

248 "How much are you asking for it?"

249 "I want a hundred million
pieces of money. 250 Because it
is continually producing money.
251 When it has finished producing some money, it produces
some more. 252 It continually
gives money," said the foolish
man sitting there.

237 Entonces se fue, se fue.
238 Así se fue. 239 Entonces,
había un árbol en el pueblo.
240 Allí se juntaba la gente.
241 En el camino que pasaba la
gente 242 había un árbol verde.
243 Todo el dinero que consiguió lo puso en el árbol.

244 —Yo tengo un árbol de
dinero —dijo.

245 Pasaron unos que habla-
ban español. 246 Allí pasaban
los que hablan español.

247 —Yo tengo un árbol de
dinero para vender a ver si lo
quieras comprar.

248 —¿Cuánto pides por él?

249 —Quiero cien millones
de dinero. 250 Porque este árbol diario da dinero. 251 Acaba
de dar dinero, y vuelve a dar
otra vez. 252 Diario da dinero
—dijo el tonto.

237 Orze' zay, zay, zay. 238 Orze' ni zi'l zay. 239 Orze' ze' zub tub yag
lat gyedz ze'. 240 Ze' rde' mbecy. 241 Ru' gyernez rded mbecy. 242 Zub tub
yag ca'. 243 Dela tiñ nu guud niy ze' nu bid pta'y ñi lo yag ze'. 244 Orze'
«Ya ricy cupa tub yag tiñ», nay.
245 Rded wan. 246 Ze' rded wan.
247 «Ya ricy cupa tub yag tiñ ben a wazir duta» na yu ton rab yuy.
248 «¿Labe la niir nii?»
249 «Nii rlagya mas tub gaaynal miyoo tiñ. 250 Gun nii zaab cya' la rbic
ñi tiñ. 251 Lazh cuic ñi tiñ, cuic ñi tuuba'. 252 Zaab rbic la nii tiñ», na yu
ton zub yu.

253 "Now look at this bag of mine. 254 I have been gathering money from it for a long time. 255 A little bit more and it will be full for me," he said.

256 His sack had gone down, because he had put some on the tree.

257 "I will buy it then," said one of them.

258 He arrived and bought the tree. 259 Now when he picked *the money on it*, the time of its having money was long over. 260 He picked the money. 261 Then there was only the tree there.

262 The foolish man got the money *for it*. 263 Then he went away and disappeared. 264 *The tale* is over.

253 —Mira mi bolsa. 254 Ya hace tiempo que recojo centavos de aquí. 255 Un poco más, y se llena —dijo.

256 Se había mermado su costal, porque había puesto algo de dinero en el árbol.

257 —Creo que sí lo compro —dijo uno de ellos.

258 Llegó y compró el árbol. 259 Cuando bajó el dinero, ya hacía tiempo que había terminado de dar dinero. 260 Él había bajado el dinero. 261 Entonces, sólo quedaba el árbol.

262 El tonto se quedó con el dinero. 263 Desde entonces se fue, y desapareció. 264 Se terminó.

253 «Na nerbid ii ne̱, güii la. 254 Bi gulas bi rac tiem rte̱' sentab loñ. 255 Na sñuu ga dzaa nii ne̱», nay.

256 Ze' yu ze' nu bet naañ ru' da' bid ze' niy nu pta'y nde' lo yag ze'. 257 Orze'

«Par zi̱ beni», na tub yu.

258 Bru'ñay wiiy yag ze'. 259 Na ornu blag yu, bi rac tiem blazh bda' tiñ loñ. 260 Blag yu tiñ. 261 Laab nde' zub yag ze'.

262 Orze' guud tiñ niy. 263 Laab nde' zay mnit yu orze'. 264 Blazh ñi.

7

Lucecita

I am told that the story of "Lucecita" is the single most requested folktale among the Texmelucan Zapotecs. Perhaps one of the reasons for this interest is that it portrays an episode in the life of a Zapotec with whom everyone can identify. In order to better understand this episode, I first give a brief sketch of the marriage custom of the Texmelucan Zapotecs.

Marriage is typically initiated by the family of the groom. The groom chooses a woman his parents approve of. Then the parents send a go-between to contract for the marriage. The ritual that the go-between performs requires several visits. The woman acts reluctant. Her parents talk about how worthless she is, and they ask if the groom is sure he wants her.

When she finally agrees, the groom's family put on an engagement ceremony in order to honor the family of the bride. The engagement ceremony is called the *lagyez* 'cigarette', because the groom's family pass out cigarettes to the brides family as a visible sign of respect. In the past the family of the bride would be seated in a row according to social rank. Opposite each member of the brides family would be seated a corresponding member of the groom's family. So the father of the bride and the father of the groom would be seated opposite each other, and so on down the line. During the parts of the ritual where the groom's family speaks, they would stand, fold their hands under their chins, and continually bow slightly foreword and back again before the bride's family. The bride's family would remain seated. In ways like these the family of the groom honors the family of the bride, because the family of the bride is thought to be

97

enduring a hardship. They are loosing a family member. The groom's family is gaining a family member.

After the engagement ceremony, the groom goes to live with the family of the bride to perform a bride service. The groom works for his father-in-law in order to earn his bride. The amount of time he works for his father-in-law is determined by the go-between in contracting for the marriage. It is typically six months to a year. During this time, if the bride's father likes the way the groom is treating his daughter, and the way in which he works, he will "deliver the bride to her husband." The groom then begins having marital relations with his wife. But if the girl's father thinks he is unsuitable, and especially if he is lazy, the father can send him home and the marriage is off.

After the bride service has been performed, the groom takes his bride home to live with his parents. They live with the groom's parents until the marriage of a younger son. Then the groom's parents, ideally, set them up in a new residence. The youngest son lives with his parents until their death. He inherits their remaining wealth.

The events described in the story of Lucecita occur during and immediately following the bride service. Lucecita is the daughter of a king. She has a husband who is from far away. Thus, the story begins with a foreign flavor. But the attitudes and following events are distinctly Zapotec. The husband is working for the king, doing his bride service. But there is a clash between the interests of the king and the interests of the husband. The king does not want to lose his daughter. The husband wants to earn a wife. So the king gives his son-in-law impossible tasks to perform. Lucecita is torn between the two sides, but it is inevitable that she go with her husband, and in doing so she must experience pain and uncertainty. She experiences pain when she is forced to kill her mother. When a woman becomes part of her husband's family, her own family no longer has any claim on her or her children. It is as if they were dead. She reveals the concern she has for the risk she is taking when she keeps asking her husband if he is sure he wants her. That same question is asked over and over again of the go-between in contracting the marriage and of the groom's father during the engagement ceremony. It is a very important question for a Zapotec woman, because when a man mistreats his wife, her family usually cannot help.

One of the most fascinating aspects of the story to me is the way in which women are portrayed. First of all, they are seen as being indispensable to men. Over and over the rhetorical question is asked, what would the young man be without Lucecita? Zapotec single men are socially restricted in that they cannot assume any political or religious office other than the very lowest and most burdensome offices. Adult single men are looked down upon and are the subject of much criticism. A man without a woman is not a whole person.

Secondly, Zapotecs believe that women do not think like men. Women are sometimes portrayed as being unreasonable. They are portrayed as not being capable of rational thought: "There is a hole that goes straight through the mind of a woman, but the road in the mind of a man takes many turns." However, the story of Lucecita portrays them as having a greater grasp on reality than men. According to Zapotec world view, things are not as they seem. The problem with men is that their thinking is too closely tied to their senses. Thus, the men in this story are made out to be fools. When situations appear to be impossible, they despair. The women, however, have a superior knowledge of the way things really are, and Lucecita is able to save her man. I think that it is because of such knowledge that some activities like those relating to curing are more often performed by women than men.

Juana Antonio gave me this tale in 1974 for no other reason than that she wanted me to have it. She recorded it on the tape recorder in her home with only her family present. Her son Claudio Martinez transcribed it and edited it slightly.

Lucecita

Se me ha dicho que la historia de Lucecita es una de las más solicitadas entre los zapotecas de Texmelucan. Este interés se debe, posiblemente, a que refleja un episodio de la vida zapoteca con el que todos se pueden identificar. Para poder entender este episodio, daré una breve descripción de lo que se acostumbra hacer cuando se trata del matrimonio entre los zapotecas de Texmelucan.

El matrimonio es iniciado, típicamente, por la familia del novio. Él escoge a una mujer que sus padres aprueben. Luego los padres contratan al mediador para que haga los arreglos. El ritual del mediador requiere varias visitas. La mujer actúa renuentemente, sus padres explican lo insignificante que es y preguntan si el novio está seguro de que la quiere por esposa.

Cuando ella accede finalmente, la familia del novio celebra una ceremonia de compromiso para honrar a la familia de la novia. La fiesta de compromiso se llama el *lagyez* "cigarro", porque la familia del novio reparte cigarros a la familia de la novia como una notoria señal de respeto. En el pasado, la familia de la novia se sentaba en una fila de acuerdo a su rango social. Opuesto a cada miembro de la familia de la novia se sentaba el miembro de la familia del novio del rango correspondiente. De esta manera, el padre del novio quedaba sentado frente al padre de la novia y así sucesivamente. Cuando la familia del novio habla en el ritual, se ponen todos de pie, juntan las manos bajo la barbilla y se inclinan ligeramente hacia adelante ante la familia de la novia una y otra vez. La familia de la novia permanece sentada. La familia del novio honra de esta manera a la familia de la novia, porque se piensa que la familia de la novia está pasando por un percance difícil. Están perdiendo un miembro de la familia. Por el contrario, la familia del novio gana un miembro más.

Después de la ceremonia de compromiso, el novio va a vivir con la familia de la novia para prestar "el servicio a la novia". El novio trabaja para el padre de la novia para ganarla. El tiempo que tiene que trabajar para su suegro es determinado por el mediador encargado del casamiento; generalmente es de seis meses a un año. Durante este tiempo si al padre de la novia le agrada el modo como el novio trata a su hija y la manera como trabaja, "le entrega" la novia al esposo. El novio empieza entonces a tener relaciones matrimoniales con su esposa. Pero si el padre ve que el muchacho no le conviene a su hija o que es flojo, lo manda a su casa y se rompe el compromiso.

Después del "servicio a la novia" que el novio ha llevado a cabo puede llevarla a su casa a vivir con sus padres. Ellos viven en la casa de los padres hasta que se case uno de los hijos más jovenes de la familia de él. Luego los padres los establecen, idealmente, en su nueva residencia. El hijo más joven vive con los padres hasta que mueren. Él hereda lo que quede de las posesiones de sus padres.

Los sucesos descritos en la historia de Lucecita se efectúan durante e inmediatamente después del "servicio a la novia". Lucecita es la hija de un rey; tiene un esposo que vino de lejos. Por eso la historia comienza con un sabor extranjero, pero el modo de pensar y los eventos siguientes son claramente zapotecas. El esposo trabaja para el rey haciendo su "servicio a la novia", pero hay un choque entre los intereses del rey y los del esposo. El rey no quiere perder a su hija, y el esposo quiere ganar a su esposa. Así que el rey da al yerno trabajos imposibles de cumplir. Lucecita está entre la espada y la pared, pero tiene que ir con su esposo, pero al hacer esto tiene que experimentar duda y dolor. Sufre cuando se ve obligada a matar a su madre. Cuando una mujer se vuelve parte de la familia del esposo, su propia familia no tiene más derecho sobre ella ni sus hijos. Es como si se hubieran muerto para ella. Ella muestra su preocupación por el riesgo que corre al preguntar constantemente a su esposo si está seguro que la quiere. Esa misma pregunta se le hace una y otra vez al mediador al arreglar el casamiento, y también al padre de la novia durante la ceremonia del compromiso. Es una pregunta muy importante para la mujer zapoteca, porque cuando un hombre maltrata a su esposa, generalmente la familia de ella no puede ayudarla.

Para mí, uno de los más fascinantes aspectos de la historia es la manera como describen a las mujeres. En primer lugar, se les considera indispensables para los hombres. Una y otra vez se pregunta retóricamente qué sería del joven esposo sin Lucecita. Los hombres solteros zapotecas están restringidos socialmente en cuanto a trabajos políticos o religiosos que pueden desempeñar o aceptar. Sólo pueden hacer los trabajos más bajos y pesados en las oficinas. A los hombres adultos solteros se les mira con desprecio y se les critica mucho. Un hombre sin una mujer no está completo.

En segundo lugar, los zapotecas creen que las mujeres no piensan como los hombres. Algunas veces se les considera irrazonables; hablan de ellas como si no fueran capaces de pensar racionalmente. "Hay un hueco que pasa directo a través de la mente de una mujer, pero el camino de la mente del hombre tiene muchas vueltas." Sin embargo, la historia de Lucecita las presenta como teniendo mejor concepto de la realidad que los hombres. De acuerdo al punto de vista del mundo zapoteca las cosas no son como parecen. El problema con los hombres es que su pensamiento está demasiado atado a sus sentidos. Así, los hombres de esta historia son presentados como tontos. Cuando las situaciones parecen ser imposibles se desesperan. Sin embargo, las mujeres tienen un mejor conocimiento de las cosas, y Lucecita es capaz de salvar a su esposo. Yo creo que es debido a esa sabiduría que muchas actividades, como las que se relacionan con curaciones, son llevadas a cabo más frecuentemente por mujeres que por hombres.

Juana Antonio me dio esta historia por la única razón de que ella quería que yo la tuviera. La grabó en una cinta magnética en su casa cuando sólo estaba presente su familia; su hijo Claudio Martínez la trancribió y le hizo pequeñas correcciones.

1 A long time ago there was a king who had a daughter called Lucecita. 2 She got a husband. 3 Now when *the king's* son-in-law arrived at *her* house, the king commanded him to go to work. 4 He was to clear the bush and plant flowering plants. 5 The king told him that on the very day he planted some flowers, on that same day he was to bring home flowers to put before *the king's* gods.[1]

6 "Okay," said the young man.

7 He went to work to clear off the bush. 8 *When he arrived*, he sat down and cried.

9 When lunch time came, Lucecita took him some food to eat. 10 When she arrived, he was sitting there crying.

11 "Why are you crying?" asked Lucecita.

---

[1]The typical Zapotec family has two houses: the god house and the kitchen. There is a altar in the god house where people put the images they call "god." This is where these flowers are to be put.

1 Hace tiempo había un rey que tenía una hija que se llamaba Lucecita. 2 Ella se casó. 3 Cuando el *nuevo* yerno del rey llegó a la casa del rey, el rey le ordenó que fuera a trabajar, 4 que hiciera el rozo y sembrara flores. 5 El rey le dijo que el mismo día que sembrara las plantitas, debería traerle las flores para que las pusiera delante de sus dioses. Le dijo él a su yerno.[1]

6 —Bueno— dijo el yerno.

7 Y se fue a hacer el rozo. 8 Entonces fue, y se sentó a llorar.

9 Cuando llegó el medio día, entonces Lucecita llegó con tortillas que él comiera. 10 Cuando llegó Lucecita, él estaba sentado llorando.

11 —¿Por qué lloras? —dijo Lucecita.

---

[1]La familia zapoteca típica tiene dos casas: la casa de dios y la cocina. Hay un altar en la casa de dios donde la gente pone las imágenes que llaman "dios". Es aquí donde se ponen estas flores.

Lusesit

1 Gulas bzu tub rey la i'ñ mi Lusesit. 2 Orze' guud ñgyeeñ. 3 Na ornu bri ngudz mi ze' yu', orze' pcaam ñii nu chañ gyicy ñi riiñ. 4 Ga'n ñi gyish nunu nuuz ñi ya gyee. 5 Laab dzi nu gnuuz ñi ya gyee ze', laab dzi ze' gri nuñ gyee nu chu' lo ñgyoozh nim, mniim gugy mi ñii.

6 «O», na fiñ ze'.

7 Zañ gyicy ñi riiñ ga'n ñi gyish. 8 Orze' zañ gusub ñi ruun ñi.

9 Na byap or cui, orze' za Lusesit za nuñ gyit goñ. 10 Ornu bru'ña Lusesit, ruun ñi zub ñi.

11 «¿Lagu ruun ru?» naa ga' Lusesit.

12 "Why should I not cry? 13 Your father said that today I am to clear the bush, and this very day I am to set fire to it, and this very day I am to plant some flowers. 14 This is what he said. 15 What should I do?" he said to Lucecita.

16 "You don't have anything to worry about. 17 Quickly go to sleep," said Lucecita.

18 "Okay," he said.

19 He laid down and went to sleep. 20 He only slept for a moment. 21 Then he arose. 22 When he looked around, the flowers were already there. 23 Then Lucecita went home.

24 *But before she went home, she said,* "Stay here for now. 25 Come home in the afternoon. 26 Then bring some flowers to put before the gods."

27 "Okay," he said.

12 —¿Cómo qué no voy a llorar? 13 Tu papá me dijo que hoy mismo hago el rozo, y hoy mismo debo quemarla, y hoy mismo debo sembrar las flores. 14 Eso me dijo. 15 ¿Qué debo hacer? —dijo a Lucecita.

16 —No tienes que preocuparte. 17 Duérmete pronto —dijo Lucecita.

18 —Bueno —dijo él.

19 Entonces se acostó a dormir. 20 Sólo durmió un ratito. 21 Y se levantó. 22 Cuando miró alrededor, vio que ya estaban crecidos las flores. 23 Entonces, se fue Lucecita.

24 —Quédate aquí ahora. 25 Y ven a la casa en la tarde. 26 Entonces, trae las flores para poner a los dioses —había dicho ella a su esposo.

27 —Bueno —dijo él.

12 «¿La wadun ya? 13 Ze' uz ru mniiy nu laab dzi na du'na gyish, nunu laab dzi na caa gyi nu nii, nunu laab dzi na nuuza ya gyee. 14 I nay. 15 ¿Ze' lac gyicya?» naañ rab ñi Lusesit.

16 «Wagad nu gyicy ru cuen. 17 Dzach zir ptaas», i na ga' Lusesit.

18 «O», na ga'ñ.

19 Orze' gugyit ñi nas ñi. 20 Tub miiñ zi'l ptaas ñi. 21 Orze' weshteñ. 22 Ornu bgüiiñ, bi nash ya gyee. 23 Orze' ya Lusesit.

24 Ze' anzir nu gyañ, orze' nam:

«Byeeñ la ru na. 25 Orze' yeed ru or gudze. 26 Orze' yeed nur gyee chu' lo ñgyoozh», i na'ñ rab ñi ñgyeeñ.

27 «O», na ga' fiñ ze' orze'.

28 He waited until it was afternoon 29 to go home. 30 Then he picked some of the flowers to take home.

31 Now when he arrived before the king, "I have brought the flowers now," he said.

32 "Did you bring them?" the king asked.

33 "I brought them," he said.

34 "If that is the case we have really acquired a competent son-in-law now," he said.

35 "What would your competent son-in-law be, if Lucecita had not done that?" asked his wife.

36 The next day dawned.

37 "Now you will go again to clear the bush. 38 You are to clear enough bush to plant about a bushel and a half of corn. 39 And you are to plant the corn this same day. 40 And this same day you are to bring fresh corn for us to eat," the king said to him.

28 Se esperó hasta la tarde 29 para ir a la casa. 30 Entonces cortó algunas flores para llevar. 31 Cuando él llegó donde estaba el rey, le dijo:

—Ya traje las flores.

32 —¿Las trajiste? —dijo el rey.

33 —Sí, las traje —dijo.

34 —Sí es así, entonces de veras tenemos ahora un yerno listo —dijo él.

35 —¿Qué habría hecho tu yerno listo si Lucecita no hubiera hecho eso? —dijo la mujer entonces.

36 Amaneció al siguiente día.

37 —Vas a ir otra vez a hacer el rozo. 38 Vas a rozar un tanto de terreno en el que se pueda sembrar una fanega de maíz. 39 Y siembras el maíz este mismo día. 40 Y este mismo día traes los elotes que comamos —dijo el rey.

28 Blez ñii gudze. 29 Orze' yaañ. 30 Gaze' nu pcyug ñi gyee ya nuñ. 31 Na ornu briiñ lo rey na orze'

«Bi yap du̱ gyee na», na'ñ.

32 «¿A yeed nur?» naa ga' rey.

33 «Yap du̱», naa ga'ñ orze'.

34 «Na gaal guud tub ngudz lily na beni», i na ga'm orze'.

35 «¿La ngudz lily ru, ti cue' Lusesit ricy ñi nde'?» i na ga' biñ mñaa ze' orze'.

36 Ze' bza' yu tuuba' dzi.

37 «Cha ga'r na ga'n ru gyish. 38 Ze' nu chu' tub ane uub ze' ga'n ru. 39 Nunu nuuz ru uub laab dzi na. 40 Nunu laab dzi na gri nur za' don», na ga'm rab mi ñii.

41 "Okay," he said.

42 He took to the trail again. 43 When he arrived in the bush, he sat down and cried. 44 He just sat there crying. 45 He did not even clear any bush. 46 Once again when lunch time came, Lucecita brought his lunch.

47 "Why are you crying?" asked Lucecita

48 "Why should I not cry? 49 Because your father has now said that I am to clear the bush today, and today I am to set fire to it, and this same day I am to plant corn, and this same day I am to take fresh corn to him to eat. 50 Whatever should I do?" he asked.

51 "You don't have anything to worry about. 52 That is not such a big thing. 53 Quickly go to sleep," she said to her husband.

54 "Okay," said the young man.

41 —Bueno —dijo.

42 Se fue otra vez. 43 Cuando llegó al monte, se sentó a llorar. 44 Sólo estaba sentado llorando. 45 Ni siguiera cortó el monte. 46 Cuando llegó la hora de la comida, otra vez llegó Lucecita con la comida.

47 —¿Por qué lloras? —le dijo.

48 —¿Cómo no voy a llorar? 49 Si tu papá dice ahora que tengo que rozar hoy, y quemar el rozo hoy, y hoy mismo sembrar el maíz, y también hoy debo llevar los elotes para que coma él. 50 ¿Qué voy a hacer? —dijo.

51 —No tienes que preocuparte. 52 No es la gran cosa. 53 Duérmete rápido —le dijo a su esposo.

54 —Bueno —dijo él.

41 «O», na'ñ.

42 Gush neza'ñ. 43 Na bru'ñañ lat gyish ze', orze' gusuba'ñ ruun ñi. 44 Nu ruun zi'l lañ zub ñi. 45 Ni gyish wanga'n ñi. 46 Byapa' or cui bru'ña ga' Lusesit nuñ cuiñ. 47 Orze'

«¿Lagu ruun ru?» naa ga' Lusesit.

48 «¿Ca wadun ya? 49 Ze' na mnii uz ru nu dzi na du'na gyish, nunu laab dzi na caa gyiiñ, nunu laab dzi na nuuza uub, nunu laab dzi na gya du za' goy. 50 ¿Ze' lac gyicya?» naa ga'ñ.

51 «Wagad nu gyicy ru cuen. 52 Walab coz ily nde'. 53 Dzach ru ptaas», i na ga'ñ rab ñi ñgyeeñ.

54 «O», na ga' fiñ ze'.

55 Once more he laid down and slept.

56 Later, "Get up," she told the young man.

57 "Okay," he said.

58 When he looked around, there was corn all over. 59 The corn was ready.

60 "Remain here for now. 61 You are to come home in the afternoon. 62 Then pick some fresh corn to bring for him to eat," she said to her husband.

63 "Okay," said the young man.

64 He was happy. 65 He remained there. 66 He waited until afternoon. 67 Then he went home.

68 Now when he arrived home, he brought the fresh corn with him.

69 "I have brought you some fresh corn to eat now," he said to the king.

55 Entonces se acostó a dormir.

56 Más tarde le dijo:
—¡Levántate!

57 —Bueno —dijo él entonces.

58 Cuando miró alrededor, había matas de maíz por todas partes. 59 Ya estaba lista la milpa.

60 —Quédate aquí por ahora. 61 Vas a la casa en la tarde. 62 Cuando vayas, cortas algunos elotes y los traes para que coma él.

63 —Bueno —dijo el joven.

64 Él estaba contento. 65 Se quedó. 66 Esperó hasta la tarde. 67 Entonces se fue a la casa.

68 Cuando llegó a la casa, trajo los elotes.

69 —Aquí traigo elotes para que comas ahora —le dijo al rey.

55 Orze' gugyita'ñ nasa'ñ. 56 Ze' na «Weshte na», na'ñ raba'ñ fiñ ze'.

57 «O», na ga'ñ orze'.

58 Ornu bgüiiñ, se zi la za gyel. 59 Bi guc la gyel orze'. 60 Orze' «Byeeñ la ru na. 61 Yeed ru or gudze. 62 Orze' cyug ru za' gyed nur gom», i na ga'ñ raba'ñ ñgyeeñ ze'.

63 «O», na ga' fiñ ze'.

64 Orze' yet lagy ñi. 65 Byeeña'ñ orze'. 66 Orze' blez ñii gudze. 67 Gaze' nu yaañ.

68 Na ornu briiñ na, bi bri nuñ za'.

69 «Ii bi yap tu za' gor na», na ga'ñ raba'ñ rey ze'.

70 "We have really acquired a competent son-in-law now," said the king again.

71 "What would our competent son-in-law be if Lucecita had not done that? 72 What would our son-in-law be?" she said again to the king.

73 But the king didn't hear her. 74 She said it under her breath.

75 Another day dawned. Lucecita had already told the young man to prepare himself.

76 "If my father tells you to go break the branches off a coconut tree, say 'Okay'. 77 Climb up the tree. 78 Break all of its branches off. 79 And you are to pick all of the ripe coconuts. 80 Only don't cut the bud at its tip, because that is me," she said.

81 "Okay," said the young man.

82 Once more *the king* told *his son-in-law*, "Go break off the branches of the coconut tree."

70 —Ahora sí tenemos un yerno listo —dijo el rey.

71 —¿Qué sería de nuestro yerno listo si Lucecita no hubiera hecho eso? 72 ¿Que sería nuestro yerno? —le dijo ella al rey.

73 Pero el rey no la oyó. 74 Ella estaba hablando en voz baja.

75 Entonces amaneció otro día. Lucecita le avisó al joven que se preparará.

76 —Si te dice mi papá que vayas a cortar las ramas de ese palmar, le dices que sí. 77 Entonces te subes al palmar, 78 cortas todas las ramas, 79 y cortas todos los cocos tiernos. 80 Pero el cogollo de punta, ése no lo cortas, porque ése soy yo —dijo ella.

81 —Bueno —dijo el joven.

82 Una vez más el rey le dijo a su yerno:

—Ve a cortar las ramas de ese palmar.

70 «Na gaal guud tub ngudz lily na na», na ga' rey.

71 «¿La ngudz lily na la ti cue' Lusesit ricy ñi nde'? 72 ¿La ngudz?» rnii ga'm raaba'm rey orze'.

73 Ni wagyeñ rey. 74 Nañ gyid ru' zi'l lam rnii ga'm nde'.

75 Orze' bza' yu tuuba' dzi na, orze' Lusesit bi mniiñ lo fiñ gyeey ze' orze' nu gzu lily ñii.

76 «Benu nii uza̱ nu char lag ru yaa ya coc re, orze' 'O' la niir. 77 Orze' chup ru lo ya coc. 78 Glag ru dela yaañ. 79 Nunu dela coc re'ñ re glag ru. 80 Par stub ngüicy loñ, nde' cue' shi'ñ ru, gun nde' ya̱», naañ.

81 «O», na ga' fiñ gyeey ze' orze'.

82 Orze' na ga' mi ze' nu

«Char lag ru yaa ya coc», na'm rab mi ngudz mi orze'.

83 "Okay," he said.

84 He went and climbed the coconut tree. 85 When he arrived at the top, he broke off all of the branches of the coconut tree. 86 He picked all of the ripe coconuts. 87 The only thing he didn't break off was the bud at the tip. 88 He grabbed hold of the bud tightly. 89 He sat on it.

90 "I have really acquired a competent son-in-law now. 91 Might he not win Lucecita?" said the king.

92 "What would your competent son-in-law be if not for Lucecita? 93 What would your son-in-law be?" she said again.

94 Another day, "Go beat that mule," said the king.

95 "Okay," he said.

83 —Bueno —le dijo.

84 Se fue y se subió al palmar. 85 Llegando, quebró todas las ramas del palmar. 86 Bajó todos los cocos tiernos. 87 Lo único que no bajó fue el cogollo de la punta. 88 Lo agarró con fuerza. 89 Se sentó sobre él.

90 —Ahora si tengo un yerno listo. 91 ¿No ganará a Lucecita? —dijo el rey.

92 —¿Qué sería tu yerno si no fuera por Lucecita? 93 Qué sería de tu yerno —decía la viejecita.

94 Otro día dijo el rey:
—Ve a golpear a esa mula.
95 —Bueno —dijo él.

83 «O», na ga'ñ orze'.

84 Zañ gup ñi lo ya coc. 85 Orze' bru'ñañ blag ñi dela yaa ya coc. 86 Dela coc re'ñ blag ñi. 87 Stub ngüicy loñ, nde' wanlag ñi nde'. 88 Nicy bdu' yaañ ngüicy. 89 Lo nde' zub ñi. 90 Orze' la

«Na gaal la guud ngudz lilya. 91 Na gaal la wabee ga' na gyicy yu gan Lusesit», i na ga'm orze'.

92 «¿La ngudz lily ru la ti cue' Lusesit? 93 ¿La ngudz ru?» rnii ga'm orze'.
94 Ze' na tuuba' dzi orze'
«Gua gaaz ru muly re», na ga' rey orze'.
95 «O», na'ñ.

96 He went to beat the mule. 97 Yes, Lucecita had already told him to not remove its bridle, but only to beat it. 98 It had a saddle. 99 He was to remove all of the tack and cast it aside. 100 Lucecita said that only the bridle was not to be cast aside. 101 He did this. 102 He went and beat it. 103 How he began to beat it and beat it! 104 He cast aside all of the tack.

105 "Remove its bridle and cast it aside," said the king.

106 He didn't say anything. 107 But he more strongly adhered to the bridle as he stood there. 108 How he beat it! 109 He hit all over its head, all over its ears, all over those places. 110 After that it was over.

111 "We have really acquired a competent son-in-law now. 112 Might he not succeed in possibly taking our Lucecita?" the old man said once more.

96 Fue a golpear a la mula. 97 La misma Lucecita lo había dicho que no le quitara el freno de la mula, síno que nada más le pegara. 98 La mula estaba ensillada. 99 El iba a quitar toda la montura y tirarla. 100 Lucecita le dijo que sólo el freno no debía tirar. 101 Así lo hizo él entonces. 102 Fue y golpeó a la mula. 103 Empezó golpearla y golpearla. 104 Tiró toda la montura.

105 —Quita el freno y tíralo —le dijo el rey.

106 Él no contestó nada. 107 Pero se asió con fuerza del freno mientras estaba parado allá. 108 ¡Cómo golpeó a la mula! 109 Le pegó en la cabeza, las orejas y en todas partes. 110 Y después, terminó.

111 —Ahora sí tenemos un yerno listo. 112 Ahora sí creo que será posible que se lleve a nuestra Lucecita —dijo el rey una vez más.

96 Za'ñ za gaaz ñi muly. 97 Laaba' Lusesit bi bee ga'ñ rishloñ orze' nu cue' nu coñ fren ni ma ze' nu gaaz zi'l lañ ma ze'. 98 Yu' shily ma ze'. 99 Dela shily ze', dela co zañ ne'ñ. 100 Par se tub fren ni ma ze' cue' ne'ñ, mnii Lusesit. 101 Ni bicya'ñ orze'. 102 Gua'ñ bgaaza'ñ ma ze' orze'. 103 La brugyi' rgaaz ñi ma, rgaaz ñi ma. 104 Dela shily dela mne'ñ.

105 «Bloo fren ni ma mne'», na ga' rey ze'.

106 Wagnii lañ. 107 Orze' fert zi'l nash ñii fren ze' zuñ. 108 Par ti laca' la bgaaz ñi ma ze'. 109 Dela too ma, dela lo gyidag ma, dela pshet ñi. 110 Orze' ni zi'l bded nde' orze'.

111 «Na gaal la guud tub ngudz lily na. 112 Labee na la wabee gyicy yu gan cha nuy Lusesit nin», rnii ga' biñ gyeey ze' orze'.

113 "What would your son-in-law be, if Lucecita had not done that? 114 What would he be to you?" she said. 115 That is what she said. 116 "What would he be to you?" she had said.

117 But again the old man didn't hear her. 118 That was the end of all of that.

119 Then *Lucecita and her husband* began to agree that they should go to his house. 120 Once more the old man said to him, "Go dry the well with a broken water jug."

121 "I will go," he said.

122 The next day he took to the trail. 123 He went. 124 When he got there, he sat down. 125 He sat there crying. 126 When lunch time came, his lunch arrived. 127 He was sitting there crying.

128 "Why are you crying?" asked Lucecita.

113 —Qué fuera de tu yerno si no hubiera hecho Lucecita eso? 114 ¿Qué sería para ti? —dijo ella. 115 Eso es lo que decía ella—. 116 ¿Qué sería para ti? —decía ella.

117 Pero, una vez más, el viejo no la escuchó. 118 Y así terminó todo eso.

119 Entonces empezaron ellos a ponerse de acuerdo para irse a su casa. 120 Una vez más volvió a decir el rey:

—Ve a secar ese pozo con un cántaro roto.

121 —Ya voy —dijo.

122 El siguiente día se fue otra vez. 123 Se fue. 124 Llegando allí, se sentó. 125 Se sentó a llorar. 126 Cuando llegó la hora de la comida, llegó su comida. 127 Estaba sentado llorando.

128 —¿Por qué lloras? —le dijo Lucecita.

113 «¿La ngudz ru la ti cue' Lusesit ricy ñi nde'? 114 ¿la ru?» na ga' mi ze'. 115 Ni raj. 116 «¿La ru?» rnii ga'm orze'.

117 Orze' ni zi'l, biñ gush ze' wagyeñ mi. 118 Orze' na ni zi'l blazh dela nu nde'.

119 Orze' nu brugyi' rsaap fiñ ze' riidz nu Lusesit nu gya deñ yu'ñ. 120 Ze' na mnii ga'm nu

«Char cuiigy ru zo re nu tub re' la'», naa ga'm raaba'm ñii.

121 «Cha», naa ga'ñ orze'.

122 Gush neza'ñ zañ tuuba' dzi. 123 Orze' zañ. 124 Bri'ñ ze', gusuba'ñ. 125 Ruuna'ñ zuba'ñ ze'. 126 Byap or cui na, bru'ña ga' cuiñ. 127 Ruun ñi zuba'ñ.

128 «¿Lagu ruun ru?» naa ga' Lusesit.

129 "How should I not cry? 130 *Your father* said that I should dry the well of water with a broken water jug. 131 What should I do? 132 This is a broken water jug. 133 What will I do for the well to dry up?" he asked.

134 "You don't have anything to worry about. 135 Eat your food fast. 136 After that you are to go to sleep," said Lucecita.

137 "Okay," he said.

138 He ate his food. 139 After eating, "Go to sleep now," said Lucecita.

140 "Okay," he said.

141 He laid down and slept. 142 He only slept for a little bit. 143 Then Lucecita woke him up. 144 When he looked around, the well had already dried up.

129 —¿Cómo no voy a llorar? 130 Él dijo que tengo que secar el pozo de agua con un cántaro roto. 131 ¿Qué voy a hacer? 132 Este es un cántaro roto. 133 ¿Cómo le voy a hacer para secar el agua del pozo? —dijo.

134 —No tienes que preocuparte. 135 Come las tortillas rápido. 136 Terminando eso, te duermes —dijo Lucecita.

137 —Bueno —dijo.

138 Comió sus tortillas. 139 Después de comer, le dijo Lucecita: —Duérmete ahora.

140 —Bueno —dijo. 141 Se acostó a dormir. 142 Nada más durmió un ratito. 143 Entonces lo despertó Lucecita. 144 Cuando miró alrededor, ya estaba seco el pozo.

129 «¿Ca wadun ya? 130 Ze' mniiy nu cuiigya nis nu re' la'. 131 Ze' ¿lac gyicya? 132 Ze' re' la' nu nii. 133 ¿Lac gyicya cuigy nis ii?» na ga'ñ.

134 «Wagad nu gyicy ru cuen. 135 Dzach ru bdow gyit. 136 Lazh ze' gas ru», naa ga' Lusesit orze'.

137 «O», na'ñ.

138 Orze' bdowa'ñ gyit. 139 Blazh bdoñ gyit «Ptaas na», na Lusesit.

140 «O», na'ñ.

141 Gugyit ñi nas ñi. 142 Tub miiñ zi'l ptaas ñi. 143 Orze' pcueeñ Lusesit ñi. 144 Ornu bgüiiñ, bi bigy zo ze'.

145 "Remain here now. 146 You are to come home in the afternoon. 147 Then you are to say to him that the water has all dried up," she said.

148 "Okay," said the young man.

149 He was very happy. 150 He stayed there. 151 He waited until the afternoon. 152 Then he went home. 153 Now when he arrived home, *he said,* "The water has dried up."

154 "We have really acquired a competent son-in-law now," said the old man.

155 "What would your son-in-law be if not for Lucecita? 156 What would your son-in-law be?" said the old woman.

157 So he finished doing all of that.

158 "Now let's go to my home, because now I have finished all of the things that your father told me to do."

145 —Quédate ahora. 146 Entonces vas a la casa en la tarde, 147 y le dices a él que ya se secó el agua —dijo ella.

148 —Bueno —dijo el joven.

149 Estaba muy contento. 150 Se quedó. 151 Esperó hasta la tarde. 152 Y entonces se fue a la casa. 153 Cuando llegó, dijo:
—Se secó el agua.

154 —Ahora sí tenemos un yerno listo —dijo el rey.

155 —¿Qué sería de tu yerno si no fuera por Lucecita? 156 ¿Qué sería tu yerno? —dijo la vieja.

157 Así, él terminó de hacer todas esas cosas.

158 —Ahora vamos a mi casa, porque ya terminé todas las cosas que me dijo tu papá que hiciera —dijo él.

145 «Byeeñ la ru na. 146 Orze' or gudze yeed ru. 147 Orze' niir lom nu bi bigy nis», na ga'ñ.

148 «O», na ga' fiñ gyeey ze'.

149 Yet lagy ñi. 150 Byeeñ ñi orze'. 151 Blez ñii gudze. 152 Gaze' nu yaañ. 153 Na ornu briiñ na,
«Bigy nis», i na ga'ñ.

154 «Na gaal la guud tub ngudz lily na beni», naa ga'm.

155 «¿La ngudz ru la ti cue' Lusesit? 156 ¿La ngudz ru?» rnii ga'm.

157 Orze' ni zi'l dela nde' blazh bicy ñi.

158 Orze' la nu
«Par na gyan na, gun na blazh dela coz nu mnii uz ru bicya», naañ.

159 "Let's go then," said Lucecita. 160 "But will you really take me home with you? 161 Isn't it the case that you are lying to me? 162 The day might come when you will forget me."

163 "But why should I forget you? 164 I came seeking you because that is what is in my heart. 165 And your father did unreasonable things to me for that reason. 166 Why should I forget you?" he said to Lucecita.

167 "Let's go then. 168 Go find a thin horse, one that is as thin as can be. 169 Put a saddle on it, so that we can ride it, because then my father will not catch up with us."170 "Okay," said her husband.

159 —Vamos pues —dijo Lucecita—. 160 ¿Pero de verdad me llevas a tu casa? 161 ¿Qué no me estás engañando? 162 Llegará un día en que te olvidarás de mí —dijo Lucecita.

163 —¿Pero por qué me voy a olvidar de ti, 164 siendo que yo quise venir a buscarte? 165 Y por eso, ¡cuántas cosas hizo tu papá conmigo! 166 ¿Por qué me voy a olvidar de ti? —le dijo él a Lucecita.

167 —Vamos, pues. 168 Entonces ve a buscar un caballo, el más flaco que haya. 169 Lo ensillas, porque lo vamos a montar, para que no nos vaya a alcanzar mi papá —le dijo ella a su esposo.

170 —Bueno —dijo su esposo.

159 «Gyan beni», na Lusesit. 160 «¿Par a lyar rishli gya nur ya? 161 ¿A walab nu rguur ya? 162 Shuub dzi nit lagy ru ya», na Lusesit.

163 «Par ¿lagu nit lagya ru? 164 Par nde' ru' nu pcaa lagya nu byap yuba ru. 165 Nunu par nde' nu blazh coz nu bicy uz ru nuy ya. 166 ¿Lagu nit lagya ru?» na ga'ñ raba'ñ Lusesit.

167 «Gyan beni. 168 Orze' char cha yub ru tub cuay rit nu blaazha' la cuay rit. 169 Cu'r shily ma, gun orze' gyub na ma, gun cue' nu cyid cheel uza uub na», na ga'ñ raba'ñ ñgyeeñ.

170 «O», na ga' ñgyeeñ ze'.

171 But he didn't obey her.
172 He caught a fat horse.
173 He put a saddle on it.
174 Then they took to the trail
and went on their way. 175 *Before they left*, she put her saliva in
three places. 176 She put it on
the door post to her room.
177 Then they took to the trail
and went.

178 Now when the old woman
knew, she began to say *to her husband*: "Get up and look in on Lucecita, because she has left."

179 "How could she have
gone? 180 She is lying there quietly sleeping. 181 You are acting
bad," he said.

182 "She has gone I say," said
the woman.

183 "She is lying there I say,"
said the man.

184 He began to yell for
Lucecita.

185 "Lucecita," he said.

186 "What is it?" she said.

187 "Are you there?" he said.

171 Pero él no la obedeció.
172 Cogió un caballo gordo,
173 y lo ensilló. 174 Entonces se
fueron. 175 Ella puso saliva en
tres lugares. 176 Puso su saliva
debajo de la puerta de su
cuarto. 177 Entonces se fueron.

178 Pero cuando lo supo la
mujer, empezó a decir a su
esposo:

—Levántate a ver a nuestra
hija, Lucecita, porque ya se fue.

179 —¿Cómo puede ser que
se haya ido? 180 Está durmiendo tranquilamente allá.
181 Eres mala —le dijo a su
mujer.

182 —Ya se fue, te digo —le
dijo la mujer.

183 —Está acostada, te digo
—le contestó el hombre.

184 Entonces empezó a llamar a gritos a Lucecita.

185 —Lucecita —decía.

186 —Qué quieres? —contestaba ella.

187 —¿Estás allí? —decía.

171 Na fiñ ze' wangyeñ ñi. 172 Cuay re'ñ bdub ñi. 173 Orze' bdu'ñ shily
ma ze'. 174 Gaze' nu gush nez deñ yaañ. 175 Guañ pshuñ chon se'.
176 Pshuñ nis yeñ ñi nañ ya ro' niñ. 177 Gaze' nu gush nez ñi yaañ.

178 Na ornu gud lagy biñ mñaa na, orze' la brugyi' rniim nu:

«Weshte güiir Lusesit nin, gun bi yaañ», rniim rab mi ñgyeem.

179 «¿La gya' fiñ ze'? 180 Nas ñi ri byub. 181 Shiñ riib ru», naa ga'm
raaba'm biñ mñaa ze'.

182 «Bi yaañ rnee», rnii ga' biñ mñaa ze'.

183 «Riib ñi rnee», rnii ga' biñ gyeey.

184 Orze' brugyi' rbish ti num Lusesit.

185 «Lusesit», rnii ga'm.

186 «¿Lagu?» rnii ga'ñ.

187 «¿A riib ru?» rnii ga'm.

188 "I am here," she said.

189 But it was only her saliva *speaking*. 190 It was speaking from inside the door posts. 191 Little by little as her saliva dried, she began to speak weakly.

192 "Fool! 193 You sure are a fool. 194 Get up. 195 Look in on Lucecita," I say.

196 "Unfortunately, you are the fool. 197 Where would Lucecita go? 198 Well, I say that she is there. How could she be speaking *if she has gone*?" he asked.

199 "They are not there I say. 200 Why has her speech become so weak then? 201 Hurry up! 202 Go look. 203 She is not there." 204 "Okay," said the man.

205 Then he *got up* and went to look in her room. 206 When he looked, who would still be there? 207 Only her saliva was there. 208 And that was already drying. 209 The woman acted very upset.

188 —Sí, aquí estoy —decía ella.

189 Pero sólo estaba la saliva de ella. 190 Hablaba como si estuviera debajo de la puerta. 191 Poco a poco, conforme se iba secando la saliva, la voz sonaba más débil.

192 —¡Que tonto eres! 193 De veras eres muy tonto. 194 Levántate. 195 Mira a nuestra hija Lucecita —le dijo entonces.

196 —¡Ah! Tonto éste. 197 ¿A dónde se iría Lucecita? 198 Yo te digo que está acostada allí. ¿Si no, por qué habla ella pues? —dijo el rey.

199 —Te digo que no está aquí. 200 ¿Por qué ya habla más quedo ahora, pues? 201 Rápido. 202 Ve a verla. 203 No está allá.

204 —Bueno, pues —dijo el hombre.

205 Y se fue a ver al cuarto de ella. 206 Cuando miró él, no había nadie. 207 Nada más la saliva estaba. 208 Y ya estaba secándose. 209 Entonces la mujer se enojó mucho.

188 «Riba», rnii ga'ñ orze'.

189 Se' nis yeñ ziñ ze'. 190 Rnii nde' nguaañ nañ ya ro'. 191 Niga, niga ornu bi rbigy nis yeñ ñi, shni rnii ga'ñ orze'. 192 Orze' la «A pendef. 193 Dzi ga pendef nar. 194 Weshte. 195 Güiir Lusesit nin rnee», naa ga'm.

196 Orze' «Maasa' zir pendef ru. 197 ¿Ca za Lusesit? 198 Gunca ya rnee riib ñi rnee la, ¿lagu rniiñ beni?» naa ga'm.

199 «Saca'ñ rnee. 200 ¿Lagu byashni rniiñ beni? 201 Dzach ru. 202 Yaa güiir. 203 Saca'ñ.»,

204 «O beni», naa ga' biñ gyeey ze'.

205 Gaze' nu gush nez mi ya güiim nañ cuart niñ. 206 Ornu bgüiim, ¿cyu ru' cuic ñi? 207 Se nis yeñ ziñ nguaa ze'. 208 Bi rbigy la nde' orze'. 209 Orze' la nu rdza' biñ mñaa la dzi ricy mi.

210 "As quick as possible, 211 Follow her now. 212 Catch a thin horse. 213 Go now, so that you might catch up with them," she said.

214 "Okay," said the man.

215 Then he caught a thin horse. 216 He put a saddle on it. 217 He took to the trail and went. 218 He went and went and went. 219 It dawned. 220 Then the sun came up. 221 He went thinking that there was no way he would meet Lucecita. 222 Then he arrived *at a place*. 223 When noon came, he arrived *at a place* where there was an orange tree. 224 He thought, "Ah, orange tree, you sure are pretty sitting here. 225 As for me, I am so unfortunate. 226 I am so sad. 227 Where has my daughter Lucecita gone? 228 If you could only speak, you would advise me. 229 Did my daughter Lucecita pass by here?"

210 —Lo más pronto que puedas, 211 anda a seguirla. 212 Lleva el caballo flaco. 213 Anda ahora, y trata de alcanzarla —dijo ella.

214 —Bueno —dijo el hombre.

215 Despues, él agarró el caballo flaco, 216 lo ensilló. 217 Tomó el camino y se fue. 218 Caminó, caminó, y caminó. 219 Llegó el amanecer. 220 Poco a poco salió el sol. 221 Siguió sin esperanza de alcanzar a Lucecita. 222 Llegó *a un lugar*. 223 Al mediodía, llegó a donde estaba un naranjal. 224 Entonces pensó —¡Hay naranjal! Que chulo estás. 225 Pero yo, ¡pobre de mí! 226 Tengo mucho remordimiento. 227 ¿A dónde se fue mi hija Lucecita? 228 Si tú pudieras hablar, me dirías. 229 ¿Por aquí pasó mi hija Lucecita? —le dijo al naranjal.

210 «Dzach zir. 211 Gua ca iich ñi na. 212 Bdub cuay rit. 213 Gua na, gun trat nu dzeel ruñ», na ga'm orze'.

214 «O», na ga' biñ gyeey.

215 Gaze' nu bdub mi cuay rit ze'. 216 Bdu'm shily ma ze'. 217 Gush nez mi zam. 218 Za mi, za mi, za mi, zam. 219 Bza' yu. 220 Niga briib doo. 221 Zam ni mod la nu dzeel mi Lusesit. 222 Ze' na gaze' nu bru'ñam. 223 Byap or wi doo, bru'ñam zub tub ya lazh. 224 Orze' rsa' lagy mi: «Ah ya lazh, cyit ga na ru zub ru. 225 Par ya, dzi ga cuaa. 226 Dzi ga ricya sentiir. 227 ¿Ca za Lusesit ne? 228 Be bicy na nu ru nu gac niir, gyoor riidz. 229 ¿A ii bded Lusesit ne?» na'm rab mi ya lazh.

230 He was very sad as he looked at the orange tree. 231 He looked at where the orange tree sat. 232 There was only one orange on it. 233 "If only that orange would come down so I could eat it. 234 What should I do for it to come down? 235 It is so hot," he thought as he sat there.

236 His horse was standing by him as he sat there.

237 "Ah orange tree, you sure bring enjoyment with you as you sit here. 238 But I sure am sad in my heart because my daughter has gone away," he said. 239 "It would be best if I go home. 240 I am so unfortunate. 241 I will not go on, because I will not meet her again. 242 She has gone away. 243 I will not meet her again," he said.

230 Estaba muy triste mirando al naranjal. 231 Miraba hacía donde estaba el naranjal. 232 Sólo tenía una naranja. 233 "¡Cómo quisiéramos que cayera esa naranja! 234 ¿Qué haremos para que caiga? 235 Hace mucho calor" pensaba él mientras estaba sentado allí.

236 Su caballo estaba junto a él.

237 —¡Hay naranjal, que dichoso estás aquí! 238 Pero yo tengo mucha tristeza en mi corazón, porque se fue mi hija —decía él—. 239 Sería mejor que me fuera a casa. 240 ¡Pobre de mí! 241 Ya no seguimos, porque ya no la alcanzaremos. 242 Ya se fue. 243 Ya no la alcanzaremos —dijo.

230 Orze' shni ricya'm rgüii ga'm lo ya lazh ze' orze'. 231 Rgüiim zub ya lazh. 232 Tub zi la lazh niñ ca. 233 Orze' «dzi la bi bet lazh re don. 234 ¿Lac gyicy na gyet nde? 235 Tanta' nu zig», rsa' lagy mi zub mi orze'.

236 Zu cuay nim lom zub mi.

237 «Ah ya lazh, dzi ga nur gusht ga zub ru ii. 238 Par ya dzi ga shni rac nañ lardoo nu za i'ña», naa ga'm orze'. 239 «Nap zir nu gya la ub na. 240 Cuaa ya. 241 Waya ga'n, gun wadzeela' ub na fiñ ze'. 242 Bi za fiñ ze'. 243 Wadzeela'n ñi», na ga'm.

244 He returned home with his horse. 245 The orange tree remained behind. 246 After that, he went home. 247 He arrived home that very same day. 248 Now when he first arrived, "Did you meet her?" asked the old woman.

249 "I didn't meet her," he said. 250 "I didn't see anything. 251 I met no one, not a single person. 252 I only saw a single orange tree sitting in the roadway. 253 I rested underneath it. 254 When noon came, I rested underneath it. 255 That is all I saw," he said.

256 "Oh fool! 257 Why didn't you speak to it so that you could bring it home? 258 Because that was our daughter Lucecita. 259 The orange tree was the young man. 260 The orange was Lucecita. 261 You should have beaten it, or you should have picked the orange and brought it home.

244 Entonces regresó a su casa con su caballo. 245 El naranjal se quedó atrás. 246 Y se fue a casa. 247 Llegó a la casa ese mismo día. 248 En cuanto llegó, le dijo la mujer:

—¿La alcanzaste?

249 —No la alcancé —dijo él—. 250 No vi nada. 251 Ni gente vi, a nadie encontré. 252 Sólo vi un naranjal que estaba en el camino. 253 Debajo de él descansé. 254 Cuando llegó el mediodía, descansé debajo del naranjal. 255 Eso fue lo único que yo vi —dijo él entonces.

256 —¡Qué tonto! 257 ¿Por qué no hablaste con el naranjal para que lo trajeras? 258 Porque esa naranja es nuestra hija Lucecita. 259 El naranjal es el hombre. 260 Y esa naranja era Lucecita. 261 Lo hubieras golpeado, o hubieras traído esa naranja.

244 Orze' bish cya'm ya nu'm cuay nim orze'. 245 Byeeñ ya lazh ze' orze'. 246 Ni zi'l yam. 247 Orze' brim yu' laab dzi ze'. 248 Na laab brim na, orze'

«¿A bdzeel ruñ?» na ga' biñ mñaa?

249 «Wancheela ñii», na ga'm orze'. 250 «Se la la coz bzaaca. 251 Ni mbecy, ni se cyu la bdzeela. 252 Nomaas tub zi la ya lazh zub ñi gyernez. 253 Gyi' nde' bzu lagya. 254 Ornu byap or wi doo bzu lagya gyi' nde'. 255 Nomaas nde' bzaaca», naa ga'm orze'.

256 «A pendef! 257 ¿Lagu wannii nur nde' ñgyeed nur ñii? 258 Gun nde' Lusesit nin. 259 Ya lazh ze', nde' na fiñ gyeey ze'. 260 Ze' lazh ze', nde' Lusesit. 261 Nde' ngaaz ruñ o lazh ze', nde' nlag ru ñgyeed nur.

262 If the young man did not want to come, at least you should have brought back our daughter Lucecita. 263 You should have at least brought our daughter Lucecita back. 264 You should have beaten it. 265 Then it would have turned into a person. 266 You should have brought her back. 267 You sure are a fool!" she said.

268 "But I will go," she said.

269 "Whatever you say. 270 If you are going, then go. 271 But I will not go, because we will not meet her again," he said.

272 "I will go," said the woman

273 Again, she caught a thin horse. 274 Again, she put on its saddle. 275 Then she took to the trail and went a long way. 276 Now when she was very close to where Lucecita was, Lucecita knew that she was approaching. 277 Then she said to her husband,

262 Por lo menos hubieras traído Lucecita, si el hombre no quería regresar. 263 Debías haber traído a nuestra hija Lucecita. 264 Le hubieras pegado el naranjal. 265 Entonces se hubiera convertido en gente. 266 La hubieras traído. 267 ¡Qué tonto eres! —dijo la mujer entonces.

268 —Ahora, yo voy —dijo ella entonces.

269 —Lo que tú digas. 270 Si quieres ir, anda. 271 Pero yo, ya no voy, porque ya no los alcanzaremos —dijo él entonces.

272 —Ya me voy —dijo la mujer.

273 Agarró el caballo flaco. 274 Lo ensilló. 275 Tomó el camino, y se fue, anduvo y anduvo. 276 Cuando estaba muy cerca del lugar donde estaba Lucecita, Lucecita supo que ella andaba cerca. 277 Entonces le dijo a su marido:

262 Mas ñuu Lusesit nin ñgyeed nur, benu wangalagy fiñ gyeey ze' ñgyeed ñi.

263 Par mas ñuu Lusesit nin ñgyeed nur. 264 Ngaaz ruñ. 265 Orze' ñgyac fiñ ze' mbecy. 266 Ñgyeed nur ñii. 267 Dzi ga pendef nar», naa ga' biñ mñaa ze' orze'.

268 «Par cha ya», naa ga'm orze'.

269 «Ru nar. 270 Benu char, gua. 271 Par ya waya ga', gun wadzeela' ub na fiñ ze'», na ga' mi ze' orze'.

272 «Cha», naa ga' biñ mñaa.

273 Bduba'm tuuba' cuay rit. 274 Orze' bdu' ga' lam shily ma. 275 Gush neza' lam, za mi, za mi, za mi, za mi. 276 Na ornu tanta' la nu bi rgaab mi ze' nu za Lusesit, orze' fiñ ze' bi gud lagy ñi nu za gaab mi. 277 Orze' nañ rab ñi ñgyeeñ:

"You sure are foolish! 278 Why did you catch a fat horse? 279 I said that you were to bring a thin horse, because then they would not have caught up with us, I say. 280 Now mother is already coming."

281 "Now what should we do?" he asked.

282 "What should we do? 383 I will decide what to do," said Lucecita.

284 She had a new comb with her. 285 Taking it out she put it down on the trail. 286 Then they went away. 287 They were able to continue *on their journey*.

288 Now when the old woman arrived, "Why is the sensitive plant growing in the roadway?" *she thought.* 289 Then she began to beat the sensitive plant.

290 "Lucecita you fool, let's go home. 291 Why are you sitting *there* like that? 292 Let's go as quickly as possible," she said.

—¡Qué tonto eres! 278 ¿Por qué agarraste el caballo gordo? 279 Yo te dije que trajeras un caballo flaco, porque así no nos hubieran alcanzado. 280 Ahora ya viene mi mamá— le dijo a su marido.

281 —¿Qué vamos a hacer ahora? —decía el hombre entonces.

282 —¿Qué haremos? 383 Ya veré como hago —dijo Lucecita.

284 Ella tenía un peine nuevo. 285 Sacando ella el peine nuevo, lo puso en el camino. 286 Y siguieron su camino. 287 Lograron seguir.

288 Cuando llegó la mujer, dijo:

—¿Por qué hay espina vergonzosa en el camino? 289 Y allí empezó ella a pegarle a la espina vergonzosa.

290 —Lucecita tonta. ¡Vámonos ! 291 ¿Por qué estás sentada así? 292 Vámonos lo más pronto posible —dijo ella.

«Dzi ga ton nar. 278 ¿Lagu cuay re'ñ bdub ru? 279 Gunca ya̱ rnee cuay rit ñgyiid nur, gun orze' wayid cheel dem uub na rnee. 280 Na bi yad la ña̱a na», na ga'ñ raba'ñ ñgyeeñ.

281 «¿Par lac gyicy na na?» na ga' fiñ gyeey orze'.

282 «¿Lac gyicy na? 383 Ya̱ güii̱ lac gyicya̱», naa ga' Lusesit.

284 Orze' ze' bi nuuñ tub beg cub. 285 Bloo za laañ beg cub briish lañ gyernez orze'. 286 Za deñ orze'. 287 Bicy deñ gan zañ.

288 Na ornu bru'ña biñ mñaa ze' na, orze' ¿lagu gyech to' lo nash ñi gyernez? 289 La ze' la brugyi' rgaaz mi gyech to' lo.

290 «Lusesit pendef, yaa gyan. 291 ¿Lagu ni zub ru? 292 Dzach zir yaa», na ga'm.

293 She beat the sensitive plant. 294 She beat the sensitive plant. 295 It wouldn't become a person at all.

296 "Fool! You sure are bad. 297 I have come to take you *home*, I say. 298 Now you are being troublesome by not wanting to come home," she said.

299 She exerted herself and passed through the sensitive plant. 300 She went on her way. 301 All the while Lucecita was going along. 302 The old lady went along ways. 303 Now she was very close to Lucecita. 304 Then Lucecita said,

"You unfortunate fellow. 305 Will you really take me home with you? 306 Will my mother now die because of you? 307 Because my mother is now approaching close by. 308 There appears to be no other way out. 309 We do not have anywhere to hide. 310 Are you sure that you have really decided to take me home with you? 311 Because my mother will die now because of you," she said.

293 Y le pegó a la espina vergonzosa. 294 Le pegó a la espina vergonzosa. 295 Pero, con todo, no se convertía en gente.

296 —Tonta, que mala eres, 297 porque yo vengo a traerte. 298 Ahora estás jugando conmigo porque no quieres ir —decía.

299 Hizo un esfuerzo para pasar entre las espinas vergonzosas. 300 Y siguió su camino. 301 Mientras tanto, Lucecita seguía su camino. 302 La vieja seguía el camino largo. 303 Ya se iba acercando ella a Lucecita. 304 Entonces dijo Lucecita:

—Pobre de ti. 305 ¿De veras me llevarás a casa contigo? 306 ¿Se morirá por tu causa mi mamá? 307 Porque ella ya viene cerca. 308 Parece que no hay forma de escapar. 309 Ya no hay donde ir a escondernos —dijo ella a su marido—. 310 ¿De veras has decidido llevarme a casa contigo? 311 Porque por tu causa se va a morir mi mamá —dijo ella a su esposo.

293 La rgaaz mi gyech to' lo. 294 Rgaaz mi gyech to' lo. 259 Tanta' nu wagyac ñi mbecy.

296 «Ah pendef dzi ga nar. 297 Gunca ya̱ yap te̱ ru rnee̱. 298 Ii na ricy ras ru nu walagy ru gyar», naa ga'm orze'.

299 Bicy mi fers bdeda'm lat gyech to' lo ze'. 300 Zam orze'. 301 Dub ni za Lusesit. 302 Za mi, za mi, zam. 303 Tanta' bi rgaab mi Lusesit na. 304 Orze' la nu nañ:

«Lashta ru. 305 ¿A lyar rishli yad nur ya̱? 306 ¿A par nu nac ru gat ñaa na? 307 Gun ñaa bi yad gaab mi. 308 Ze' na wabee ga' na. 309 Wada' ca cha cach lon», nañ rab ñi ñgyeeñ. 310 «¿A lyar rishli nap psa' lagy ru yad nur ya̱? 311 Gun par nu nac ru gat ñaa na», nañ rab ñi ñgyeeñ orze'.

312 "I have decided *to bring you home.* 313 Why would I have brought you if I had not thought about it? 314 I thought hard about bringing you home. 315 Why do you imply that I might abandon you? 316 What else would I do with you?" he asked.

317 "That is nothing, because my mother will die because of you," she said to her husband.

318 "What could we to do if she is to die? 319 If she is to die, there is really no other way. 320 It is best for us to go home," he said.

321 "Okay then," she said.

322 Her mother was already closely approaching. 323 Lucecita had a bar of new soap with her. 324 She took out the soap. 325 She put it on the ground. 326 Then she told him,

312 —Lo decidí. 313 ¿Por qué te traje si no lo hubiera pensado? 314 Pensé bastante en traerte. 315 ¿Por qué dices que te voy a dejar? 316 ¿Qué más voy a hacer contigo? —dijo el hombre entonces.

317 —Eso no es nada, porque mi mamá va a morir por medio de ti —dijo ella a su esposo.

318 —¿Qué haremos si se muere ella? 319 No hay remedio si se va a morir. 320 Será mejor que nos vayamos a casa —dijo el hombre entonces.

321 —Bueno pues —dijo ella.

322 Su mamá ya estaba muy cerca. 323 Pero Lucecita tenía una pieza de jabón nuevo. 324 Sacó el jabón nuevo. 325 Lo puso en el suelo. 326 Entonces dijo a su esposo:

312 Nap psa' lagya. 313 Par ¿lagu yap tu ru benu ya wanrusha shcab? 314 Nap brush ya shcab nu yap tu ru. 315 ¿Lagu nar nu gzaana ru? 316 O ¿la gyicy du ru?» na fiñ gyeey ze'.

317 Orze' «Se la la nde' beni, gun ya gat ñaa nu nac ru», na'ñ raba'ñ ñgyeeñ orze'.

318«La, ¿la gyicy na benu gat mi? 319 Nde' gaal la sac mod niñ benu gat mi. 320 Nap zir nu ub na cha lan», na ga' fiñ gyeey orze'.

321 «O beni», naañ.

322 Tanta' nu bi ya gaab ñaañ. 323 Orze' bi nuuñ tub cu'ñ yashtily cub. 324 Bloo lañ yashtily cub ze'. 325 Briish lañ za. 326 Orze' nañ rab ñi fiñ gyeey ze':

"You will become a frog. 327 You will be across the way there. 328 I will be on this side. 329 When she arrives, whatever she says, what ever she does, all you are to do is go, 'croak, croak, croak', on the lake. 330 Because this soap will become a lake," she said to her husband.

331 "Okay then," they said.

332 She put the new soap on the ground. 333 The *two of them* became frogs. 334 They settled on the lake. 335 The lake was already there when the old woman arrived. *She said to the lake,*

336 "O Lucecita, why are you here like this? 337 Let's go as quickly as possible."

338 She began to break off a switch to beat the lake. 339 She beat the lake. 340 She beat the lake for a long time. 341 But in no way would *Lucecita* become a person. 342 But the frogs went "croak, croak, croak" from each side of the lake.

—Te vas a convertir en rana. 327 Vas a estar al otro lado. 328 Y yo voy a estar en este otro lado, aquí. 329 Y cuando llegue ella, entonces cualquier cosa que ella diga, cualquier cosa que ella haga, entonces dices: "cua, cua, cua." 330 Porque este jabón se va a convertir en laguna —le dijo ella a su marido.

331 —Bueno pues —dijeron.

332 Ella puso el jabón nuevo en el suelo. 333 Entonces se convirtieron ellos en ranas. 334 Se metieron a la laguna. 335 Ya estaba la laguna allá cuando llegó mamá.

336 —¡Ay Lucecita! ¿por qué estás aquí? 337 Vámonos lo más pronto que puede —le dijo ella a Lucecita.

338 Cortó un palo y le pegó a la laguna. 339 Ella le pegó a la laguna. 340 Le pegó por mucho rato. 341 Pero de ninguna manera se convertía en gente. 342 Las ranas decían: "Cua, cua, cua". Estaban cada una al lado de la laguna.

«Ru gyac ru bigy. 327 Cuir tub la' ga' dzu re. 328 Ze' ya cui tub la' ga' ii. 329 Gun ornu ru'ñam, orze' mas la zi'l rniim, mas la zi'l ricy mi, orze' niir 'ngaay, ngaay, ngaay', zi'l gyicy ru cuir lo lagun ze' orze'. 330 Gun orze' yashtily ii, nii gyac ñi lagun», na ga'ñ raba'ñ ñgyeeñ.

331 «O beni», na deñ.

332 Briish lañ yashtily cub ze' za. 333 Orze' byac la deñ bigy. 334 Guchu' lañ lo lagun. 335 Bi ri lagun ornu bru'ña biñ mñaa ze'.

336 «A Lusesit, ¿lagu ni rir ii? 337 Dzach zir yaa gyan», nam rab mi Lusesit.

338 Brugyi' la rcyug mi laspeed rgaaz mi lagun. 339 Rgaaz mi lagun. 340 Tanta' nu guchi rgaaz mi lagun. 341 Orze' la ni mod la nu gyac ñi mbecy. 342 Bigy ze' «ngaay, ngaay, ngaay», ricya' ma ze' yu' ga' ma tub la' ga ru' lagun.

343 They didn't become people at all. 344 So the old lady put her mouth to the lake. 345 She drank from it. 346 She drank from the lake. 347 But the lake would not dry up at all. 348 Her belly burst. 349 She died right there.

350 Then the young ones turned into people again. 351 They took to the trail and went along. 352 They went along. 353 They went along. 354 Now when they were close to arriving at his home, *he said,* "Stay here, and I will go get a car, for us to get in to go to my father."

355 "I will not stay *here.* 356 Why should I? 357 Up until now we have come by foot. 358 We will arrive *at the place* where you are going. 359 It would be better if we went as we are," said Lucecita.

343 No se convertían en gente. 344 Entonces la mamá puso su boca en la laguna. 345 Estaba bebiéndose la laguna. 346 Estaba bebiéndose la laguna. 347 Pero no se acababa la laguna. 348 Se le reventó el estómago. 349 Allí nada más se murió.

350 Entonces ellos se convirtieron otra vez en gente. 351 Se pusieron en camino, y siguieron. 352 Se fueron. 353 Y se fueron. 354 Cuando ya estaban cerca de su pueblo entonces, dijo el esposo:

—Te quedas aquí, porque yo voy a traer el coche porque iremos en él hasta donde está mi papá —dijo él a su esposa.

355 —No me quedo. 356 ¿Por qué me voy a quedar? 357 Ya venimos a pie. 358 Llegaremos hasta donde tú vas. 359 Mejor que llegaremos así nada más —dijo Lucecita entonces.

343 Orze' tanta' nu wagyac ñi mbecy. 344 Orze' briib la ru'm lo lagun ze'. 345 Ro'm lagun. 346 Ro'm lagun. 347 Tanta' nu wacuigy lagun. 348 Briich lañ nañ mi. 349 Orze' ze' ga la gut mi orze'.

350 Orze' byaca' la de fiñ ze' mbecy. 351 Gush neza' la deñ yaañ orze'. 352 Yaa ñi. 353 Yaa ñi. 354 Na ornu bi bgaab nu griiñ ledz ñi na, orze' «Gyiyeeñ ru ii, gun ya cha cha gyi coch, gun chu'n gun gyan lo uza», naañ rab ñi mñaañ ze'.

355 «Wayiyeeña. 356 ¿Lagu ze'? 357 Nil bi yap ub na gyi'n. 358 Gri ub na gal ze' nu gya ru. 359 Nap zir nu gya lan i zi'l», na ga' Lusesit ze' orze'.

360 "No. Rather remain here.
361 Because it would be better
if we were in a car. 362 We
would enjoy the trip more. 363 I
will go to get the car. Then my
father and mother will come to
meet you. 364 I'll take a mes-
sage to my family so that they
bring the car," he said.

365 "Go then. 366 But you
will forget me when you arrive
at your house. 367 You will not
remember me any more," she
said to her husband.

368 "Why should I forget
you? 369 I want you to come
with me. 370 Why should I forget you?" he said.

371 "So you say, but let's see
if you will forget me or not," she
said.

372 "I will not forget," he
said.

360 —No, mejor quedate aquí.
361 Porque ser mejor si vamos en
coche. 362 Así lo gozaremos más.
363 Voy por el coche, para que
entonces vengan mi papá, y mi
mamá a encontrarte. 364 Voy a
dejar la razón a mi familia, para
que vengan con el coche —dijo
el.

365 —Ve entonces. 366 Pero
tú te vas a olvidar de mí cuando
llegues a tu casa. 367 Ya no te vas
a acordar de mí —dijo ella.

368 —¿Por qué me voy a olvidar de ti? 369 Yo quise que vinieras conmigo. 370 ¿Por qué me
voy a olvidar de ti? —dijo él
entonces.

371 —Tú dices eso, pero vamos a ver —dijo ella entonces.

372 —No me voy a olvidar de
ti —dijo él.

360 «A' par byeeñ la ii. 361 Gun nap zir cuin nañ coch. 362 Gusht zir
gyan orze'. 363 Gya la ya gya gyi coch, gun orze' niga cyid uza cyid ñaa,
cyid dey cyid cheel yu ru. 364 Gya la gya du rasoo lo de famil ne, gun cyid
nuy coch», na ga'ñ.

365 «Gyar beni. 366 Par ru nu gnit lagy ru ya ornu grir yu'r.
367 Wayeza' ga' lagy ru ya», naañ rab ñi ñgyeeñ.

368 «¿Lagu nit lagya ru? 369 Par nde' ru' nu rcaa lagya ru yap tu ru.
370 Ze' ¿lagu nit lagya ru?» na ga'ñ orze'.

371 «Na ub ru beni ze' benu nit lagy ru ya», naa ga'ñ orze'.

372 «Wanit lagya», naañ.

373 "Then I will stay. 374 Go on. 375 But when you arrive at your house, don't stand around and allow even one of your family to embrace you. 376 They should not embrace you," she told her husband. 377 "Don't allow them to embrace you, because if they embrace you, you will forget me," she said.

378 "Okay," he said.

379 He took to the trail going home. 380 Now when he arrived home, all his family came out to greet him. 381 He would not allow them to embrace him. 382 However, a servant came up behind him. 383 She embraced him from behind. 384 She caused him to forget Lucecita. 385 He completely forgot *her*. 386 It was as if his wife had never existed.

387 So he stayed in the house of his father. 388 He stayed at the house of his father for a long time. 389 Then his parents began to suggest that they should seek a wife for him.

373 —Me quedo pues —dijo ella. 374 Ve tú. 375 Pero eso sí, cuando llegues a tu casa, no permitas que te toque niguno de tu familia. 376 Que no te agarren —dijo ella a su esposo—. 377 No dejes que te agarren, porque si te agarran, entonces te olvidarás de mí —dijo.

378 —Bueno —dijo él.

379 Se fue a su casa.

380 Cuando llegó él a la casa, entonces todos los de su familia salieron a saludarlo. 381 Él no permitió que lo tocaran ellos. 382 Pero por detrás de él llegó un criado. 383 Lo agarró por detrás. 384 Eso hizo que se olvidara de Lucecita. 385 Se olvidó completamente. 386 Como si no tuviera esposo entonces.

387 Así estuvo él en la casa de su papá. 388 Ya tenía mucho tiempo de estar en la casa de su padre. 389 Entonces empezaron los viejos a decir que iban a pedir una esposa para él.

373 «Gyiyeeñ la̱ beni. 374 Yaa la ru», nañ orze'. 375 «Par esii ornu grir yu'r, a̱' zaan ru nu cu' yaa ni tub la de famil nir. 376 Cue' cu' yaam ru», na'ñ raba'ñ ñgyeeñ ze'. 377 «Cue' la zaan ru nu cu' yaa dem ru, gun ze' benu cu' yaam ru, orze' nu gnit lagy ru ya̱», naañ.

378 «O», na fiñ ze'.

379 Gush nez ñi yaañ. 380 Na ornu briiñ yu' na, orze' dela de famil niñ bruum nu rnii num ñii ñgyoozh. 381 Wansaan ñi nu ngu' yaa dem ñii. 382 Lac par ich ñi bru'ña tub criad. 383 Mi ze' bdu' yaam ñii par ich ñi. 384 Orze' nu bicy ñi nu mnit lagy ñi Lusesit. 385 Orze' mnit la lagy, mnit la lagy ñi. 386 Consefer wansu laa mñaañ orze'.

387 Ni zi'l zuñ yu' uz ñi. 388 Orze' tanta' nu gules zuñ yu' uz ñi. 389 Orze' nu brugyi' mnii ga' de biñ gush ze' nu yub mi mñaañ. 390 Orze'

390 "Okay," he said agreeing to get another wife.

391 After that they had the engagement ceremony.

392 Now Lucecita arrived at the town where the young man was. 393 She borrowed a house close by to live in. 394 After the engagement ceremony, she took to the trail and went to her mother-in-law. 395 When she arrived, *she said to her mother-in-law,* "I heard tell that there is a groom here who recently got married. 396 Therefore, give me *some cloth* so I can sew his clothing. 397 But don't take his measurements. 398 I will take the cloth just like it is. 399 I will cut it out over there."

400 But *the woman* didn't know that *Lucecita* was her daughter-in-law.

401 "Okay," she said.

390 —Bueno —dijo él estando de acuerdo en tener otra mujer.

391 Después se terminó la ceremonia del compromiso.

392 Entonces Lucecita llegó al pueblo donde estaba él. 393 Alquiló una casa para estar cerca. 394 Terminada la ceremonia del compromiso, entonces ella fue a la casa de su suegra. 395 Llegando allá , dijo:

—Supe que aquí está un novio que ya está para casarse. 396 Así que, dame la ropa de él para coserla. 397 Pero no le tomes la medida. 398 Así como está la tela la llevo. 399 Allá voy a cortarla —le dijo a su suegra.

400 Pero ella no sabía que era su nuera.

401 —Bueno —dijo la suegra.

«O», mnii ga'ñ nu psheta' ic ñi nu gad tuuba' mñaañ.

391 Orze' ni zi'l la bya' lo gu' lagyez gu'.

392 Na Lusesit bi briiñ gyedz ze' nu zu fiñ ze' orze'. 393 Nunu garee ga bdiiña'ñ yu' pcyiiña'ñ orze'. 394 Bded nu gu' lagyez, orze' gush nez ñi zañ lo ñaa gud ñi. 395 Bru'ñañ ze'

«Ya güeña riidz nu ii zu tub nob nu sa chelaa. 396 Nde' nu cuic ru shaab ñi cha du diba. 397 Par esii cue' la gash beey ruñ. 398 Gal nu na zi'l la negy ze', cha du. 399 Gashtal re shi'ña», naañ rab ñi ñaa gud ñi ze'.

400 Ze' mi ze' shtee lam ti shis mi nu nde'.

401 «O», na ga' mi ze'.

402 She gave her some cloth to take. 403 Now when she arrived home, she measured the cloth to make clothing for the young man. 404 She cut it out. 405 After she cut it out, she sewed it. 406 After she sewed it, she delivered it. 407 Now when she arrived, the young man put it on. 408 It was just his size. 409 Then they said *to the young man*, "What a very clever person you are. 410 Why did it turn out just your size?" they said. 411 "Why is her eye so accurate? 412 Could she have already seen your clothing? 413 Why is that?"

414 They didn't know the reason why the clothing came out that way. 415 Anyway *the young man* married *his bride*. 416 They had the wedding feast. 417 On the day of the wedding feast, Lucecita went and asked for the hat of the groom in order to tell his fortune.

402 Y le dió la tela para llevar. 403 Cuando llegó a su casa, tomó la medida de la ropa de él, 404 y la cortó. 405 Cuando terminó de cortarla, la costuró. 406 Cuando terminó de coserla, fue a dejarla. 407 Cuando llegó, se la puso. 408 Estaba a su medida. 409 Entonces le decían:

—¡Pero qué persona tan listo eres! 410 ¿Cómo es que la ropa salió tan a tu medida? —le dijeron a él—. 411 ¿Cómo es que pudo hacerla tan bien? 412 ¿Qué, siempre ha visto tu ropa? 413 ¿Por qué? —decían ellos.

414 Así que no se dieron cuenta por qué salió así la ropa. 415 Y se casaron. 416 Hubo fandango. 417 El día del fandango, fue Lucecita a pedir el sombrero del novio para hacer una suerte.

402 Briica'm negy ze' za nu ga'ñ. 403 Na briñ yu'ñ na, orze' gush beey ñi shab fiñ ze'. 404 Pshi'ñ ñi nu nde'. 405 Blazh pshi'ñ ñi, gaze' nu bdib ñi. 406 Blazh bdib ñi nu nde', byazeñ ñi. 407 Na ornu briiñ na, bzu fiñ gyeey ze' nde'. 408 Beey zi'l lañ nu nde'. 409 Orze' nu na dem nam:

«Par dzi nu laca' lily na ru. 410 ¿Lagu ga' dzi beey shab ru bruu?» na ga' dem raba'm ñii. 411 «¿Lagu ga' dzi loñ, lagu ga'? 412 ¿A nil rzac ñi shab ru? 413 ¿Lagu nde'?» na ga' dem.

414 Ni zi'l wancuica' dem ras<u>oo</u> lagu nu ni bruu negy ze' orze'. 415 Ni zi'l pchelaa deñ. 416 Orze' gu' fandang. 417 Dzi nu gu' fandang ze', orze' nu gua Lusesit gua tiiñ ñi shimbely nob ze' nu gyicy ñi suert orze'.

418 "I have come to see if you would give me the groom's hat in order for me to tell his fortune tomorrow," she said to her mother-in-law.

419 "I'll give it *to you*," she said.

420 Now the wedding feast was at dawn. 421 *Lucecita* arrived. *She said,*

422 "For the last time, will you lend me the groom's hat?"

423 "I'll lend it *to you*," said *the woman.*

424 She already had a fine quality bowl with her. 425 There were two dove eggs in it. 426 She put her bowel down on the groom's table. 427 She took hold of the hat. 428 She put it over the bowl. 429 Now when she lifted the hat, there were two doves under it. 430 They began to fight with one another.

418 —Vine a pedirte que me des el sombrero del novio para que yo haga una suerte mañana —le dijo a su suegra.

419 —Te lo daré —dijo ella.

420 El fandango fue al amanecer. 421 Entonces llegó ella.

422 —Por la última vez dame el sombrero del novio —dijo.

423 —Voy a dar —dijo ella.

424 Ella ya tenía un plato muy fino 425 en el que estaban dos huevos de paloma. 426 Entonces puso ella el plato fino en la mesa del novio. 427 Tomó el sombrero. 428 Lo puso sobre el plato. 429 Cuando levantó el sombrero, allí ya estaban dos palomas. 430 Empezaron las palomas a pelear una con otra.

418 «Ya yapa nu yap nee ben a wabic ru shimbely nob nu gyicya ñuu tub suert ina», nañ rab ñi ñaa gud ñi ze'.

419 «Grica», naa ga' mi ze'.

420 Na ornu bza' yu na, yu' fandang. 421 Bru'ñañ orze'.

422 «Por fii shimbely nob, ¿a cuic gaal lar diña beni?» naañ.

423 «Rica», nam.

424 Orze' bi nuuñ tub gya'n chiñ. 425 Ze' ri cyup nguu begy. 426 Orze' bzuub lañ gya'n chiñ niñ lo mez ni nob. 427 Pshet la yaañ shimbely. 428 Briib ñi too nu nde'. 429 Na ornu pshes nañ ñi shimbely ze', ze' bi ri cyup begy. 430 Orze' la nu brugyi' rucoo ma nu losa' ma.

431 "Do you remember one day, one time, the day when my father ordered you to go clear the bush? 432 You planted flowers. 433 Now when I arrived with food for you to eat, you were sitting there crying. 434 If not for me, what would you be?" said a dove to its companion.

435 "I don't remember at all," said the male dove.

436 Again: "Do you remember one day, one time, the day when my father ordered you to go plant corn? 437 He said that on that same day you were to bring back fresh corn. 438 You were to bring it, he said. 439 Now when I came to deliver food for you to eat, you were sitting there crying. 440 If it were not for me, what would you be?" said the dove.

441 "I don't remember at all," said the male dove.

431 —¿Te acuerdas un día, un tiempo, el día que te mandó mi papá a hacer un rozo? 432 Sembraste flores. 433 Y cuando fui a dejar las tortillas para comieras, estabas llorando. 434 Si no hubiera sido por mí, ¿qué sería de ti? —decía la paloma a su compañero.

435 —No me acuerdo de nada —decía la paloma macho.

436 Entonces,—

¿Te acuerdas un día, un tiempo, el día que te mandó mi papá a sembrar la milpa? 437 Dijo que ese mismo día llegaras con los elotes. 438 Que deberías traerlos, te dijo. 439 Cuando fui a dejar las tortillas para que comieras, estabas sentado llorando. 440 Si no hubiera sido por mí, ¿qué sería de ti? —decía la paloma.

441 —No recuerdo nada —decía la paloma macho.

431 «¿A zu lagy ru tub dzi, tub tiem, dzi nu pcaa uza ru nu guar gu'n ru gyish? 432 Mnuuz ru ya gyee mnuuz ru. 433 Na ya, ornu byap tu gyit gor, ruun ru zub ru. 434 Par ti cue' ya, ¿la ru?» rnii ga' begy ze' raba' ma losa' ma.

435 «Rila nu gyeza' lagya», rnii ga' begy guzeey ze' orze'.

436 Orze' la ze' ga' na:

«¿A zu lagy ru tub dzi, tub tiem, dzi nu pcaa uza ru guar mnuuz ru gyel? 437 Mniim nu laab dzi ze' ri nur za'. 438 Ri nur, mniim. 439 Na ornu byap seeña gyit gor, ruun ru zub ru. 440 Par ti cue' ya, ¿la ru?» rnii ga' begy ze'. 441 Orze'

442 Again, "Do you remember one day, one time, the day when my father ordered you to climb up the coconut tree? 443 You picked all of the ripe coconuts. 444 You broke off all of its branches. 445 The only thing you didn't break off was the bud on the tip of the tree. 446 Do you remember that?" asked the female dove.

447 "I don't remember at all," said the male dove.

448 Again, "Do you remember one day, one time, the day when my father ordered you to beat the mule? 449 You removed all of its tack. 450 You cast it all aside. 451 Wherever did you put it? 452 If not for me, what would you be?" said the female dove.

453 "I don't remember at all," said the male dove.

442 Y otra vez:

—Te acuerdas un día, un tiempo, el día que te mandó mi papá a subirte al palmar? 443 Cortaste todos los cocos tiernos que tenía. 444 Todas las ramas cortaste. 445 Pero el único que no cortaste fue el cogollo de la punta. 446 ¿Te acuerdas de eso? —decía la paloma hembra.

447 —No recuerdo nada —decía la paloma macho.

448 Y otra vez:

—¿Te acuerdas tú un día, un tiempo, el día que te mandó mi papá a que le pegaras a la mula? 449 Quitaste la montura. 450 La tiraste. 451 ¿Dónde le pusiste? 452 Si no hubiera sido por mí, ¿qué sería de ti? —le decía la paloma hembra.

453 —No me acuerdo nada —decía la paloma macho.

«Rila nu gyeza' lagya̱», rnii ga' begy guzeey. 442 Ze' ga' na «¿A zu lagy ru tub dzi, tub tiem, dzi nu pcaa uza̱ ru nu chup ru lo ya coc? 443 Blag ru dela coc re'ñ niñ. 444 Dela yaañ dela blag ru. 445 Par se tub ngüicy loñ, nde' wanlag ru. 446 ¿A zu lagy ru nu nde'?» rnii ga' begy gus ze'.

447 «Rila nu gyeza' lagya̱», rnii ga' begy guzeey ze'. 448 Ze' ga' na

«¿A zu lagy ru tub dzi, tub tiem, dzi nu pcaa uza̱ ru nu bgaaz ru muly? 449 Bloor dela shily ni ma. 450 Dela mne'r. 451 Ti ca' gal mne'r. 452 Par ti cue' ya̱, ¿la ru?» rnii ga' begy gus.

453 «Rila nu gyeza' lagya̱», rnii ga' begy guzeey. 454 Ze' ga' na

454 Again, "Do you remember the day when my father ordered you to dry the well with a broken water jug? 455 Now when I arrived with food for you to eat, you were sitting there crying. 456 If not for me, what would you be?" said the female dove.

457 "I don't remember at all," said the male dove.

458 "You bitch! 459 So this is what you are like."

460 Wham, it struck the male dove on the head. 461 Then *the young man* suddenly remembered his wife.

462 "This is my first wife. 463 I will take possession of my wife now. 464 I will leave this other bride," he said.

465 The *second* bride remained behind at the table. 466 He took possession of his wife. 467 Then he took his wife into another room. 468 His second wife remained behind. 469 The old people were there looking around.

454 Y otra vez:

—¿Te acuerdas un día que te mandó mi papá a que secaras un pozo con un cántaro roto? 455 Cuando fui a dejar las tortillas para que comieras, estabas sentado llorando. 456 Si no hubiera sido por mí, ¿qué sería de ti? —le decía la paloma.

457 —No recuerdo nada —decía la paloma macho.

458 —¡A sinvergüenza! 459 ¿Así eres tú siempre? —le dijo entonces.

460 ¡Chas! le pegó en la cabeza a la paloma macho. 461 Entonces de repente se acordó ese hombre de su mujer.

462 —Esta es mi esposa; esta es mi primera esposa. 463 Recibiré a mi esposa ahora. 464 Dejaré a la otra novia —dijo.

465 Entonces dejó a la novia en la mesa. 466 Y recibió él a su esposa. 467 Se fue a otro cuarto con su esposa. 468 La nueva novia se quedó atrás. 469 Entonces los viejos estaban mirando por todos lados.

«¿A zu lagy ru dzi nu pcaa uza̱ ru pcuiigy ru zo nu tub re' la'? 455 Na ornu byap tṵ gyit gor zub ru ruun ru. 456 Par ti cue' ya̱, ¿la ru?» rnii ga' begy gus ze'.

457 «Rila nu gyeza' lagya̱», rnii ga' begy guzeey.

458 «Ah put. 459 I la na ru beni», naa ga' ma orze'.

460 Chaa la pshet ma too begy guzeey ze'. 461 Orze' la trii la byeza' lagy fiñ ze' mñaañ orze'.

462 «Nii nu mñaa ya̱, nii mñaa loga ya̱. 463 Gyash ya̱ mñaa̱ na. 464 Gzeeña̱ tuuba' nob ii», nañ.

465 Orze' zub ga la nob ze' lo mez. 466 Byash lañ mñaañ orze'. 467 Gush nez ñi yaañ nañ tuuba' cuart nuñ mñaañ orze'. 468 Zu ga la nob cub ze' orze'. 469 Orze' dri' zi lo de biñ gush yu'm.

470 The bridal party were there just looking around. 471 The young man found his wife. 472 He remembered all of the things that happened to them.

473 "The tragedy I experienced with my wife is just like the animal said. 474 Where is my wife if this is not her? 475 Yes this is my wife. 476 The tragedy I experienced with my wife is just like this animal said."

477 Then he remembered that she was his wife. 478 He found his wife Lucecita.

470 La familia de ella estaba mirando por todos lados. 471 Encontró él a su esposa. 472 Recordó él todas las cosas que le habían sucedido.

473 —Así como dice este animal, así fue la desgracia que sufrí con mi esposa —dijo—. 474 ¿Dónde estuviera mi esposa si no fuera ésta? 475 Ésta es mi esposa. 476 Así como dice este animal, así fue la desgracia que sufrí con mi esposa —dijo él.

477 Entonces recordó que ella era su esposa. 478 Encontró a su esposa Lucecita entonces.

470 De biñ guzan ze', se dri' zi'l lo dem yu'm orze'. 471 Byad mñaa fiñ ze' orze'. 472 Byeza' lagy ñi dela coz nu bzac ñi.

473 «Gal nu rnii ma ii, ni na gyel zi nu bzaca du mñaa. 474 ¿Ca cha mñaa nu walab ñi nu nii? 475 Laab mñaa ya nu nii. 476 Gal nu rnii bañcyug ii, i na gyel zi nu bzaca du mñaa», naañ orze'.

477 Gaze' nu byeza' lagy ñi nu nde' mñaañ orze'. 478 Byada' Lusesit niñ orze'.

8

Cuerposulal

Once a man asked me if I knew where the center of the world was, because, he said, the Texmelucan Zapotecs believe that Mexico City is the center of the world, and the farthest edge of the world is on the other side of the seventh ocean. Then to prove his point he told me the story of Cuerposulal.

Actually, there is no mention of Mexico City in the story of Cuerposulal at all. But it does take us to the other side of the seventh ocean where supernatural things so often happen.

The story begins with a young man who wants to get married. His father warns him against marrying, because Cuerposulal is going about, and he may come some night and take the bride away. Cuerposulal's identity is very vague. The word clearly comes from Spanish, but its etymology is unclear. Claudio Martinez suggests that it may come from *cuerpo sin alma* 'body without soul' because his spirit is separate from his body. It might also come from *cuerpo zu alma* 'body exist soul' because he is an empty body that collects the souls of brides. At any rate, he seems to be a personification of death and a symbol of the tenuous nature of life.

The young man marries against the advice of his father, and as is always the case in Zapotec folklore, the old man's wisdom proves to be right. Cuerposulal comes and takes the man's wife away. The man sets out to get his wife back. His journey takes him to the seventh ocean, because Cuerposulal's spirit is in a rock at the bottom of the seventh ocean.

The story reminds me of a Zapotec teaching about the spirit. They believe that when a person experiences strong emotion like fear, anger, or frustration his spirit may become trapped in the ground. He may live for many years without realizing this. Then one day he may become sick. The diviner may tell him he is sick because he was once afraid of a dog, or because he was angry with a person who harmed him. Then a number of possible cures might be performed. One of the riskiest cures is to call the person's spirit in the middle of the night to return to its body. It is risky, because the spirit will turn into an animal. If it turns into a large animal, it will most likely make the trip home to its body safely. But it may turn into a small animal. It may be eaten or killed before it is reunited with its body. Then the person will surely die.

The situation with Cuerposulal's spirit is similar. It is bound in a rock, but it does not seem to affect the activities of his body. When it is released, it turns into a dove. A hawk eats the dove, and Cuerposulal dies.

The story of Cuerposulal is very popular among the Texmelucan Zapotecs. I have heard it many times. This version was told to me by an elderly lady, Antonia Marcial de Sumano in 1973 during a visit in her home. I recorded it on the tape recorder. Several years later, I asked Claudio Martinez to transcribe it for me.

Cuerposulal

Una vez un hombre me preguntó si sabía yo dónde estaba el centro del mundo, porque, dijo, los zapotecas de Texmelucan creen que la Ciudad de México es el centro del mundo y que la más remota orilla del mundo es al otro lado del séptimo océano. Luego, para probar su punto de vista, me contó la historia de Cuerposulal.

En realidad, la Ciudad de México no se menciona en lo absoluto en el cuento de Cuerposulal. Pero nos lleva al otro lado del séptimo océano donde suceden frecuentemente cosas sobrenaturales.

La historia comienza con un hombre joven que se quiere casar. Su padre está en contra de que se case porque Cuerposulal anda rondando por ahí y puede llegar alguna noche a llevarse a la novia. La identidad de Cuerposulal es muy vaga. La palabra viene claramente de español, pero su etimología no es clara. Claudio Martínez sugiere que viene de "cuerpo sin alma", porque su espíritu está separado de su cuerpo. Puede que venga también de "cuerpo su alma" porque es un cuerpo vacío que colecciona las almas de las novias. En todo caso, parece ser la personificación de la muerte, y un símbolo de la naturaleza tenue de la vida.

El joven se casa en contra de la voluntad de su padre, y como sucede siempre en los cuentos folklóricos zapotecas, el padre tiene la razón. Cuerposulal llega y se lleva a la esposa. El joven sale a rescatarla. Su viaje lo lleva al séptimo océano, porque el espíritu de Cuerposulal está en una roca en el fondo del séptimo océano.

La historia me recuerda a un zapoteca que da clases acerca de los espíritus. Ellos creen que cuando una persona experimenta fuertes emociones, como miedo, coraje o frustración su espíritu puede quedar atrapado en la tierra. Puede que viva por muchos años sin darse cuenta de esto. Entonces, puede que un día se enferme. Puede que el adivino le diga que está enfermo porque una vez le tuvo miedo a un perro, o porque estaba enojado con una persona que le causó ese daño. Después puede que sea sometido a una serie de "curas". Una de las más arriesgadas es la de llamar al espíritu de la persona a medianoche para que regrese a su cuerpo. Es arriesgado porque el espíritu se puede convertir en animal. Si se convierte en un animal grande habrá más probabilidad de que haga el regreso de vuelta a su cuerpo sano y salvo. Pero puede ser que se transforme en un animal pequeño. Puede que se la coman o la maten antes de que se reúna con su cuerpo. Entonces la persona se morirá con seguridad.

La situación del espíritu de Cuerposulal es parecida. Está atado a una roca, pero esto no parece afectar las actividades de su cuerpo. Cuando lo sueltan se convierte en una paloma. Una águila se come la paloma y Cuerposulal muere.

La historia de Cuerposulal es muy popular entre los zapotecas de Texmelucan. La he oído muchas veces. Esta versión me la contó en 1973 una señora anciana, Antonia Marcial de Sumano, cuando fui a visitarla en su casa. En esa ocasión grabé el cuento. Varios años después le pedí a Claudio Martínez me la transcribiese.

1 There once was a person 2 who wanted to get a wife for his son.[1]

3 "I should get a wife," said the young man.

4 "Don't get a wife, because Cuerposulal is going about. 5 He will take away your wife," said the old man.

6 "I will get one," said the young man.

7 "But could you overcome you sleepiness and *stay awake at night* if you got a wife?" asked the old man.

8 "I will overcome it," he said.

9 The old man went to ask for a wife for his son. 10 He went to ask for a wife for his son.

---

[1]I assume that this sentence is an error. His son wants to get a wife. The man below appears to be against it. It should read *rlagy i'ñ mi gad mñaay* 'his son wanted to get a wife'.

1 Había una vez un hombre 2 que quería conseguir una mujer para su hijo.[1]

3 —Debo tener una esposa —dijo el joven.

4 —No busques mujer, porque anda rondando el Cuerposulal. 5 Te va a quitar a tu mujer —dijo el viejo.

6 —Voy a buscarla —dijo el joven.

7 —¿Pero te aguantarás el sueño si tienes mujer? —dijo el viejo.

8 —Aguantaré —dijo.

9 Entonces fue a pedir mujer para su hijo. 10 Fue a pedir una mujer para su hijo.

---

[1]Supongo que esta oración es un error. El hijo quiere buscar esposa. El hombre abajo parece estar en contra de ello. Debe leerse *rlagy i'ñ mi gad mñaay* 'su hijo quería conseguir una esposa'.

Rishtoo ni Cuerposulal

1 Zu tub mbecy. 2 Rlagy mi gad mñaa i'ñ mi.

3 «Gad mña̱a̱», i nañ.

4 «Cue' gad mñaar, gun rded Cuerposulal. 5 Coy mñaar», nam.

6 «Gad la ne̱», naañ.

7 «¿Par a gagyer pcaal benu gad mñaar?» nam.

8 «Gagye̱», naañ.

9 Orze' gua lam gua tiiñ mi mñaa i'ñ mi. 10 Orze' guam gua tiiñ mi mñaa i'ñ mi.

11 Now on the first night *after the marriage* the son overcame his sleepiness *and didn't sleep.* 12 On the second night he overcame it. 13 He guarded his wife *all night long.* 14 He had gotten a wife. 15 But Cuerposulal was going about 16 taking wives from their new husbands.

17 "You should not get a wife", the old man had said.

18 "I will get a wife," the young man said.

19 "Okay then," the old man said.

20 Then he had gotten a wife. 21 It was only the third night when he fell asleep. 22 Then Cuerposulal took his wife and went away with her. 23 At dawn,

"Now look! 24 My wife has gone away. 25 My wife has gone," he said.

26 "Has she gone?" asked the old man.

27 "She has gone," he said.

11 Después, la primera noche él aguantó el sueño. 12 La segunda noche aguantó también. 13 Cuidaba a su mujer. 14 Él tuvo esposa. 15 Pero Cuerposulal andaba alrededor. 16 Venía a quitarles las esposas a los novios.

17 —No debías tener mujer —dijo el viejo.

18 —Yo tendré mujer —dijo él.

19 —Está bien, pues —dijo.

20 Después tuvo mujer. 21 Era la tercera noche nada más, cuando le agarró el sueño. 22 Entonces Cuerposulal quitó a su mujer. Se le llevó. 23 Cuando amaneció,

—¡Ahora, mira! 24 Se fue mi mujer —dijo—. 25 Se fue mi mujer —dijo.

26 —¿Se fue? —dijo su papá.

27 —Se fue —dijo él.

11 Ze' na gaze' nu rel tub rel loga zi'l la gugyeeñ pcaal. 12 Nu cyup ze' gugyeeñ. 13 Mñaañ mñaañ. 14 Guud la mñaañ orze'. 15 Par Cuerposulal rded mi. 16 Ryiid boom mñaa nob.

17 Gaze' nu «Cue' gad mñaar», nam.

18 «Gad la mñaa», naañ.

19 «O beni», nam.

20 Gaze' nu guud mñaañ. 21 Rel chon zi'l, ornu gush pcaal ñi. 22 Orze' bloo Cuerposulal mñaañ za num orze'. 23 Or bza' yu, orze' gaze' nu «Na na güii la. 24 Za mñaa na», nañ. 25 «Za mñaa», naañ.

26 «¿A zañ?» nam.

27 «Zañ», nañ.

28 "Didn't I tell you not to get a wife? 29 Now look *at what you have done!* 30 You went to sleep," his father said.

31 "But I will go follow her," he said.

32 "Will you go?" said the old man.

33 "I will go," he said.

34 Then he saddled his burro. 35 He went to get bread and chicken. 36 He put them in a basket. 37 He took to the trail. 38 He put his supplies on a donkey to go follow his wife. 39 After that, he went on his way.

40 When he arrived at the edge of a river, there was a little girl fishing there.[2]

41 "What are you doing, little girl?" he asked.

42 "I am catching fish for my mother to eat," she said.

43 "Let me see what they are like?" he said.

[2]In women's speech the Zapotec word *[fiñ] nguzh* could refer to a young boy or a young girl.

28 —¿Qué, no te dije que no tuvieras mujer dije? 29 ¡Ahora, mira lo que pasó! 30 Te agarró el sueño —dijo su papá entonces.

31 —Pero voy a seguirlo —dijo.

32 —¿Vas a ir? —dijo el padre.

33 —Sí, voy —dijo.

34 Después aparejó su burro. 35 Fue a traer pan y una gallina. 36 Los puso en una canasta. 37 Y se fue por el camino. 38 Cargó el burro para seguir a su esposa. 39 Entonces se fue.

40 Cuando llegó a la orilla de un río, vio que estaba allí una niña pescando.[2]

41 —¿Qué haces, niña? —le dijo.

42 —Estoy pescando para que coma mi mamá —dijo.

43 —Permítame verlo —le dijo.

[2]En el lenguaje de la mujer *[fiñ] nguzh* puede significar niño o niña.

28 «¿A walab ga ya rnee cue' gad mñaar rnee? 29 Na güii la. 30 Gush pcaal ru», na uz ñi orze'. 31 Gaze' nu
«Par cha cha ca iich ñi», i nañ.
32 «¿A char?» nam.
33 «Cha», naañ.
34 Gaze' nu bdu'ñ shab bur niñ. 35 Gua gyiiñ gyishtily, gua gyiiñ gyid, gua gyiiñ. 36 Bdu'ñ nañ chicyiw. 37 Gush nez ñi. 38 Pcaañ suu bur zañ za cañ ich mñaañ. 39 Gaze' nu blazh ze' na, gaze' nu zañ.
40 Ornu bru'ñañ tub ru' gyoow, ze' ri tub fiñ nguzh rub ñi bel. 41 Ze' ga gaze' nu
«¿La ricy ru fiñ nguzh?» nañ.
42 «Ii rduba bel gow ñaa», naañ.
43 «Na ma güii ben», na mi ze'.

44 "Okay," she said.

45 She went *to him* and gave him her gourd to look into.

46 "The poor animal of God. 47 Let it go, because it is so unfortunate," he said.

48 He turned the little girl's gourd over. 49 He set the fish free. It went way.

50 The girl stood there crying. 51 Then he said,

"Don't cry. 52 Here is a chicken for you to take to your mother to eat," the man said.

53 "Okay then," she said.

54 She took the chicken. 55 She got a chicken to take home with her. 56 The fish was let go. 57 It went away in the river.

58 He went a little farther. 59 There were some ants there fighting. 60 The ants were fighting.

61 "The unfortunate animals of God. 62 They are fighting because they are hungry," he said.

44 —Bueno —dijo la niña.

45 Fue y le dio su coco para que viera él.

46 —¡Pobre animal de Dios!

47 Déjalo lo que se vaya, porque da lástima —dijo.

48 Y volteó el coco de la niña. 49 Dejó que el pez se fuera.

50 La niña se puso a llorar. 51 Entonces dijo él:

—No llores. 52 Aquí hay una gallina para que le lleves a tu mamá —dijo el hombre.

53 —Está bien —dijo ella.

54 Y tomó la gallina. 55 Tenía una gallina para llevar. 56 Soltaron al pez. 57 Y se fue en el río.

58 Se fue. 59 Habían unas hormigas peleando. 60 Las hormigas estaban peleando.

61 —¡Pobres animales de Dios! 62 Están peleando porque tienen hambre —dijo él.

44 «O beni», naañ.

45 Gua lañ briic lañ cyug niñ bgüii mi ze'.

46 «Cuaa pro bañcyug ni Ñgyoozh. 47 Blaa ma ii cha ma, gun cuaa ma», i nam.

48 Bzu tiily lam cyug ni fiñ nguzh. 49 Blaam bel za ma.

50 Ruun fiñ nguzh zuñ. 51 Orze' nam:

«Cue' gun ru. 52 Ii tub gyid yaa nu gow ñaar», i na mbecy ze'.

53 Orze' gaze' nu «O beni», naañ.

54 Gush ñi gyid. 55 Guud gyid ya nuñ. 56 Orze' bdulaa bel. 57 Za ma gyoow.

58 Za ga'm, za ga'm. 59 Ze' la bi yu' bree rucoo ma. 60 La rucoo bree. 61 Gaze' nu

«Cuaa bañcyug ni Ñgyoozh. 62 Nu ran ma ii, nde' nu ni rucoo ma», nam.

63 Once more he put bread out before them. 64 He had crumbled the bread.

65 He walked a little farther. 66 There were leaf—cutter ants there fighting.

67 "The poor animals of God. 68 They are hungry," he said.

69 Again he crumbled the bread before the leaf-cutter ants. 70 He put the bread before them. 71 He went a long ways.

72 "Caw," said a hawk.

73 "Ah, animal of God. 74 Why are you whistling? 75 You are whistling because you are hungry," he said.

76 He took hold of a chicken. 77 He threw it to the hawk. 78 The hawk ate it. 79 The hawk ate the chicken.

80 Again he went along ways. 81 There was a burro tied up there. 82 There was a burro tied up on bare ground there. 83 It was tied up on bare ground.

63 Puso pan frente ellas. 64 Hizo pedazos el pan.

65 Caminó otro poco. 66 Allí habían hormigas arrieras peleando.

67 —¡Pobres animales de Dios! 68 Tienen hambre —dijo.

69 Despedazó el pan para las arrieras. 70 Puso el pan frente a ellas. 71 Se fue, se fue y se fue.

72 —Piw —dijo el águila.

73 —¡A animal de Dios! 74 ¿Por qué chiflas tú? 75 Chiflas porque tienes hambre —dijo él.

76 Cogió la gallina. 77 Y se la tiró al águila. 78 El águila se comió. 79 El águila se comió la gallina.

80 Y se fue, se fue, se fue, se fue. 81 Entonces allí estaba atado un burro. 82 Allí estaba atado el burro en el terreno baldío. 83 Estaba atado en el terreno baldío.

63 Orze' la pcuaa ga'm gyishtily lo ma ze'. 64 I psug mi gyishtily.

65 Bza ga'm se ñuu. 66 Ze' la rucoo ga' byub yu' ma.

67 «Cuaa pro bañcyug ni Ñgyoozh. 68 Nu ran ma ii nguaa ma», naa ga'm.

69 Psuga'm gyishtily lo byub ze'. 70 Pcuaa ga'm gyishtily lo ma. 71 Za ga'm, za ga'm, za ga'm. 72 Orze'

«Piw», na la psi.

73 «Ah bañcyug ni Ñgyoozh, 74 ¿lagu rgyiiw ru? 75 Nu ran ru, nde' nu rgyiiw ru», nam.

76 Bdu' ga' yaam tub gyid. 77 Mne' lam lo psi. 78 Bdowa' psi ze'. 79 Bdowa' psi gyid ze'.

80 Za ga'm, za ga'm, za ga'm, za ga'm. 81 Orze' ze' la bi ca bur. 82 Ze' bi ca bur lo yu yaagy la. 83 Lo yu yaagy la ca ma.

84 "Ah, animal of God, you are there crying because you are hungry, aren't you?" he said.

85 He lowered the horse's pack. 86 He took some hay from his pack and threw it to the donkey. 87 He went on his way. 88 Then there was a sheep tied at a rock. 89 It was tied at a rock. 90 Then he said,

"How unfortunate is this poor animal of God."

91 The sheep was there crying.

92 "How unfortunate you are. 93 You sure are hungry, aren't you? 94 That is why you are crying like this," he said.

95 Again he removed hay from in his pack to put before the sheep.

96 He took to the trail again. He went a long ways. 97 Then it became apparent where his wife was. 98 Then he knew where his wife and Cuerposulal were. 99 Then he sat down and cried. 100 What should he do in order to get his wife away? 101 Then the ants arrived.

84 —Ay, animal de Dios, estás llorando porque tienes hambre, ¿verdad? —le dijo.

85 Bajó el aparejo. 86 Entonces sacó el zacate en su aparejo y se lo tiró al burro. 87 Y siguió su camino. 88 Después se encontró un borrego atado en una piedra. 89 Estaba atado a la piedra. 90 Y le dijo:

—¡Pobre animal de Dios!

91 El borrego estaba llorando.

92 —¡Pobre de ti! 93 Tienes mucha hambre, ¿verdad? 94 Por eso estás llorando —le dijo.

95 Sacó el zacate de su aparejo y se lo dio al borrego.

96 Entonces siguió su camino otra vez. Se fue, se fue. 97 Después supo dónde estaba su esposa. 98 Ahora supo él dónde estaba su esposa y Cuerposulal. 99 Entonces se sentó a llorar. 100 ¿Cómo haría él para que se escapara su esposa? 101 Entonces llegaron las hormigas.

84 «Ah bañcyug ni Ñgyoozh, ¿ruun ru car shiñ, nu ran ru?» na'm.

85 Psheta'm paref. 86 Orze' bloom gyizh nañ paref nim mne'm lo bur ze'. 87 Za ga'm, za ga'm. 88 Orze' gaze' nu ze' ca tub shily lo gyita'. 89 Ma ze' ca ma lo gyita'. 90 Gaze' nu na ga'm:

«Ca cuaa pro bañcyug ni Ñgyoozh»,

91 Ruun shily ze' ca ma. 92 Gaze' nu

«Ca cuaar. 93 Dzi ga ran ru ¿shiñ? 94 Nde' nu ni ruun ru», naa ga'm.

95 Bloo ga'm gyizh nañ paref za ga' lo shily ze'.

96 Orze' gush neza'm zam, zam. 97 Orze' gaze' nu byu' bee nu ca ri mñaam. 98 Par na gud lagy mi ca gal ri mñaam nu Cuerposulal ze'. 99 Gaze' nu gusub mi ruun mi. 100 ¿Lac gyicy mi nu gruu mñaam? 101 Gaze' nu bru'ña bree. 102 Orze' gaze' nu

102 "Why are you crying?" asked the ants.

103 "Why should I not cry? 104 My wife is over there. 105 What should I do to get her away?" said the recently married man.

106 "Don't worry. 107 You did us a favor when you gave us food to eat on the day in which we were hungry. 108 You gave us bread to eat. 109 Now we will get into her clothing. 110 When she comes out to shake out her clothing, be quick to speak with her," said the ants.

111 "Okay then," he said.

112 When the ants entered the brides clothing, she left at a run to go shake them out of her clothing. 113 Then the man went to speak with his wife.

114 "You unfortunate man! 115 Go quickly lest he kill you, because he is ready to kill you," she said.

116 "But where is his spirit?" he asked.

102 —¿Por qué lloras? —dijeron las hormigas.

103 —¿Cómo no voy a llorar? 104 si allí está mi esposa. 105 Pero ¿qué haré para que salga ella? —dijo el novio.

106 —No te preocupes. 107 Nos hiciste un favor al darnos de comer el otro día que teníamos hambre. 108 Nos diste pan para comer. 109 Ahora, vamos a meternos en su ropa. 110 Entonces cuando ella salga a sacudir su vestido, te pones listo para hablar con ella —dijeron las hormigas.

111 —Bueno —dijo.

112 Cuando se metieron las hormigas en la ropa de la novia, salió ella corriendo para sacudirse la ropa. 113 Entonces llegó el hombre que fue a hablar con su esposa.

114 —¡Pobrecito de ti! 115 ¡Vete rápido para que no te mate, porque él está listo para matarte! —le dijo ella.

116 —¿Pero dónde está su alma? —dijo él.

«¿Lagu ruun ru?» na bree.

103 «¿Ca wadun ya? 104 Ze' re ri mñaa. 105 ¿Par lac gyicya gruuñ?» na nob ze'. 106 La orze' gaze' nu

«Cue' sug ic ru. 107 Faboor nu bicy ru nur ya, nu briic ru nu daw dzi ze' rana nguaa de. 108 Briic ru gyishtily daw. 109 Par na ya cha gzu nañ shab ñi. 110 Orze' ornu gruuñ nu cyib ñi shab ñi, orze' dzach zur nii nur mñaar», na bree.

111 «O beni», nam.

112 Orze' ornu bzu laa bree nañ shab nob mñaa, orze' bruuñ carer za tib ñi shab ñi. 113 Orze' bru'ña la biñ gyeey ze' biid nii num mñaam. 114 Orze'

«Lashta' ru. 115 Dzach ru yaa nis cut ñi ru, gun zuñ cut ñi ru», nañ.

116 «¿Par ca ri lardooy?» nam.

117 "His spirit is very far away. 118 His spirit is all the way in the middle of the seventh ocean," she said.

119 Then the leaf-cutter ants arrived. 120 The regular ants had not caused her to get away *from Cuerposulal.* 121 Then the leaf-cutter ants arrived,

"Why are you crying?" they asked.

122 "Why should I not cry? 123 My wife is over here."

124 "Now we will go carry off her corn. 125 We will go into her corn basket, 126 and carry her corn away. 127 Then she will come out *of the house* striking at us with a torch. 128 She will strike at us with a torch to kill us. 129 Then be quick to speak with her," said the leafcutter ants. 130 "You did us a favor when you gave us something to eat one day of God when we were hungrily sitting there. 131 Whatever the case, you gave us bread to eat.

117 —Su alma está muy lejos. 118 Está en medio del séptimo mar —dijo ella.

119 Después llegaron las arrieras. 120 Las hormigas no lograron que se escapara. 121 Después llegaron las arrieras,

—¿Por qué lloras? —dijeron las arrieras.

122 —¿Cómo no voy a llorar? 123 Mi esposa está aquí.

124 —Ahora vamos a acarrear su maíz. 125 Vamos a meternos en el costal de su maíz. 126 Después vamos a acarrear su maíz. 127 Entonces ella nos va a pegar con una tea de fuego de ocote. 128 Nos va a pegar con el fuego de ocote para matarnos. 129 Entonces ponte listo para hablar con ella —le dijeron las arrieras—. 130 Nos hiciste un favor cuando nos diste de comer el otro día de Dios cuando teníamos hambre. 131 Pero nos diste pan para que comiéramos.

117 «Uju zet tona' la ri lardooñ. 118 Gashtal gazel la lo nisyudoo gagy ri lardooñ», i nam.
119 Gaze' nu bru'ña ga' byub. 120 Wancyuum ni bree. 121 Gaze' nu bru'ña ga' byub:
«¿Lagu ruun ru?» na ma.
122 «¿Ca wadun ya? 123 Ze' mñaa, ii riñ.» 124 Gaze' nu
«Na cha saa uub niñ. 125 Chu' ru' da' bid uub niñ. 126 Gaze' nu csaa uub yap du. 127 Gaze' nu ruuñ cyiñ gyi gyegy too. 128 Cyiñ gyi gyegy too cut ñi ya. 129 Orze' gaze' nu dzach zur nii nur ñii», na ga' byub. 130 «Faboor nu bicy ru nur ya, nu briic ru nu daw tub dzi ni Ñgyoozh rana nguaa de. 131 ¿Par la gyicy ru? briic ru gyishtily daw.

132 Because of that we have come to carry *her* corn away so that she will come out *of the house*. 133 She will come out to kill us. 134 She will put fire on us," said the leaf-cutter ants.

135 "Okay then," said the young man.

136 Then his wife came out. 137 He asked *her* where Cuerposulal's spirit was.

138 "Where is that man's spirit to be found?"

139 "His spirit is way in the middle of the seventh ocean," she said.

140 "I will go see where his spirit is," he said.

141 The recently married man took to the trail and went on his way. 142 He went a long ways until he arrived at the edge of the seventh ocean. 143 The spirit of Cuerposulal was way over there. 144 Then he arrived. 145 He sat down on the shore of the ocean. 146 He sat there crying and crying.

132 Por eso venimos para acarrear maíz ahora, porque así va a venir ella. 133 Ella va a venir a matarnos. 134 Va a poner fuego de ocote sobre nosotros.

135 —Bueno pues —dijo el hombre.

136 Después llegó su esposa. 137 Él le preguntó dónde estaba el alma del Cuerposulal.

138 —¿Dónde se puede encontrar el alma de ese hombre?

139 —Su alma está en medio del séptimo mar muy lejos —dijo la mujer.

140 —Voy a ver hasta donde está su alma —dijo él.

141 El novio volvió a su camino y se fue. 142 Caminó hasta que llegó a la orilla del séptimo mar. 143 Hasta allí estaba el alma de Cuerposulal. 144 Entonces llegó. 145 Se sentó a la orilla del mar. 146 Estaba llorando mucho.

132 Par na nde' na nu yapa̱ na csa̱a̱ uub na, gun orze' cyid ñi. 133 Cyid tut ñi ya̱. 134 Griib ñi gyi gyegy to̱o̱», na byub.

135 "O beni," na ga' mbecy ze'.

136 Gaze' nu bruu mñaam. 137 Bdiñ riidz mi ca ri lardoo Cuerposulal. 138 Gaze' nu

«¿Ca gyad lardoo fiñ re?»

139 «Ze' gashtal gazel lo nisyudoo gagy, gazel ze' ri lardooñ», na biñ mñaa ze'. 140 Orze'

«Cha̱ cha güi̱i̱ ben ca gal ri lardooy», i nam.

141 Gush nez nob ze' zam. 142 Za mi, za mi, za mi gashtal brim ru' nisyudoo gagy. 143 Gashtal ze' ri lardoo Cuerposulal. 144 Gaze' nu bru'ñam. 145 Gusub mi ru' nisyudoo ze'. 146 Ruun mi, ruun mi zuba'm. 147 Orze'

147 "What should I do?" he said.

148 Slowly a fish arrived. 149 That animal was the one he had set free. 150 That was the fish that arrived.

151 "Why are you crying?" it asked.

152 "How am I not going to cry? 153 The spirit of Cuerposulal is way in the middle of this ocean. 154 He took my wife away. 155 That is why I have come get *his spirit*. 156 But how can I cause it to come forth?"

157 "You don't have anything to cry about. 158 You did me a favor when you set me free in the river. 159 If not for that, I would have already gone into hot water. 160 But you set me free in the river. 161 I will go and remove it *from the water*. 162 Take hold of it quickly when it is found," said the fish.

163 "Okay," he said.

147 —¿Qué debo hacer? —decía.

148 Lentamente llegó el pez. 149 Ese pez era el pez que él había liberado. 150 Ese fue el pez que llegó.

151 —¿Por qué lloras? —le dijo el pez.

152 —¿Cómo no voy a llorar? 153 El alma de Cuerposulal está lejos en medio de este mar. 154 Él vino con mi esposa. 155 Por esa razón vengo a sacarlo. 156 Pero, ¿cómo hago para que salga?

157 —No tienes que llorar por eso. 158 Me hiciste el favor de soltarme en el río. 159 Si no hubiera sido por eso, ya me hubiera caído al agua caliente. 160 Pero me salvaste en el río. 161 Ahora, yo voy a sacar a ése. 162 Te pones listo para agarrarlo cuando lo encuentre —dijo el pez.

163 —Bueno —dijo él.

«¿Lac gyicy<u>a</u>?» nam.

148 Orze' dze dze la bru'ña bel. 149 Orze' ma ze' bañ nu blaam ze'. 150 Bru'ña la bel ze'. 151 Orze'

«¿Lagu ruun ru?» na ma.

152 «¿Ca wadun y<u>a</u>? 153 Gashtal gazel nisyudoo ii ri lardoo Cuerposulal. 154 Yad nuy mñ<u>aa</u>. 155 Nde' na nu bicy nu yap<u>a</u> yap l<u>oo</u> ñii na. 156 ¿Par lac gyicy<u>a</u> ruuñ?»

157 «Wagad nu gun ru. 158 Faboor nu bicy ru nur y<u>a</u> blaar y<u>a</u> gyoow. 159 Ti cue' ni, bi za y<u>a</u> lo nis zig. 160 Par blaar y<u>a</u> gyoow. 161 Par nu ch<u>a</u> cha l<u>oo</u> nu nde'. 162 Dzach zur cu' yaar ñii ornu gyad ñi», na bel.

163 «O», nam.

164 Then the fish went on its way. 165 After a long while, there was the continual noise of the fish coming with a quartz rock this big. 166 It was continually lifting it with its head. 167 It was continually lifting it with its head bringing it along. 168 It arrived. 169 Then the young man took hold of it. 170 The recently married man took hold of the rock.

171 "You should break this *rock* open to see if Cuerposulal's spirit is inside it," said the fish.

172 "Okay," he said.

173 He sat right down there to cry. 174 He was crying, because what could he do to break open the rock? Because inside it was the spirit of Cuerposulal.

175 "Be quick when I arrive with *the rock* in order to see what comes out of it when it comes out. 176 Don't allow it to get away. 177 Don't cry lest it get away. 178 You are to take hold of it," *the fish had said.*

179 "Okay," he had said.

164 Entonces se fue el pez. 165 Y lo que pasó más tarde fue que el pez volvió con una piedra blanca muy grande. 166 La levantaba con la cabeza. 167 Lo levantaba con la cabeza mientras la traía 168 hasta que llegó allí. 169 Entonces la agarró el esposo. 170 El novio agarró esa piedra.

171 —Debes quebrar esta piedra para ver si está adentro el alma de Cuerposulal —dijo el pez.

172 —Bueno pues —dijo.

173 Allí se sentó a llorar. 174 Estaba llorando porque ¿cómo iba a quebrar la piedra? Porque en ella estaba el alma del Cuerposulal.

175 —Te pones listo cuando llegue con esta piedra a ver que cosa va a salir de adentro. 176 No lo dejes que se vaya. 177 No llores para que no se escape. 178 Tienes que agarrarlo.

179 —Bueno pues —dijo él.

164 Gaze' nu ya bel. 165 Or guchi, la se i la rac, se i la rac yad bel nuu ma i la na gyita' gyigyis. 166 Orze' se i la rlaagy too ma. 167 Se i la rlaagy too ma yad nu ma. 168 Orze' bru'ña la ma ze'. 169 Orze' bdu' la yaa mbecy ze' nde'. 170 Bdu' la yaa nob ze' gyita' ze'.

171 «Nu nii gla'r na ben nañ nu nii ri lardoo Cuerposulal», na ma.

172 «O beni», nam.

173 Ze' gusuba'm ruun mi. 174 Ruun mi nu lac gyicya'm gla'm gyita' ze' orze', gun nañ nde' ri lardoo Cuerposulal.

175 «Par nunu dzach zur ornu gru'ña du̱ ñii, gun ben la coz gruu nañ ñi ornu ruuñ. 176 Cue' zaan ru nu chañ. 177 Cue' gun ru, gun nis chañ. 178 Cu' yaar nu nde'».

179 «O beni», nam.

180 *The young man* had arrived. 181 He sat down to cry. 182 Then the donkey and the sheep arrived. 183 Those animals arrived.

184 "Why are you crying?" they said.

185 He was crying because *the rock* wouldn't be broken open. 186 He was crying.

187 "Don't cry. 188 You did me a favor. 189 You gave me hay to eat on the day when I was tied up there hungry. 190 On that day you gave me something to eat. 191 When, if not now, should I break this open? 192 Don't worry," said the donkey to the young man.

193 The donkey began to use its feet. 194 "Bam," *it* struck out. 195 "Bam," the sheep struck it with its forehead. 196 They broke the rock in two. 197 Then a dove flew out *of it*. 198 It came to rest way up on top of a large pine tree. 199 The dove came to rest *there*. 200 A very large dove came out of it. 201 It flew away.

180 Entonces llegó.181 Entonces se sentó a llorar. 182 Y llegó el burro con el borrego. 183 Esos animales llegaron.

184 —¿Por qué lloras? —le dijeron.

185 Estaba llorando porque no podía quebrarla. 186 Seguía llorando.

187 —No llores —dijo el burro—. 188 Hiciste un favor conmigo. 189 Me diste zacate para comer cuando tenía hambre. 190 Ese día me diste de comer. 191 ¿Cuando si no ahora, es la ocasión de ya voy a quebrar esto? 192 No te preocupes —le dijo el burro al hombre.

193 El burro comenzó a usar sus patas. 194 "Paa", pegaba el burro. 195 El borrego con su frente: "paa" pegaba. 196 Quebraron en dos pedazos la piedra. 197 Entonces voló la paloma. 198 Fué a pararse hasta la punta de un pino grande. 199 Se sentó la paloma. 200 Entonces salió una paloma grande. 201 Se fue.

180 Gaze' nu orze' bru'ñam. 181 Orze' gusub mi ruun mi. 182 Orze' bru'ña bur nu ma shily. 183 Orze' bru'ña ma ze' na. 184 Gaze' nu
«¿Lagu ruun ru?» na ma.
185 Ruun mi nu wagac dula' nde' nim. 186 Ruun mi. 187 Gaze' nu
«Cue' gun ru. 188 Faboor nu bicy ru nur ya. 189 Briic ru gyizh daw dzi nu ca rana. 190 Dzi ze' briic ru nu daw. 191 ¿Par gul dzi ti walab na ya gla' nu nii? 192 Cue' sug ic ru», na bur rab ma mbecy ze'.
193 Bur za ma nu gyi' ma. 194 Paa, rshet bur. 195 Shily nu cyuga ma, paa rshet shily. 196 Bicy cyup la' ma gyita' ze'. 197 Orze' ornu wes nañ la begy, 198 gusub ma gashtal lo ya gyerdoo. 199 Gusub begy. 200 Na tub begy ily bruu ma nañ ñi. 201 Za ma.

202 Then he sat down and cried. 203 Once again he cried.

204 "Caw, why are you crying?" asked the hawk arriving.

205 "Why should I not cry? 206 I have come here to get the spirit of Cuerposulal, I say. 207 Now look at *what happened*! 208 It got away. 209 Just look at *what happened*! 210 It went way up there. 211 What can I do to make it come down?" he said.

212 "You don't have to cry. 213 You did me a favor. 214 I was hungrily traveling around. 215 You gave me a chicken to eat. 216 Now I will do you a favor. 217 *The dove* is not a large animal. 218 I will eat it," said the hawk.

219 "Okay," he said.

202 Entonces él se sentó a llorar. 203 Una vez más se puso a llorar.

204 —"Piw", por qué lloras? —dijo el águila llegando.

205 —¿Cómo no voy a llorar? 206 Vine a sacar el alma del Cuerposulal. 207 ¡Mira ahora! 208 Se escapó. 209 ¡Mira! 210 Hasta allá se fue. 211 ¿Cómo lo hago para que baje ese animal? —dijo.

212 —No tienes que llorar. 213 Me hiciste un favor. 214 Tenía hambre cuando viniste. 215 Me diste una gallina para comer. 216 Ahora voy a hacerte un favor. 217 Ése no es un animal muy grande. 218 Me voy a comer a ese animal —dijo el águila entonces.

219 —Bueno pues —dijo él.

202 Orze' gusuba'm ruun mi. 203 Ruuna'm. 204 Orze' «¿Lagu ruun ru?» na la, "Piw la", na psi bru'ña ma. 205 Orze' «¿Ca wadun ya raa? 206 La ii bruu yap loo lardoo Cuerposulal nee. 207 Na güii ñuu la. 208 Bruuy. 209 Güii la. 210 Gashtal re zay. 211 ¿Lac gyicya gyet ma re na?» nam.

212 «Wagad nu gun ru. 213 Faboor nu bicy ru nur ya. 214 Rana yapa. 215 Briic ru tub gyid daw. 216 Par na gyicya faboor. 217 Walab la bañ ily nu nde'. 218 Ya daw ma re», na psi.

219 Orze' «O beni», na mi ze'.

220 *The hawk* fell on the dove right as it was sitting on top of the large pine tree. 221 It fell on the dove. 222 It ate it. 223 *The young man* was delighted that the hawk got the dove and ate it. 224 Then he took to the trail and went home.

225 When he arrived at where he had been with his wife, Cuerposulal had already died. 226 He was no longer there. 227 The nine days after Cuerposulal's death had already been observed. 228 He went home. 229 He found his wife. 230 He went home. 231 He went home with his wife.

220 Entonces el águila cayó sobre la paloma allí donde estaba, sobre el pino grande. 221 Bajó el águila sobre la paloma 222 y se la comió. 223 Él estaba contento que el águila cogió a la paloma para comer. 224 Después tomó su camino y se fue a su casa.

225 Cuando llegó a donde estaba su mujer, ya Cuerposulal había muerto. 226 Ya no estaba él. 227 Y se habían completado los nueves días desde que Cuerposulal había muerto. 228 Entonces se fue a su casa. 229 Y encontró a su esposa. 230 Se fue a su casa. 231 Y llevó a su esposa con él.

220 Orze' gaze' nu beet la psi too begy ze' gaal zi'l nu zub ma lo ya gyerdoo ze'. 221 Bet la psi too begy ze'. 222 Orze' la bdow ma ma ze'. 223 Gaze' nu cyit nim nu guud begy ze' bdow psi ze'. 224 Gaze' nu gush nez mi yam.

225 Ornu yam nu brim lo mñaam, bi gut Cuerposulal. 226 Saca'm orze'. 227 Bi bza' gaa dzi ni Cuerposulal. 228 Orze' yam. 229 Byad mñaam. 230 Yam orze'. 231 Ya num mñaam.

9

The World of the Dead

The story of "The World of the Dead" is a story of two worlds. The first world is the earth, the world of the living. The word for it, *gyishlombecy*, appears to be derived from the expression *rgyish lo mbecy* 'people hope'. Zapotecs believe that they can only experience happiness, contentment, and enjoyment during this life. Death is final. After death there is no hope. The second world in this story is the world of the dead. The word for it, *gyibaa*, appears to be made up of two morphemes. I cannot identify the first morpheme with any certainty. The second morpheme, *baa*, is the word for 'sky' and for 'grave'. *gyibaa* is also the word used when referring to the Christian concept of heaven, although the description here does not resemble what we think of as the Christian teaching. A few comments about what Zapotecs think happens after death might be helpful in understanding the story.

When a person dies, his body lies at home for at least one full night. During this time his family and others gather around to watch over him. At this time he is thought to be conscious of what is going on around him. But already some changes have occurred. He is no longer referred to by the name he had when he was living. He is referred to as *añ* [from the Spanish *anima*], which is also the word for 'heart'. One never says, "the *añ* called John." When referring to his past activities one could say *gyitoo Waa* 'the late John', or *gyitoo uza* 'my late father'. But when referring to him in his present or future state, one merely says *añ*, the same as every dead person. It is as if he has lost his individuality.

153

If the person is wealthy his family might butcher a cow and put on a feed so that the dead man can take it with him. If they butcher a cow, they bury him with several blades of bamboo grass for the cow to eat. If the dead person is a child, people are told not to cry, because if they do, the child will take the water of their tears with him. A lot of water would burden him down. The world of the dead is a mirror image of this world. There are houses. There are churches. There are animals. People buy and sell. The two worlds are the same in appearance, but different in other ways. In this story the bodies of the dead appear normal, but are corrupt. Dead people eat by smelling. Even social relations are corrupt. The dead woman in the story is married to a weasel who torments her.

After the dead man has lain in his house, people take him to the church. From there they bury him. When they walk seven meters from the church on the way to the graveyard, he is said to "forget." I am not sure what all this expression encompasses. He is no longer thought to be conscious of the world of the living. People are not even sure that he remembers his family and acquaintances or has any affection for them. Anyway he is taken to the graveyard and put in the ground. The entrance to the world of the dead in the story is through a cave in the ground, which Claudio Martinez says is on the other side of the seventh ocean.

In the story the two worlds are similar in appearance. They are also organically connected. When the man burns down his house in the world of the dead, his house in the world of the living burns down, too. And the two worlds come together once each year, during the week of All Saints.

All Saints is a celebration of the family past and present. People butcher turkeys, bake bread, and collect fruit for the celebration. For several days they put out food on the table of the dead. When the table is prepared they say, "You dead people, it is already ready for you to come." On October 31 those who died while they were young are thought to come and partake of the food. The evenings of November 1 to November 3 other dead are thought to come. Each morning, the women recook the food and the living partake. Also on November 1 people begin going to the houses of every family member who is of higher social standing than they are: parents, aunts, uncles, godparents, etc. They take them gifts of food which always include special bread which they call "grandfather." All Saints is a time for reaffirming social relations, it is a point of contact for all family members. The story is offered as an explanation as to how Texmelucan Zapotecs know that the dead return at All Saints.

This story was given to me by Claudio Martinez in 1976 when he was twenty-five years old. He wrote it in practical orthography.

El mundo de los muertos

Ésta es la historia de dos mundos. El primero es la Tierra, el mundo de los vivos. La palabra zapoteca para este mundo es *gyishlombecy,* que parece ser una derivación de la palabra *rgyish lo mbecy 'gente espera'.* Los zapotecas creen que sólo pueden experimentar felicidad, alegría y satisfacción en esta vida. La muerte es final. Después de la muerte no hay esperanza.

El otro mundo en esta historia es el mundo de los muertos. La palabra para nombrarlo *gyībaa,* parece haberse formado de dos morfemas. No puedo identificar con certeza el primer morfema. El segundo, *baa,* es la palabra para cielo o tumba. También se usa *gyībaa* para referirse al concepto cristiano del cielo, aunque la descripción aquí no se asemeja a lo que nosotros conocemos como enseñanza cristiana. Algunos comentarios acerca de lo que piensan los zapotecas pasa después de morir puede que ayuden a entender la historia.

Cuando una persona muere, su cuerpo se conserva en su casa por una noche cuando menos. Su familia y amistades se reúnen esa noche a guardar vigilia junto a su cuerpo. Se piensa que él está consciente de lo que sucede a su alrededor durante todo este tiempo, pero ya se notan algunos cambios: Ya no se habla de él con el nombre que tenía cuando estaba vivo. Se habla de él como *añ,* del español *'ánimo',* que también es la palabra para *corazón.* Uno nunca dice "el *añ* que se llamaba Juan." Cuando uno se refiere a sus actividades pasadas, debe decir *gyitoo waca* 'el finado Juan', o *gyitoo uza* 'mi difunto padre'. Pero cuando se habla de él en su presente o futuro estado, solamente se dice *añ,* lo mismo que al referirse a cualquier otra persona muerta. Es como si él hubiera perdido su personalidad.

Si la persona gozaba de buena posición, puede que su familia mate una res y la prepare para que el muerto se la lleve. Si descuartizan una res, la entierran con algunas hojas de bambú para que la res coma. Si el muerto es un niño, se le pide a la gente que no llore, porque si lo hacen, el niño se llevar el agua de sus lágrimas con él. Mucha agua es una carga pesada para él. El mundo de los muertos es un espejo de este mundo. Hay casas, hay iglesias, hay animales, gente que compra y vende. Los dos mundos son iguales en apariencia, pero diferentes en otros aspectos. En la historia, los cuerpos de los muertos parecen normales, pero están corrompidos. La gente muerta come al oler. Aun las relaciones sociales están corrompidas. La mujer muerta en la historia está casada con una comadreja que la atormenta.

Después que el hombre muerto ha sido velado en su casa, lo llevan a la iglesia. De ahí, lo llevan a enterrar. Cuando ya han caminado siete metros de la iglesia hacia el cementerio o el lugar en donde lo van a sepultar, se le dice que "olvide." No estoy seguro del significado de esta expresión. Se piensa que él ya no está consciente del mundo de los vivos. Tampoco están seguros de si él recuerda a su familia y conocidos o de si tiene alguna estimación por ellos. De cualquier manera, lo llevan al panteón y lo entierran. La entrada al mundo de los muertos en esta historia es una cueva en la tierra, lo que, según Claudio Martínez, es al otro lado del séptimo océano.

En la historia, los dos mundos son similares en apariencia. Están también conectados orgánicamente. Cuando el hombre quema su casa en el mundo de los muertos, su casa en el mundo de los vivos también se quema. Y los dos mundos se juntan una vez al año, durante la semana de Todos los Santos.

Todos los Santos es la celebración de la familia, tanto la pasada como la presente. La gente mata guajolotes, hace pan y colecciona toda clase de fruta para la celebración. Por varios días ponen comida en la mesa para los muertos. Cuando preparan la mesa, dicen: "Muertos, ya está listo todo para que vengan." Se cree que el 31 de octubre vienen a comer los que murieron cuando aún eran niños. En las noches del 1.o y 2 de noviembre se piensa que vienen a comer los adultos. Todas las mañanas las mujeres calientan la comida para que los vivos participen de ella. El 1.o de noviembre van a las casas a visitar a los parientes que están en posición social superior a la de ellos: padres, tíos, tías, padrinos, etc., llevando regalos de la comida que incluye el famoso pan de muerto al que ellos llaman "abuelo." Todos los Santos es el tiempo de consolidar relaciones sociales y una costumbre para reunirse en familia con todos los parientes. Ofrecemos esta historia como una explicación de cómo los zapotecas de Texmelucan piensan que los muertos regresan en Todos los Santos.

Esta historia me la dio Claudio Martínez en 1976 cuando tenía 25 años. Fue escrita con su puño y letra.

1 There once was a person 2 who had a wife. 3 However, his wife died. 4 He began to be very sad because she died. 5 He wanted to see her a lot. 6 So he went to seek a spiritualist to see if he would know what to do so that he could see his wife. 7 The spiritualist told *him* that he knew where the door to heaven is. 8 Then he set a day to accompany the man whose wife died to take him to see where the door to heaven is. 9 But before they went, the spiritualist said that the man whose wife died should prepare, chiles, cotton *thread*, and many more things to take with him to sell in heaven, 10 because while he is there selling those things, he would see his wife.

1 Había una vez un hombre 2 que tenía esposa. 3 Un día se murió su esposa. 4 Empezó a entristecerse mucho porque había muerto su esposa. 5 Quería mucho ver a su esposa. 6 Entonces se fue a buscar a un espiritista a ver si podía decirle como hacer para ver a su esposa. 7 Entonces el espiritista dijo que sabía dónde estaba la puerta del cielo. 8 Después fijó un día en el que iba a llevar al hombre que se le había muerto la esposa para mostrarle dónde estaba la puerta del cielo. 9 Pero antes de irse, dijo el espiritista que el hombre debía preparar chiles, algodón y muchas otras cosas más para llevar a vender al cielo. 10 Porque mientras él vendía esas cosas, iba a ver a su esposa.

Ze' nu yu' mbecy gut

1 Bzu tub mbecy. 2 Zu mñaay. 3 Lac orze' gut mñaay. 4 Brugyi' tona' la ricy shniy nu gut mñaay. 5 Tanta' nu rlagy yu gzac yu mñaay. 6 Gaze' nu gua yub yu tub mbecy siñ nu ben a wad lagy yu lac gyicy yu nu gzac yu mñaay. 7 Orze' mbecy siñ ze' mniiy nu rad lagy yu ca zub ro' gyibaa. 8 Gaze' nu bzuy tub dzi nu cha nuy yu nu gut mñaa ze' cha lyuuy loy ca zub ro' gyibaa. 9 Tees anzir nu cha dey, mnii mbecy siñ ze' nu zu ye yu nu gut mñaa ze' gyiiñ, iily, nu zañ zir coz nu gya nuy cut yu gyibaa. 10 Gun lat nu gzub yu cut yu de nde', gzac yu mñaay.

11 Now when the day arrived for them to go, they took to the trail and went. 12 When they arrived, there was a cave in the rock at the door to heaven. 13 Then the spiritualist said to the person whose wife died,

"Go now. 14 When you arrive, mass will be half over. 15 Go sit at the door to the church. 16 Act like you are selling your things. 17 Because your wife will arrive there. 18 But if she doesn't want to come home, leave *her* alone. 19 Don't force her," he said.

20 "Okay" said the man whose wife died.

21 Then he took to the trail and entered the hole in the rock. 22 Now when he arrived in the other world, there was a church there. 23 Inside it mass was half over. 24 Then he started out and went to sit in front of the Church. 25 He took out his things and set them out in front of him. 26 Now when the mass was over, people began to come out from inside the church.

11 Cuando llegó el día que tenían que ir, se fueron. 12 Cuando llegaron, había una cueva allí, en la puerta del cielo. 13 Entonces dijo el espiritista al hombre a quien se le había muerto la esposa:

—Ve ahora. 14 Cuando llegues, la misa estará a la mitad. 15 Entonces te sientas a la puerta de la iglesia 16 como si estuvieras vendiendo tus cosas. 17 Porque allí va a llegar tu esposa. 18 Pero si no quiere venir a la casa, entonces déjala. 19 No la fuerces —dijo.

20 —Está bien —dijo el hombre a quien se le había muerto la esposa.

21 Después tomó su camino y se fue por el hoyo de la piedra. 22 Cuando llegó al otro mundo, vio una iglesia allí. 23 La misa estaba a la mitad. 24 Entonces se fue a sentarse en frente de la iglesia. 25 Sacó sus cosas y las puso delante de él. 26 Cuando terminó la misa, empezó la gente a salir de la iglesia.

11 Ornu pshuub dzi nu cha dey na, orze' gush nez dey zay. 12 Ornu bru'ña dey, ca tub gyita' blyuu ze' ro' gyibaa. 13 Gaze' nu na mbecy siñ ze' rab yu mbecy nu gut mñaa ze':

«Gyar na. 14 Or rir cyaal la yu' mizh. 15 Orze' char gzub ru ro' wedz. 16 Gyicy ru nu cut ru de coz nir. 17 Gun ze' ru'ña mñaar. 18 Tees benu walagy ñi gyed ñi, orze' zaan lar. 19 Cue' gyicy ru fers nur ñii», nay.

20 «O», na yu nu gut mñaa ze'.

21 Gaze' nu gush nez yu yay gyergyita' ze'. 22 Na ornu briy tuuba' gyishlombecy na, zub tub yu' wedz ze'. 23 Cyaal la rac mizh nañ ñi. 24 Gaze' nu gush nez yu zay gusub yu ro' wedz ze'. 25 Blooy de coz niy pcuaay loy. 26 Na ornu bded mizh na, brugyi' druu mbecy ich yu' wedz.

27 The women began to come out. 28 In this way his wife should appear. 29 It wasn't until all the people finished leaving *the church*, at the very end *of the line*, that his wife came out.30 Now when he saw her, he pulled out the handkerchief in which he kept his money and put it close to where she would pass by. 31 But when she passed by, she didn't pay any attention to the handkerchief. 32 He saw that she did not pay any attention to the handkerchief. 33 Then he stood up. 34 He went to speak with her. 35 He said to her,

"Let's go home."

36 "I will not go home, because I don't have permission to go home any more," she said.

37 He insisted on fetching her *home*, but she did not want to go. 38 Then he approached her intending to take hold of her hand.

27 Empezaron a salir las mujeres. 28 Y esperaba que saliera su esposa así, como las otras. 29 Pero no fue sino hasta que salió toda la gente, que al final venía su esposa. 30 Cuando él la vio, sacó el paño de su dinero y lo puso cerca de donde ella iba a pasar. 31 Pero cuando ella pasó, no le hizo caso al paño de dinero. 32 Él vio que ella no le hizo caso al ˙ paño. 33 Entonces, se paró. 34 Y fue a hablar con ella. 35 Y le dijo:

—Vamos a casa.

36 —No voy, porque no tengo permiso para ir —dijo ella.

37 Él insistió en llevarla, pero ella no quería ir. 38 Después se acercó él a ella tratando de agarrarle la mano.

27 Brugyi' druu biñ mñaa. 28 Tees mñaay ni mod la nu ruu zac mi. 29 Gal blazh la bruu dela mbecy, laab nde' la gal ich la gal ze' zaab mñaay. 30 Ornu bzaac yum na, orze' bloo lay bay tiñ niy briish yu gaab ze' nu ded mi. 31 Tees ornu bded mi, wangyicy cuen lam bay tiñ ze'. 32 Rgüiiy nu wangyicy cuen mi bay ze'. 33 Gaze' nu wes suy. 34 Za nii nuy mi. 35 Orze' nay rab yum:

«Yaa gyan», nay.

36 «Waya̱, gun wada' rishbeey nu gya̱», nam.

37 Fert la zuy nu rteey mi, tees wangalagy mi. 38 Gaze' nu becha'y lom nu ricy peey cu' yaay yaam.

39 But she ran for home. 40 As she ran, he followed right along behind her pleading with her to come with him into the world. 41 Now when her house was close by, she said to him,

"Quickly turn around and go home lest my husband find out. 42 He might kill you."

43 Then *that man*, her real husband replied,

"Who is your husband? 44 Am I not your husband? 45 Could you really have another husband? 46 Do me a favor, let's go home, because our children are so sad," he said.

47 She said to him,

"How can you want me to go home *with you* 48 when God commanded me to come here? 49 It will *not* be until All Saints' Day that I will come home. 50 I cannot go home now."

51 Then he said to her,

39 Ella se puso a correr. Se fue. 40 Mientras ella corría, él la seguía rogándole que regresara con él a este mundo. 41 Cuando ya estaba cerca de la casa de ella, ella dijo a él:

—Regresa lo más pronto antes que se dé cuenta mi esposo. 42 Él te va a matar —le dijo ella.

43 Entonces dijo su verdadero esposo:

—¿Quién es tu esposo? 44 ¿Qué no soy yo tu esposo? 45 ¿A poco tienes otro esposo? 46 Vamos, hazme el favor. Porque nuestros hijos están muy tristes —dijo él.

47 Entonces le dijo ella a él:

—¿Cómo quieres tú que yo vaya? 48 Porque Dios ya dispuso que venga yo aquí. 49 Sin embargo cuando llegue Todos Santos, entonces sí creo que voy. 50 Pero ahora no puedo ir —dijo ella.

51 Después le dijo él a ella:

---

39 Orze' gush lam carer yam. 40 Dub gal yam, dub ni zaab ga lay ya cay ich mi nu rnishbaay lom nu gyed num yu par gyishlombecy. 41 Na ornu bi rgaab ze' nu zub yu'm na, orze' nam rab mi yu:

«Dzach zir bish cya yaa, gun nis gad lagy ñgyee. 42 Orze' cut ñi ru», nam.

43 Orze' na ñgyee gaal mi ze':

«¿Cyu ñgyeer? 44 ¿A walab ya ñgyeer? 45 ¿Walab gaal zu tuuba' ñgyeer?» nay. 46 «Bicy faboor yaa gyan, gun dzi shni ricy de yu nguzh nin», nay.

47 Orze' nam rab mi yu:

«¿Ca rlagya' ru nu gya ya? 48 Ze' Ñgyoozh bi bicy mi mandaar nu yapa par ii. 49 Baay be gal sicytoo, orze' gac dzi yapa. 50 Tees na la wac gya», nam.

51 Gaze' nu nay rab yum:

"Are you sure that you will come home on All Saints' Day?"

52 "I will surely come. 53 You should prepare quite a bit for us to eat," she said.

54 Then he said,

"I want for us to go home right now."

55 He took hold of her intending to take her with him by force. 56 Now when he took hold of her, her *flesh* crumbled away. 57 Her bones scattered all around. 58 Fleas, flies, and mosquitoes could be heard arriving. 59 They all arrived there, 60 and landed on the bones. 61 Then she became a person again. 62 She became like she was. 63 Then she said to her husband,

"Have you seen now? 64 Didn't I tell you that we can not go home? 65 But you would not listen. 66 You *had to* take hold of me. 67 How can I go home with you? 68 God has decreed that I should come here."

—¿Seguro que vas a ir en Todos Santos?

52 —Seguro que sí. 53 Debes preparar bastante cosas para comer —dijo ella.

54 Después dijo él:

—Pero yo quiero que vayamos ahora —dijo.

55 La agarró porque quería llevarla a la fuerza. 56 Pero cuando la agarró, ella se deshizo. 57 Sus huesos estaban regados por todas partes. 58 Después se oyó el ruido de mosquitos, moscas y zancudos que llegaban. 59 Todos llegaron juntos. 60 Se pararon sobre los huesos. 61 Entonces, ella se volvió gente otra vez. 62 Así como era ella antes, así volvió a ser. 63 Entonces le dijo a su esposo,

—¿Ya viste? 64 ¿No te dije que no podemos ir? 65 Pero tú no entiendes. 66 Me agarraste. 67 ¿Cómo puedo ir contigo? 68 Dios ya dijo que yo venga aquí.

«¿Par a segur la gyar benu gal sicytoo?» nay.
52 «Segur la yapa. 53 Orze' sheñ ñuu la coz zu yer don», na'm orze'.
54 Gaze' nu nay:
«Tees ya na la rlagya gyan», nay.
55 Bdu' la yaay mi nu ricy peey nu gyed nuy mi por fers la. 56 Na ornu bdu' yaay mi na, bzuun lam. 57 Brush las la rit mi nguaañ. 58 Gaze' nu rzigy la bru'ña be'y, shcyeg, plecy. 59 Dela ma ze' bru'ña ma ze'. 60 Bgo ma too de rit. 61 Orze' byaca'm mbecy. 62 Gal na zi'l mi byaca'm. 63 Gaze' nu nam rab mi ñgyeem ze':
«¿A bzaac ru na? 64 ¿A walab ya rnee wac gyan rnee? 65 Par ru wangyeñ ru. 66 Bdu' yaar ya. 67 ¿Ca gaca' gya du ya ru? 68 Ze' Ñgyoozh bi mniim nu yapa par ii», nam.

69 The man began to be very sad, because his wife did not want to come home with him. 70 He continually pleaded with her. 71 As she went to her house he followed behind her. 72 When her house was close by, she said to him,

"Be careful lest my husband find out *that you are here*. 73 He might kill you," she said.

74 Then the man said,

"Who is your husband? 75 Am I not your husband?"

76 "But I have another husband over here," she said.

77 But he didn't pay any attention *to her*. 78 He followed along behind her. 79 When he arrived at her house, it was just like their house in this world. Her house in that place was exactly the same. 80 Then she entered the house. 81 The man followed her into *the house*. 82 She said to him,

"Be careful, because my husband may arrive. 83 He might kill you."

69 Entonces empezó a ponerse muy triste el hombre, porque su esposa no quería ir con él. 70 Él seguía rogándole a ella. 71 Cuando ella se fue a su casa, él la siguió. 72 Cuando la casa de ella estaba cerca, entonces ella le dijo a él:

—Cuidado, porque se va a dar cuenta mi esposo. 73 Entonces, él te puede matar —dijo ella.

74 Después dijo el hombre,

—¿Quién es tu esposo? 75 ¿Qué no soy yo tu esposo?

76 —Pero yo tengo otro esposo por aquí —dijo esa mujer.

77 Pero él no le hizo caso. 78 Se fue trás de ella. 79 Cuando llegó a la casa de ella, que es como la casa que ellos tenían en este mundo; así es la casa de ella allí. 80 Después entró ella a la casa. 81 Entonces el hombre entró también. 82 Y le dijo ella a él:

—Cuidado, porque va a llegar mi esposo. 83 Y te va a matar.

69 Orze' brugyi' tona' la ricy shni yu gyeey ze' nu walagy mñaay gyed num yu. 70 Zaab yu rnishbaay lom. 71 Dub gal yam yu'm dub ni ya cay ich mi. 72 Ornu bi rgaab yu'm, orze' nam rab mi yu:

«Cuidad, gun nis gad lagy ñgyee. 73 Orze' cut ñi ruɯ», nam.

74 Gaze' nu na yu gyeey ze':

«¿Cyu ñgyeer? 75 ¿A walab ya ñgyeer?» nay.

76 «Tees ya zu tuuba' ñgyee par ii», na biñ mñaa ze' orze'.

77 Tees yu ze' wangyicy cuen lay. 78 Zaab lay ich mi yay. 79 Ornu briy yu'm na, gal na gåal la yu' dey nu zub par gyishlombecy ii, ni' zi'l na yu'm zub gal ze'. 80 Gaze' nu gu'm nañ yu'. 81 Dub ni zaab ga la yu gyeey ze' gu'y. 82 Orze' nam rab mi yu:

«Cuidad, gun ri ñgyee. 83 Orze' cut ñi ruɯ», nam.

84 "But I am your husband. 85 You have no other husband *beside me*," he said.

86 Then he began to look around *to see* where her husband would come from. 87 He wondered what he would be like. 88 Now when the woman knew that her husband was coming, she said to her real husband,

"Hide as quickly as possible, because he is coming now. *Do this* lest he kill you."

89 There were a group of mats *rolled up* in the corner. 90 The man got in among them. 91 He peeped out in order to see what the husband of his wife was like. 92 When her husband appeared coming, he was a weasel. 93 That animal was her husband. 94 It was coming with a load of firewood on its back. 95 On top of *the firewood* sat a mouse.

84 —Pero yo soy tu esposo. 85 Tú no tienes a otro esposo —dijo el hombre.

86 Después empezó él a mirar de dónde vendría el esposo de ella. 87 '¿Cómo será él?', pensaba el hombre. 88 Cuando supo la mujer que ya venía su esposo, le dijo a su mero esposo:

—Escóndete lo más pronto posibile, porque ya viene él. Y te puede matar.

89 Había unos petates en el rincón. 90 El hombre entró en esos petates. 91 De allí estaba espiando a ver como era el esposo de su esposa. 92 Cuando apareció el esposo, vio que era una comadreja. 93 Ese animal era el esposo de ella. 94 Traía un tercio de leña en su espalda. 95 Sobre el tercio estaba sentado un ratón.

84 «Tees ya̱ ñgyeer. 85 Ru saca' zir ñgyeer», na' yu ze' orze'.
86 Gaze' nu brugyi' dri' loy ca yeed ñgyeem. 87 ¿La nay? psa' lagy yu. 88 Na ornu gud lagy la biñ mñaa ze' nu bi yeed ñgyeem na, orze' nam rab mi ñgyee gaal mi ze':
«Dzach zir pcach lo, gun bi yeed ñi, nis cut ñi ru», nam.
89 Gaze' nu zu tub nac da' gyi' yu. 90 Orze' gu' la yu gyeey ze' nañ da' ze'. 91 Rsiiñ yu ben la na ñgyee mñaay. 92 Ornu bruu za laa ñgyeem yeed ma, ca tub nguaa. 93 Ma ze' nac ñgyeem. 94 Ca ich ma tub yuu yag yeed ma. 95 Gal too ze' zub tub bziñ.

96 As soon as it arrived, it dropped the firewood. 97 Then it went into the house. 98 As soon as it entered the house, it sensed the smell of a person. 99 Then it said to the woman,

"Why is there such a strong odor of a person from the world here?"

100 It began to go about all over inside the house seeking the person. 101 But it didn't find him. 102 Then it began to beat the woman. 103 It entered her mouth three times. 104 It emerged from her buttocks. 105 In that way it beat the woman.

106 When the man understood that he would not be able to bring his wife home, he took out a match. 107 He struck it. 108 He set her house on fire. 109 When that was over, he took to the trail and came back to this world. 110 When he arrived at the entrance, there where the spiritualist waited, the spiritualist asked him,

96 Al llegar, luego dejó caer su leña. 97 Después se metió a la casa. 98 En cuanto entró a la casa, luego sintió el olor de una persona. 99 Después, le dijo ese animal a su esposa:

—¿Cómo es que huele mucho a gente del mundo aquí? —dijo el animal.

100 Y empezó a andar por todas partes de la casa buscando al hombre. 101 Pero no lo encontró. 102 Después empezó a pegarle a su mujer. 103 Tres veces le entró por la boca 104 Y le salió por la nalga. 105 De esa manera le pegó a ella.

106 Cuando ese hombre se dio cuenta de que ya no podía llevar a su esposa, sacó un cerillo. 107 Lo prendió. 108 Y le prendió fuego a la casa de ella. 109 Cuando terminó, se vino para este mundo. 110 Cuando llegó a la puerta, donde se había quedado el espiritista, le dijo el espiritista a él:

96 Laab bri ma, ni gaal pshet lag ma yag ze' ni ma. 97 Gaze' nu gu' ma nañ yu'. 98 Cuanzir gu' ma nañ yu', lueg la gu' gyidi'ñ ma nu ti' mbecy. 99 Gaze' nu na ma rab ma biñ mñaa ze':

«¿Ca dzi ti' mbecy nu bruu gyishlombecy ii?» na ma.

100 Brugyi' rded ma dutuub la nañ yu' ryub ma mbecy ze'. 101 Tees wangyad yu ni ma. 102 Gaze' nu brugyi' rgaaz ma biñ mñaa ze'. 103 Chon tir gu' ma ru'm. 104 Briib ma par rit iiñ mi. 105 Ni mod bgaaz ma biñ ze'.

106 Ornu bdu' yu gyeey ze' pon nu waca' gyed nuy mñaay, orze' gush za laay seri. 107 Blooy gyi. 108 Pcaay gyi yu'm. 109 Blazh ze', gaze' nu gush nez yu yeed yu par gyishlombecy ii. 110 Ornu briy gyero' ze' nu byeeñ mbecy siñ ze', orze' na mbecy siñ ze' rab yuy:

"What happened? 111 Did you meet your wife?"

112 Then *the man* answered,

"I met her. 113 But she did not want to come home. 114 I set fire to her house, because she didn't want to come home with me."

115 Then the spiritualist said,

"Why did you do that? 116 Now your house will have already been burned down when you arrive home, because the same house that is here *in this world* is also there *in that world*."

117 Then the man who went to fetch his wife was very sad. 118 Right at the edge of the rock, there where the spiritualist waited, they took out some mescal to drink. 119 They drank many portions of mescal at that place. 120 Then they took to the trail and went home.

—¿Qué sucedió? 111 ¿Encontraste a tu esposa? —dijo.

112 Entonces le contestó:

—Sí, la encontré. 113 Pero ella no quiso venir. 114 Entonces le prendí fuego a su casa, porque no quiso venir conmigo —dijo.

115 Entonces dijo el espiritista:

—¿Por qué hiciste eso? 116 Ahora, seguro que cuando llegues a tu casa ya se quemó, porque la misma casa que tienes aquí, es la que tiene ella allá —dijo.

117 Entonces se entristeció mucho el que fue por su esposa. 118 Después en el mismo lugar de esa piedra, en donde esperó el espiritista, sacaron mezcal para tomar. 119 Tomaron muchas medidas en ese lugar. 120 Después se fueron a la casa.

«¿La guc? 111 ¿A bdzeel ru mñaar?» nay.

112 Orze' nay:

«Bdzeela̱ ñii. 113 Tees wangalagy ñi ñgyeed ñi. 114 Orze' pca̱a gyi yu'ñ, gun wangalagy ñi ñgyeed nuñ ya̱», nay.

115 Orze' na mbecy siñ ze':

«¿Lagu ni bicy ru? 116 Ze' na segur la bi wic yu'r ornu rir, gun laab yu' ru nu zub ii zub gal ze'», nay.

117 Orze' tona' la bicy shni yu nu gua te mñaa. 118 Gaze' nu laab ru' gyita' ze', ze' nu blez mbecy siñ ze' bloo dey mashcaly go'y. 119 Zañ medid mashcaly go' dey lugaar ze'. 120 Blazh ze' gaze' nu gush nez dey yay.

121 Now when the man who went to fetch his wife arrived home, his house had really been on fire. 122 All of his children were just sitting at the foot of a tree when he arrived. 123 He asked his children,

"At what time did the house catch fire?"

124 His children told him what time the house caught fire. 125 At the exact time when he set fire to his wife's house, at that exact time his house caught fire in this world. 126 So he knew that the same house a person has in this world he has in heaven.

127 After that he waited until All Saints' Day. 128 Because his wife said that she would come home then. 129 But she told him to tell her children that they were not to be afraid when she came. 130 And she said that they should put a basin of water in the middle of the room for her to bathe in. 131 And they were to prepare a steam bath for her to enter.

121 Cuando llegó el que fue por su mujer, vio que era cierto que ya se había quemado su casa. 122 Al pie de un árbol estaban sus hijos cuando llegó. 123 Entonces dijo a sus hijos:

—¿A qué hora se quemó la casa? —dijo.

124 Entonces sus hijos le dijeron a que hora se había quemado la casa. 125 En la hora que él había quemado la casa de su esposa, esa misma hora se había quemado la casa que tenía en este mundo. 126 Entonces supo él que la casa que tiene una persona en esta mundo, es la misma que tiene en el cielo.

127 Así esperó hasta Todos Santos. 128 Porque era cuando dijo su esposa que iba a regresar. 129 Pero ella le había dicho que él dijera a sus hijos que no tuvieran miedo cuando ella llegara. 130 Y había dicho ella que pusieran una cazuela de agua para que ella se bañara dentro de la casa. 131 Y que preparen un temascal para que esté ella.

121 Na ornu bri yu nu gua te mñaa ze' na, ni gaal bi pca la gyi yu'y. 122 Se gyi' tub yag zi yu' de i'ñ yu ornu briy. 123 Orze' nay rab yu i'ñ yu:

«¿La or pca gyi yu'?» nay.

124 Orze' mnii i'ñ yu la or pca gyi yu' ze'. 125 Gal or la nu pcaay gyi yu' mñaay ze', ni' la or pca gyi yu'y nu zub par gyishlombecy ii. 126 Orze' gud lagy yu nu laaba' yu mbecy nu ricy cup yu gyishlombecy ii, laaba' nde' ricy cup yu gyibaa.

127 Gaze' nu ni zi'l blez yu gal sicytoo. 128 Gun orze' mnii mñaay nu gyed mi. 129 Tees mniim nu niiy lo de i'ñ mi nu cue' dzib dey ornu gyed mi. 130 Nunu mniim nu gzu dey tub casuel nis laagy mi gazel nañ yu'. 131 Nunu gzu lily dey tub ya nu cuim.

132 Now when All Saints'
Day came, that man did these
things. 133 He prepared all of
the things that she said, the
things that his wife said to be
precise. 134 He prepared all of
the things that people prepare
on All Saints' Day. 135 He put
all of those things on the altar.
136 Then he went to meet his
wife. 137 There was a small
mountain. 138 He sat down
there to see what time his wife
would arrive 139 When he
looked, a thick crowd of people
were approaching. 140 His wife
was traveling among them coming. 141 She had her shawl on
her head. 142 She came carrying a basket with a handle.
143 All of the many people who
were coming, each of them
went to the houses of their family. 144 Then immediately the
man ran home. 145 He went to
tell his children that his wife
was coming. 146 He said,
"Quick, get ready to eat, because mom is already on the
way."

132 Cuando llegó Todos Santos, así lo hizo ese hombre.
133 Preparó todas las cosas que
dijo ella; lo que su esposa había
dicho. 134 Preparó todas las cosas que prepara la gente en Todos
Santos. 135 Puso todas las cosas
en el altar. 136 Después se fue a
encontrar a su esposa. 137 Había
una lomita. 138 Allí se sentó él
mirando a qué hora llegaría su esposa. 139 Cuando se dio cuenta,
venía mucha gente. 140 Entre la
gente venía su esposa. 141 Tenía
su rebozo en la cabeza. 142 En la
mano venía trayendo una canasta
de asa. 143 Toda la muchedum-
bre que venía, cada quien se fue a
la casa de su respectiva familia.
144 Entonces inmediatamente el
que esperaba a su esposa se fue
corriendo a la casa. 145 Fue a
avisar a sus hijos que ya venía su
esposa. 146 Entonces dijo:
—Rápido preparen la comida,
porque ya viene mamá —dijo.

132 Na ornu bri sicytoo na, ni bicy yu gyeey ze'. 133 Bzu yey dela coz
nu mniim ze', de coz nu mnii mñaay ze' por cuen. 134 Bzu yey dela de coz
nu rzu ye mbecy sicytoo. 135 Pcuaay dela coz ze' lo nuun. 136 Gaze' nu zay
za cheel yu mñaay. 137 Zub tub bicy mi'. 138 Ze' gusub yu rgüiiy la or gruu
za mñaay gyed mi. 139 Ornu bgüiiy, nicy la yeed mbecy. 140 Lat ze' ca cha
mñaay ze' yeed mi. 141 Riib toom bay nim. 142 Zaab yaam tub chicyiw
zub yag ru' yeed mi. 143 Dela de mbecy zigy nu yeed ze', tub ga la dey yay
yu' famil niy. 144 Orze' a' zu lagy yu nu rbez mñaa ze' gush yu carer yay.
145 Ya niiy lo de i'ñ yu nu bi yeed mñaay. 146 Orze' nay:
«Dzach zi der bzu ye dow na gyit, gun bi yeed la ña'», nay.

147 Right away they prepared food to eat. 148 Now when they looked, a very large snake appeared coming. 149 All of their chickens, their turkeys, their dogs, all of them were afraid when they saw the snake. 150 Then the snake entered the house. 151 It began to go about smelling all of the things that were on the table. 152 When it finished smelling all of the things that were on the altar, it stopped and bathed in the basin they had put there. 153 After it finished bathing in the basin, it went into the steam bath. 154 It entered *the steam bath*. Then it began to roll around. 155 It was inside it rolling around. 156 After it finished doing that, then it took to the trail going home. 157 It went to the same place it came from. 158 Then the man took to the trail to go see where the animal was going.

147 Entonces luego prepararon la comida. 148 Cuando se dieron cuenta, era una culebra grande que venía. 149 Entonces todas las gallinas, guajalotes, perros, y todos esos animales que tenían se asustaron cuando vieron la culebra. 150 Después entró la culebra a casa. 151 Empezó a oler todas las cosas que había en el altar. 152 Cuando terminó de oler todas las cosas que había en el altar, se bañó en la cazuela que pusieron ellos. 153 Terminando de bañarse en la cazuela, se fue al temascal. 154 Entró allí. Después empezó a revolcarse. 155 Estaba revolcándose adentro. 156 Después de hacer eso, se fue. 157 Regresó al mismo lugar de donde vino. 158 El hombre fue también para ver a donde se iba el animal.

147 Orze' na naa la bzu ye dey nu dugow gyit. 148 Na ornu bgüii dey na, na tub bily ily bruu za ma yeed ma. 149 Orze' dela gyid ni dey, cuñ ni dey, che' ni dey, dela de ma ze' gudzib ma ornu bzaac ma bily ze'. 150 Gaze' nu gu' bily ze' nañ yu'. 151 Brugyi' rded ma rzuub gyidi'ñ ma dela de coz nu nguaa lo nuun ze'. 152 Blazh bzuub gyidi'ñ ma dela de coz nu nguaa lo nuun ze', gaze' nu guti ma rlaagy ma nañ casuel nu bzu dey ze'. 153 Blazh blaagy ma nañ casuel ze', gaze' nu gush nez ma za ma nañ ya ze'. 154 Gu' ma ze', Gaze' nu brugyi' rdudub ma. 155 Rdudub ma ri ma nañ ñi. 156 Blazh bicy ma de nde', gaze' nu gush nez ma ya ma. 157 Ya ma laaba' par ze' nu bruu ma. 158 Gaze' nu gush neza' yu gyeey ze' zay za güiiy ca par ya ma.

159 After it walked about twenty meters from the door, it became a person again. 160 She became just like his wife as she went away. 161 She was burdened down. 162 She was going home in order to take the things they had prepared. 163 So he thought that the dead really do come on All Saints' Day.

159 Caminó como veinte metros de la casa, y se volvió gente. 160 Así como había sido antes su esposa, y se fue. 161 Estaba cansada. 162 Fue a llevar las cosas que prepararon. 163 Entonces él pensó que es verdad que vienen los muertos el día de Todos Santos.

159 Tub gal gaal metr bza ma nu bruu ma ro', byaca' la ma mbecy. 160 Gal na zi'l mñaay bi byaca'm yam. 161 Secyi la zum. 162 Yam nu ya num de coz nu bzu yey ze'. 163 Orze' mnii tooy nu rishli ryeed añ sicytoo.

10

An Elderly Woman Discovers the Sun and the Moon

To a Zapotec the celestial bodies are not inanimate. They are not referred to with the inanimate pronoun. The stars and the moon are referred to with the third person animal pronoun. The sun is referred to with the third person respect pronoun. In men's speech this pronoun is reserved for women of higher social rank than the speaker and for God. Of course, it is possible for a noun to belong to a gender class to which it is not semantically suited. But such is not the case for the word for sun. Its gender affiliation is not accidental, but is semantically based.

The full Texmelucan Zapotec expression for sun is *doo güidz*. *güidz* is the word that is cognate with the words for sun in other Zapotecan languages. It occurs in only one other expression, the word for Mexico City, *ru' -güidz,* which means literally 'the mouth of the sun'.

Often the Sun is simply referred to in the shortened form of the expression, as *doo. doo* refers to the class of supernatural beings I translate 'fairy'. For "The Seven Kinds of Rain" and "Matlaziwa" I argued that this word is an ancient word for god. Even today some people treat the sun as a god.

The title was given by Claudio Martinez when he transcribed the text. It seems to contradict the ending. Most people I talk to believe that the boy and girl become the sun and moon. The ending suggests that the serpent's eyes become the sun and moon. Claudio says that the boy is thought to carry the sun through the sky, and the girl is thought to carry the moon through the sky.

171

They put out flowers and light candles before it. They cross themselves when the sun comes up, and they cross themselves when it goes down.

There are people who are thought to know the *[orsyoo] ni doo güidz* 'prayer to the sun'. *[orsyoo]* refers to words that have magical powers. They may come from the church like the Lord's prayer, or the Hail Mary. These words protect people from evil. Or they may be other kinds of magical words. *[orsyoo]* are thought by some to empower vampires, witches, and some kinds of curers. The 'prayer to the sun' is thought to enable people to finish their work quickly when they work for other people. When they work for themselves, the prayer does not help. It is also thought to enable people to arrive quickly when they go on a journey.

According to Zapotec solar mythology, there was a time before the sun came up, when people lived in darkness. When the sun came up people were so afraid that they ran in all directions trying to escape. Some people fell in the water. They became frogs. "An Old Lady Discovers the Sun and the Moon" is a very old and widespread tale that explains how the sun and the moon first came up. It was recorded on a tape recorder by Juana Antonio in 1976 in the presence of her family in her home. Her son Claudio Martinez later transcribed it in practical orthography. There are some missing episodes. Whatever supplemental information I was able to obtain I included in footnotes.

Una vieja encontró al Sol y a la Luna

Para los zapotecas los cuerpos celestiales no son inanimados. No hablan de ellos con un pronombre inanimado. Se refieren a las estrellas y a la luna con pronombre de animal de tercera persona. Se refieren al sol con el pronombre formal de tercera persona. En el habla masculina, este pronombre se reserva para mujeres de alto rango social, superior al que habla, y para Dios. Por supuesto, es posible que un nombre pertenezca a una clase de género al que no es adecuado semánticamente, pero éste no es el caso con la palabra para el sol. Su afiliación genérica no es accidental, sino que está semánticamente basada.

La expresión completa del zapoteca de Texmelucan para "sol", es *doo güidz*. *güidz* es la palabra que es pariente de las palabras para sol en otras lenguas zapotecas. Se presenta solamente en una expresión más, en la

Claudio Martínez puso el título cuando estaba transcribiendo el cuento. Pero parece que el título contradice el final del cuento. La mayoría de las personas con quienes he hablado piensan que el muchacho y la muchacha se convirtieron en el sol y la luna. Pero el final del cuento sugiere que los ojos de la serpiente se convirtieron en el sol y la luna. Claudio dice que el muchacho es el que carga el sol en el cielo y la muchacha es la que carga la luna en el cielo.

palabra para Ciudad de México *ru'-güidz,* que significa literalmente "la boca del sol."

Algunas veces se refieren al sol en la forma apocopada de la expresión, *doo. doo* se refiere a todas las clases de seres sobrenaturales que yo traduzco como "hada." Para "Las siete clases de lluvia" y "Matlaziwa" yo sostengo que ésta es una palabra antigua para decir Dios. Aun en la actualidad hay quien considera al sol como un dios. Le ponen flores y le prenden velas. Se persignan cuando sale el sol y se persignan cuando se pone.

Hay gente que se supone sabe *[orsyoo] ni doo güidz* 'la oración del sol'. *[orsyoo]* se refiere a palabras que tienen poderes mágicos. Puede que vengan de la iglesia, como el Padre Nuestro o el Ave María. Estas palabras protegen a la gente del mal. Puede que haya otras clases de palabras mágicas. *[orsyoo]* la usan para dar poder a vampiros, brujas, y a algunas clases de curaciones. Se piensa que la oración al sol ayuda a la gente a terminar su trabajo rápidamente cuando trabajan para otra persona. Cuando trabajan para ellos mismos esta oración no ayuda. También se piensa que ayuda a las personas a llegar rápido a su destino cuando salen de viaje.

Según la mitología solar zapoteca, hubo un tiempo antes que el sol saliera en que la gente vivía en tinieblas. Cuando el sol salió la gente se asustó tanto que corrió en todas direcciones tratando de escapar. Algunos cayeron al agua; se volvieron ranas. La historia de "La viejecita que encontró a la luna y al sol" es muy antigua y ampliamente conocida que explica cómo el sol y la luna salieron por primera vez.

Este cuento fue grabado en cinta magnética por Juana Antonio en 1976 en presencia de su familia, en su casa. Su hijo Claudio Martínez la escribió más tarde. Faltan algunos episodios. Toda la información adicional que pude juntar la incluí en las notas al pie de la página.

1 There once was an old woman 2 *who* was grinding *corn.* 3 A crab was going *to where she was grinding* to get some of her corn. 4 It was continually going to get *more of* her corn. 5 It went many times to get some corn. 6 Then she said to the crab,

"Ah, forked one, where are you taking my corn?"

7 She stood up and went to spy on the crab that was taking the corn. 8 The crab was traveling 9 with a piece of corn in its mouth.

10 "Oh, you devil of a forked one, where are you taking my corn?" she asked the forked one.

11 The forked one was continuing along. 12 The woman accordingly followed behind the forked one as it went along. 13 She walked and walked and walked. 14 In this way she arrived at *the place* where the forked one was going. 15 She continued on her way.

1 Había una vez una abuelita. 2 Estaba moliendo. 3 Vino un cangrejo a robarle su maíz. 4 Siempre iba ese cangrejo a robarle su maíz. 5 Iba a robarle maíz muchas veces. 6 Entonces dijo ella al cangrejo:

—Hay horqueta, ¿a donde vas con mi maíz?

7 Entonces se paró ella a espiar al cangrejo que se llevó el maíz. 8 El cangrejo siguió su camino. 9 Llevaba el maíz en su boca.

10 —Hay horqueta del diablo, ¿a dónde vas a llevar mi maíz? —le dijo ella a la horqueta.

11 La horqueta siguió su camino. 12 Ella iba de trás de la horqueta que seguía caminando. 13 Se fue, se fue, y se fue. 14 De esa manera llegó a donde estaba la horqueta. 15 Siguió su camino.

Tub Nis Biñ Bel Byad Mi Doo Güidz Nu Beey

1 Bzu tub nis biñ bel. 2 Orze' cam rom. 3 Rza be rza gyii ma uub nim. 4 I la rza be ze' rza gyii ma uub nim. 5 Tanta' guzañ tir nu rza gyii ma uub. 6 Orze' nam rab mi be:

«Ah biiz, ¿ca cha nu ru uub ya?» i na'm rab mi be.

7 Orze' wes su lam za siiñ mi ich be nu za nu ma uub. 8 Za be. 9 Zub ru' be uub za ma.

10 «Ah biiz lañ nushow, ¿ca cha nur uuba?» na'm raaba'm biiz.

11 Za biiz. 12 Dub ni zaab mi ich biiz zam. 13 Zam, zam, zam. 14 Ni mod la nu grim ze' nu za biiz. 15 Zam.

16 Then she arrived at the edge of a river. 17 She saw the forked one turn along side the river and continue going. 18 There was a rock from which water falls there. 19 It entered an opening under the rock. 20 That was where the water fell. 21 It fell from high up. 22 But just below *that rock* there was another wide rock. 23 She saw the forked one enter there. 24 That is the place it went to.

25 "Ah, forked one, why are you taking my corn so far?" 26 This is what she said.

27 She came close to the opening in the rock, when she saw that there were two babies.

28 "What will it do?" she wondered.

16 Después llegó ella a la orilla del río. 17 Vio que la horqueta entró a un lado del río y se fue. 18 Allí había una piedra de donde bajaba agua. 19 La horqueta entró de bajo de la piedra. 20 Allí bajaba agua. 21 El agua bajaba de lo alto. 22 Adentro estaba otra piedra ancha. 23 Ella vio que entró la horqueta alla. 24 Hasta allí fue.

25 —Hay horqueta, ¿por qué llevaste mi maíz tan lejos? 26 —Así decía ella.

27 Entonces se acercó a la entrada de la piedra, y vio que estaban allí dos nenes.

28 —Pero ¿qué hara ese animal? —pensaba ella.

16 Gaze' nu bru'ñam ru' gyoow. 17 I rgüiim gu' biiz cuit gyoow za ma. 18 Orze' ca tub gyita' la. 19 Gu' la ma ru' gyita' la ze'. 20 Orze' ze' yet nis. 21 Gya yet nis ze'. 22 Par nañ ze' riib tuba' gyita' she. 23 Rgüiim gu' biiz ze'. 24 Gashtal ze' ya ma orze'.

25 «Ah biiz, ¿lagu ga' dzi zet ya nur uuba̲?» 26 I na ga'm orze'.

27 Orze' mi ze' wecha'm garee ru' gyita' ze' ornu bzaac lam nu riib cyup mdoo.

28 Orze' par ¿la gyicy ma? rsa' lagy mi.

29 She stopped to spy on it. 30 When it arrived, it began to crumble the corn. 31 It put *some corn* in the mouths of each of the babies. 32 She felt sorry for the babies. 33 I have forgotten what she said to take possession of the babies.[1] But she carried the babies away. 34 She put the babies in her skirt. 35 Then she returned home.

36 While she was still far from the front door, she called to her *husband* Domingo,

"Come with my palm girdle. 37 Come with my cloth girdle, Domingo,[2] because my children have been born."

38 "Okay," said Domingo.

---

[1]Other sources indicate that she asked the crab how it was going to pay for the corn. Then she took the babies in payment for it.

[2]The cloth girdle is used to tighten and tie the palm girdle. The purpose of the women's girdles and the man's sash is to give strength and not allow them to have intestinal spasms: *cue' gash gyïb yu*. They are customarily put on by women after giving birth in order to keep air from entering the womb

29 Entonces se paró para espiarlo. 30 Cuando llegó el animal, empezó a hacer pedazos el maíz. 31 Lo echaba en la boca de cada uno de los nenes. 32 Entonces ella tuvo compasión de los nenes. 33 Se me olvidó lo que dijo ella para agarrar a los nenes.[1] Pero recogió ella a los nenes. 34 Y puso a los nenes en su enagua. 35 Entonces se fue.

36 Y le dijo ella a su esposo, Domingo, cuando todavía estaba lejos de la casa:

—Trae mi zoyate. 37 Trae mi ceñidor, Domingo,[2] porque di a luz.

38 —Está bien —dijo Domingo.

---

[1]Otras personas indican que la anciana le preguntaba al cangrejo con qui le va a pagar por el maíz. Entonces se llevó los nenes en pago por el maíz.

[2]El zoyate y el ceñidor son usados por las mujeres después de dar a luz para que el aire no le entra en la matriz.

---

29 Orze' gusum rsiiñ mi ni ma ze'. 30 Bru'ña la ma, brugyi' la rsug ma uub ze'. 31 Dri ma ru' tub ga mdoo ze'. 32 Orze' nu gushni lagy mi mdoo ze'. 33 Nde' nu mnit lagya̱ lac mniim bdu' yaam mdoo ze', tees orze' byuun mi mdoo ze'. 34 Bdu'm mdoo ze' ru' nerlom. 35 Yaa ga'm orze'.

36 Orze' nu na'm rab mi Ach nim zet ru' nu yam ro':

«Da nu daaba̱. 37 Da nu cuuñ ya̱ Achi, gun gul i'ña», naa ga'm raaba'm Achi nim orze'. 38 Orze'

«O», na ga' Achi.

39 He took the palm girdle to her. 40 He took the cloth girdle to her. 41 When she arrived, she wrapped the babies in some cloth. 42 Then she put *the babies* in their hammocks.[3] 43 I forget how they grew up. 44 I forget how the babies grew up. 45 But she succeeded in raising the babies. 46 When the children were already big she continued to baby them. 47 She went about while they were in their hammocks.

48 One day she went out to take food to her *husband* Domingo to eat *where he was working.* 49 *But first* she wrapped her babies in cloth. 50 She put them in their hammocks. 51 But she left one of her children called Paula behind 52 so that the orphans would have a companion. 52 Now they were delighted when they saw that the old woman had gone. 54 They sent Paula out onto the trail.

39 Le llevó el zoyate. 40 Le llevó su ceñidor. 41 Cuando llegó, envolvió a sus nenes en pañales. 42 Los puso en las hamacas.[3] 43 También se me olvidó cómo crecieron. 44 Se me olvidó cómo crecieran los nenes. 45 Pero ella logró que crecieran los niños. 46 Ya eran grandes, pero ella todavía los trataba como nenes. 47 Ella daba vueltas mientras los tenía en las hamacas.

48 Entonces un día fue ella a dejar las tortillas que comía su esposo Domingo. 49 Entonces envolvió ella a los nenes en pañales. 50 Los puso en las hamacas. 51 Y dejó a una de sus hijas, que se llamaba Paula, 52 para acompañar a los huérfanos. 52 Entonces ellos se pusieron contentos viendo que se iba su abuelita. 54 Y enviaron a Paula al camino.

---

[3]Babies sleep in oval beds suspended from the ceiling.

[3]Los nenes duermen en hamacas ovaladas suspendidas de techo de la casa.

39 Za num daab mi. 40 Za num cuuñ mi orze'. 41 Orze' brim ptiish mi mdoo ze' nim negy. 42 Bdu'm de nde' nim gyishtuy orze'. 43 Ni zi'l ti lac mod guuly nu nde'. 44 Nde' mnit lagya lac mod guuly mdoo ze'. 45 Tees bicy mi gan guuly mdoo ze'. 46 Bi zily la de fiñ ze' gaal zi ricy mdoom ñii. 47 Yu' de fiñ ze' nim gyishtuy rdeda'm.

48 Orze' tub dzi zam za seeñ mi gyit gow Ach nim. 49 Orze' ptiish mi mdoo negy. 50 Bdu'm ñii gyishtuy. 51 Ze' bzeeñ mi tub i'ñ mi nu la Uly. 52 Fiñ ze' bzeeñ mi nu gad losa'ñ de zi ze'. 52 Orze' na cyit ni deñ nu rgüiiñ nu za nis biñ bel ze'. 54 Orze' bzuu nez ñi Uly zañ gyernez.

55 "Go guard the trail to see what time mom will arrive home, so that we can unravel mom's yarn," they said to Paula.

56 "Okay," said Paula.

57 She took to the trail and went out onto the road way. 58 She sat down to watch *the trail* to see what hour the old lady would arrive home. 59 As Paula sat there, she got tired. 60 She slumped over face down on the road asleep. 61 She was unconscious when the old lady passed by. 62 *The old lady* put her foot right in Paula's mouth.

63 The young people were still unraveling her yarn. 64 They were delighted that she was gone. 65 They took hold of her yarn. 66 They got out of their hammocks. 67 They took hold of her yarn. 68 They began to wrap it all around the sides of the hammocks. 69 They hung it all around inside the house. 70 They did not notice when the old lady arrived home. 71 When they saw her approaching the door, they began to take up the yarn.

55 —Anda tú a cuidar en el camino a ver a qué hora llega mamá, porque vamos a desatar el hilo de ella —le dijeron a Paula.

56 —Está bien —dijo Paula.

57 Se fue ella al camino. 58 Se fue ella al camino a vigilar a qué horas llegaba la abuelita. 59 Estando Paula ahí sentada, le agarró el sueño. 60 Se acostó boca abajo en el camino a dormir. 61 No estaba despierta cuando pasó la abuelita. 62 Entonces la abuelita metió el pie en la boca de Paula.

63 Los niños estaban desenrollando los hilos de ella. 64 Ellos estaban contentos porque se había ido ella. 65 Tomaron el hilo de abuelita. 66 Se salieron de las hamacas. 67 Tomaron el hilo de ella. 68 Empezaron a enredarlo en las orillas de las hamacas. 69 Colgaron por toda la casa el hilo. 70 No se dieron cuenta de cuando llegó la abuelita. 71 Cuando miraron que ella estaba cerca de la casa, empezaron a enrollar el hilo.

---

55 «Gua ru ñar nez ben la or ri ña', gun shaagya duu laam», naañ rab ñi Uly.

56 «O», na Uly.

57 Gush nez ñi zañ gyernez. 58 Gzub ñañ nu la or gri nis biñ bel. 59 Zub ga Uly gush pcaal ñi. 60 Gugyit tiily ñi gyernez nas ñi. 61 A' zu lagy ñi ornu bded nis biñ bel. 62 Orze' mne' la gyi'm ru' Uly.

63 Orze' ni zi'l yu' la de fiñ ze' rshaagy ñi duu laam. 64 Cyit niñ nu zam. 65 Pshet la yaañ duu laa nim. 66 Bruu lañ nañ gyishtuy. 67 Pshet la yaañ duu laa nim. 68 Brugyi' la rtiish ñi dela ru' gyishtuy. 69 Dela nañ yu', dela se bzaab zi'l lañ duu laa nim. 70 Orze' wangad lagy ñi ornu bri nis biñ bel. 71 Or bgüiiñ bi yagaab mi ro' brugyi' la rshaagy deñ nu nde'.

72 They frantically took it up. 73 But they did not succeed in rolling it up. 74 Then she arrived.

75 "And I have been treating you as babies. 76 Just look at what a mess you have created now. 77 Why did you unravel my yarn? 78 Why did you play with my yarn?" she said to them.

79 "Don't get mad mom. You should buy me a machete stub, so that I can work," said the young man.

80 "Don't get mad, mom. You should buy me a grinding stone, so that I can grind *corn* and pat tortillas for you to eat," said the young woman.

81 They were a young man and a young woman.

82 When her *husband* Domingo arrived in the afternoon,

72 Lo enrollaron furiosamente. 73 Ya no pudieron de terminar de enrollarlo. 74 Entonces llegó ella.

75 —Estaba yo tratándoles como nenes. 76 Ahora miren lo que estan haciendo. 77 ¿Por qué están desenrollando mi hilo? 78 ¿Por qué están jugando con mi hilo? —les dijo ella.

79 —No te enojes mamá, porque quiero que me compres un machete chundo, porque yo voy a trabajar —dijo el que era el niño.

80 —No te enojes mamá, porque, quiero que me compras un metate, porque yo voy a moler y voy a hacer memelas para que comas —dijo la niña.

81 Eran dos jóvenes, un hombre y una mujer.

82 Cuando llegó su esposo Domingo en la tarde,

72 Loc la rshaagy deñ nu nde'. 73 Wangyicya' deñ gan nlazh nde' ntub ñii. 74 Orze' brim na.

75 «La zi ya ricya de ru nu mdoo der ricya. 76 Lac na güii la na riiñ nu ricy der. 77 ¿Lagu rshaagy der duu laa? 78 ¿Lagu rgyit nu der duu laa?» na ga'm raba'm deñ.

79 «Cue' gyedza' ru ña' gun zi ru chun ne, gun ya gyicya riiñ», na' fiñ gyeey ze'.

80 «Cue' gyedza' ru ña' gun zi ru gyech ne, gun ya do shuuba cu'ñ gow ru», na ga' fiñ mñaa ze'.

81 Tub fiñ gyeey nu tub fiñ mñaa.

82 Orze' na or bri Ach nim or gudze na,

"This is what our son said. 83 We should buy him a machete now so that he can work. 84 He will clear the bush. 85 He will help you. 86 This is what he said. 87 We should buy it now. 88 As for the young girl, she should get a grinding stone, so that she could grind *corn* and pat tortillas for us to eat. 89 This is what she said. 90 Now our children have really become useful," she said to her husband, Domingo.

91 "Okay," said Domingo.

92 He went out and bought the boy a machete stub. 93 I forget what *the boy* did with his machete stub. 94 But he did not do any good with it. 95 *His parents* were very angry with him. 96 Then he said that he should get a rifle so that he could shoot deer.

97 "Buy me a rifle, so that I can shoot deer for us to eat," he said.

98 "What good would you do? 99 Would you really be faithful even if I bought it for you?" asked the old lady.

—Así dijeron nuestro hijo. 83 Así que debemos comprar un machete para él porque va a trabajar. 84 Va a chaponear el monte. 85 Te va a ayudar. 86 Así dijo. 87 Compremos eso ahora. 88 Y la muchacha tendrá su metate, porque va a moler y a hacer memelas, para que comamos. 89 Eso fue lo que dijo. 90 Ahora sí son útiles nuestros hijos —le dijo ella a su esposo.

91 —Está bien —dijo Domingo.

92 Fue y le compró el chundo. 93 Se me olvidó cómo hizo con su machete chundo. 94 Pero no hizo nada bueno con su machete chundo. 95 Entonces se enojaron con él. 96 Entonces dijo que debía tener un rifle para ir a cazar venados.

97 —Compra un rifle para mí, porque voy a cazar venados para comer —dijo.

98 —¿Qué de bien vas a hacer? 99 ¿Vas a cumplir aunque te compre yo eso? —le dijo la abuelita.

«I na i'ñ na. 83 Na zin mandzicy niñ gun gyicy ñi riiñ. 84 Ga'n ñi gyish. 85 Locyuub ñi ru. 86 I nañ. 87 Zin nu nde' na. 88 Ze' na fiñ mñaa re gad gyech niñ gun goñ shuub ñi cu'ñ don. 89 I nañ. 90 Na gaal la byalily i'ñ na na», I nam rab mi Ach nim orze'.

91 «O», na Ach.

92 Gua ga'm wiim chun niñ. 93 Orze' nu mnit lagya lac bicy ñi nu chun niñ ze'. 94 Gun tees orze' walab nu nap bicy ñi nuñ chun niñ ze'. 95 Orze' nu bdza' ga' dem niñ. 96 Orze' nu mniiñ nu gada' gyercoo niñ nu cha coo ga'ñ dziñ mnii ga'ñ orze'.

97 «Zi ru gyercoo ne, gun cha coo dziñ don na», na ga'ñ.

98 «¿La gyicy nap ru? 99 ¿La gyicy paa ru mas zi de nu nde' nir?» na ga' nis biñ bel orze'.

100 "I will shoot deer, mom. 101 I will shoot deer, Domingo. 102 Buy me a rifle," he said.

103 So they bought *him* a rifle.

104 "Now Domingo will go to work, but I will go about hunting for deer to eat," he said.

105 "Okay," they said.

106 Now after *he* got the rifle, old Domingo went to work, 107 and he went to hunt deer. 108 Now when the sun was ready to set,[4] he had already arrived home. 109 He arrived with a deer.

110 "Now I have really shot a deer, mom," he said to the old lady.

111 "It was Domingo you shot, wasn't it?" she said.

---

[4]Claudio says that the time of day communicated by this clause is probably a mistake. The boy arrived home at dusk. He talked to his mother and went with her to the river. Then she took lunch to Domingo in the field. Since lunch is in the middle of the day, the boy should have arrived home while it was still morning.

100 —Cazaré venados, mamá. 101 Cazaré venados, Domingo. 102 Cómprame un rifle —dijo él.

103 Entonces le compraron un rifle.

104 —Ahora, que vaya Domingo a trabajar, porque yo andaré cazando venado para comer —dijo.

105 —Está bien —dijo.

106 Después de conseguir el rifle, entonces se fue Domingo, abuelo, a trabajar. 107 Y se fue el huérfano a la cazería de venado. 108 Cuando el sol se acababa de poner,[4] llegó él. 109 llegó con un venado.

110 —Ahora sí maté un venado mamá —le dijo él a la abuelita.

111 —¿No es Domingo él que mataste? —dijo ella.

---

[4]Claudio dice que la hora del día que se entiende de esta cláusula es probablemente incorrecta. El muchacho llega a la casa al anochecer, habla con su mamá y se va con ella al río. Entonces ella le lleva la comida a Domingo al campo. Siendo que la comida es al mediodía, el muchacho debía haber llegado a la casa mientras todavía era mañana.

100 «Coo dziñ ña'. 101 Coo dziñ Achi. 102 Zi lar gyercoo ne», na ga'ñ.

103 Orze' wii ga' dem gyercoo na.

104 «Par na cha laa Ach re gyicy yu riiñ, gun ya chesa guuz dziñ don», na ga'ñ.

105 «O», na ga' dem orze'.

106 Guuda' gyercoo na, orze' za laa Ach bel gyicy mi riiñ. 107 Za fiñ zi ze' guuz dziñ. 108 Na byagal zi'l doo, orze' bi briiñ. 109 Bri nuñ dziñ.

110 «Na gaal la pcoo dziñ ña'», na'ñ raba'ñ nis biñ bel.

111 «Seegaar ru, Ach pcoor ¿shiñ?» na ga'm.

112 "I said that I was going to shoot a deer. So why would I shoot Domingo?" he said.

113 "Hurry and remove its liver then, so I can roll *it* in the ashes and then I can chew it when I go to the river *to get water*," said the old lady.

114 "Okay," he said.

115 He stuck a knife into the deer. 116 He removed its liver. 117 She rolled it in the ashes. 118 She began chewing it. 119 She went to get water. 120 When she arrived at the edge of the well,

"Croak, croak. 121 Croak, Croak," went the frog. 122 "Croak, croak, you are eating the liver of your husband," said the frog.

123 Then she thought, "He must have shot Domingo. 124 Otherwise, why would it have said that?" she thought.

125 "Croak, croak, you are eating the liver of your husband," said the frog as it sat there.

112 —¿Por qué voy a matar yo a Domingo? Yo fui a cazar venados, te digo —dijo él.

113 —Entonces, rápido, saca el hígado del venado, porque quiero revolcarlo entre la ceniza para masticarlo mientras voy al río a traer agua —dijo la abuelita.

114 —Bueno —le dijo.

115 Abrió la barriga del venado con un cuchillo. 116 Le sacó el hígado. 117 Lo revolcó en la ceniza. 118 Y se puso a masticarlo. 119 Se fue a traer agua. 120 Cuando llegó ella al pozo,

—Cua, cua. 121 Cua, cua —dijo la rana—. 122 Cua, cua, estás comiendo el hígado de tu señor esposo —dijo la rana.

123 Entonces pensó ella: "Seguro que él mató a Domingo. 124 ¿Por qué dijo eso el animal? pensó ella.

125 —Cua, cua, estás comiendo el hígado de tu señor esposo —dijo la rana.

112 «¿Lagu coo ya̱ Ach?, gun dziñ gua co̱o rnee̱», na ga'ñ.

113 «Orze' dzach ru beni bloo lagy ma, gun tuba̱ lat di'ñ tub ru̱' cha̱ gyoow», na ga' nis biñ bel ze'.

114 «O», na'ñ.

115 Bzu ga' lañ gyiscyiib nañ dziñ. 116 Blooñ lagy ma. 117 Ptuba' lam lat di'ñ. 118 Rac ru'm nde'. 119 Zam gyoow. 120 Ornu bru'ña ru' zo, orze'

«Ngaa̱y, nga̱ay. 121 Orze' nga̱ay, nga̱ay», ricya' bigy. 122 «Nga̱ay, nga̱ay ror lagy shi ñgyeer», na ga' bigy orze'.

123 Orze' rnii ga' toom: «Seegaar fiñ re Ach pcooñ. 124 ¿Lagu ni rnii ma re?» rsa' ga' lagy mi. 125 Orze'

«Nga̱ay, nga̱ay ror lagy shi ñgyeer», rnii ga' bigy ri ga' ma.

126 After that she filled her water jug 127 and returned home. 128 Now when she arrived,

"You surely shot Domingo, didn't you?" she said.

129 "Enough. 130 Why should I shoot Domingo? 131 I went to shoot a deer. 132 Why should I shoot Domingo?" he asked.

133 "Why did the frog say this to me then? 134 It said, 'croak, croak, you are eating your husband.' 135 Therefore, I figure that you shot Domingo," she said.

136 "In that case let's go listen to see *if it is so.* 137 Let's go so that you can show me if that is really what it said," he said to her.

138 "Okay," she said.

139 She led the way. 140 The young man hung back. 141 On the way he picked some fruit of the copal tree. 142 Then he passed in front *of her.*

126 Después llenó ella su cántaro. 127 Y regresó a la casa. 128 Cuando llegó,

—Seguro que mataste a Domingo, ¿no?

129 —¡Basta! 130 ¿Por qué voy a matar yo a Domingo? 131 Fui a matar un venado. 132 ¿Por qué matara a Domingo? —le dijo.

133 —¿Por qué me dijo esto la rana, pues: 134 'Cua, cua, estas comiendo el hígado de tu señor esposo?' 135 Por eso pienso que mataste a Domingo —dijo ella.

136 —Pues si es así, vamos para que escuchamos qué es. 137 Vamos para que me enseñes, para ver si de veras así dice —le dijo él a ella.

138 —Bueno —dijo ella.

139 Entonces se fue ella adelante. 140 Él se fue atrás de ella. 141 En el camino, cortó frutas de copalero. 142 Entonces, pasó él adelante.

126 Ni zi'l la pchaam re' nim. 127 Orze' gush nez mi yam. 128 Na or brim na:

«¿Seegaar ru Ach pcoor ¿shiñ zi?» na ga'm orze'.

129 «Cha' ru ii. 130 ¿Lagu coo ya̲ Ach? 131 Dziñ gua̲ coo ya̲. 132 ¿Lagu coo ya̲ Ach?» na ga'ñ.

133 «¿Lagu̲ ni mnii bigy lo̲ beni? 134 Ngaay, ngaa̲y row ru lagy shi ñgyeer, na ga' bigy ri ma. 135 Nde' nu rsa' lagya̲ nu Ach pcoor», na ga'm.

136 «Nde' ru' yaa chan cha zuub gyidag na ben. 137 Yaa chan cha lyuur lo̲ ben a ni gaal ni rnii ma», na ga'ñ raba'ñ mi orze'.

138 «O», na'm.

139 Zub lom za ga'm orze'. 140 Ze' fiñ ze' zaab ñi gal ich. 141 Nez za laañ pcyug lañ uugy ni ya yaal. 142 Orze' bded lo lañ orze'.

143 "Where is it now?" he said.

144 "There it is," she said.

145 He quickly put the fruit of the copal tree in its mouth.

146 It only went "croak, croak, croak."

The young man said,

147 "Look at what it is doing now! 148 Look! 149 You are lying. 150 Look! 151 You said that it speaks. 152 Why should it speak? 153 If what you say is true, why doesn't it speak now? 154 It only makes noise with its mouth. 155 You lie. 156 Why should it speak like that?"

157 She didn't say anything more. 158 She returned home.

159 "Hurry up. 160 Remove the blood *from the deer* so that I can cook a meal[5] 161 to take to Domingo for lunch," she said.

162 "Okay," he said.

---

[5]She wants to make blood sausage *morsiily* as part of the meal to take to Domingo for lunch.

---

143 —¿Dónde está ese animal ahora? —dijo.

144 —Allí está —dijo ella.

145 Entonces, ¡chas! le puso la fruta de copalero en la boca al animal.

146 —Cua, cua, cua —nada más decía la rana.

—147 ¡Mira lo que hace ahora. 148 ¡Mira! 149 Mientes. 150 ¡Mira! 151 Tú dices que habla ese animal. 152 ¿Por qué va a hablar ese animal? 153 ¿Por qué no habla ahora? 154 La boca nada mas está sonando. 155 Mientes tú. 156 ¿Por qué va a hablar así ese animal? —Así le dijo él a la abuelita.

157 Ella no dijo nada. 158 Entonces regresó a casa.

159 —Apúrate. 160 Saca la sangre pues, para hacer la comida.[5] 161 Voy a llevarle la comida a Domingo —dijo ella.

162 —Está bien —dijo él.

---

[5]Ella quiere hacer chorizos de sangre como parte de lo que se va a comer.

---

143 «¿Ca ri ma na?» nañ.

144 «Re ri ma», na'm.

145 Orze' chaj la briñ uugy ni ya yaal ze' ru' ma orze'.

146 «Ngaay, ngaay, ngaay», zi'l ricy ma ze'. 147 Orze' «Güii la ricy ma na. 148 Güiin. 149 Rguur na. 150 Güiin. 151 Ze' ru nar rnii ma nar. 152 ¿Lagu nii ga' ma re? 153 ¿Lagu na wagnii ma beni? 154 Ru' zi'l ma psiigy ma. 155 Nu rguu ru. 156 ¿Lagu ni nii ma re?» i nañ raba'ñ nis biñ bel orze'.

157 Wanii ga'm. 158 Orze' bish cyam yam.

159 «Bicy lal. 160 Bloo reñ beni, gun cyi' comid. 161 Cha du cui Ach», i na ga'm.

162 «O», na'ñ.

163 He began to prepare the deer. 164 He removed the blood for her to cook. 165 She went out again. 166 Lunch time came. 167 She went to take Domingo his lunch. 168 She went along on one side *of a ravine*. 169 She saw Domingo like a white patch lying among the bean plants.

170 "Why are you sleeping Domingo?" she called to her husband Domingo as she went along one side *of the ravine.*

171 She yelled like that at Domingo as she went along. 172 But Domingo did not wake up. 173 She arrived at where Domingo was.

174 "Get up, Domingo. 175 You sure are sleeping a lot. 176 *Get up* because our son has shot a deer," she said.

177 She slapped Domingo on the back. 178 When the wasps emerged from inside Domingo's clothing, they got all over the old lady. 179 She began to tumble down the hill. 180 She continually rolled, over and over. 181 An opossum was sitting on one side *of the ravine.*

163 Entonces empezó a arreglar el venado. 164 Sacó la sangre para que ella la cociera. 165 Entonces se fue ella. 166 Llegó la hora de comer. 167 Y se fue ella a llevarle la comida a Domingo. 168 Se fue al otro lado. 169 Miró a Domingo como una mancha blanco acostado entre el frijolar.

170 —¿Por qué estás durmiendo Domingo? —le dijo ella a su Domingo yéndose al otro lado.

171 Así se fue gritando a Domingo mientras caminaba hacia él. 172 No despertó Domingo. 173 Ella llegó a donde estaba Domingo.

174 —Levántate Domingo. 175 Duermes mucho. 176 Nuestro hijo mató un venado —dijo ella.

177 Le pegó en la espalda a Domingo con la mano. 178 Cuando salieron las avispas de dentro de la ropa de Domingo, se atacaron las avispas a la abuelita. 179 Ella empezó a revolcarse rodando por la colina. 180 Rodó, rodó y rodó. 181 Un tlacuache estaba al otro lado.

163 Orze' brugyi' bicy nap ñi dziñ. 164 Blooñ reñ pcyi'm. 165 Orze' gush nez mi za'm. 166 Byap or cui. 167 Gush nez mi zam za num cui Ach. 168 Zam tub la' dzu. 169 Rgüiim se caacy Ach mbisha'm lat lya'.

170 «¿Lagu nas ru Ach?» na'm raba'm Ach nim za'm tub la' dzu.

171 Ni zi'l rbish ti num Ach zam. 172 Wancyish la Ach yaa. 173 Bru'ñam lo Ach.

174 «Weshte Ach. 175 Dzi raas ru. 176 Gun pcoo i'ñ na dziñ», na'm.

177 Briich la yaam ich Ach. 178 Ornu briib la bez nañ shab Ach, bzu laa ma nis biñ bel. 179 Brugyi' la rzu la tyeñ mi zam par gyoow. 180 Se la rdudub mi zam. 181 Orze' zuba' lez tub la' dzu.

182 "Into the water, lady. 183 Into the water, lady," said the opossum while sitting on one side *of the ravine.*

184 The wasps stayed with the unfortunate woman, rolling her along, they were so active. 185 The orphan had filled the inside of Domingo's clothing with wasps. 186 It had seemed to her that Domingo was sleeping. 187 But instead he was lying there with wasps inside his clothing. 188 That was all.

189 I forget what happened next. 190 Perhaps she went to speak *with the children.* 191 She might have gone to fight with the young people. 192 Whatever. 193 But they were angry and therefore scattered. 194 They went away. 195 Who knows who they met? 196 But *whoever they were* they told the young children not to take the trail to the left, because the proud mouthed bird was there. 197 They warned them. 198 But the young people would not listen. 199 They took the road to the left.

182 —Al agua, señora. 183 Al agua, señora —decía el tlacuache que estaba al otro lado.

184 Las avispas le hicieron revolcar así mientras la picaban. 185 El huérfano había puesto puras avispas dentro de la ropa de Domingo. 186 Ella pensaba que estaba durmiendo Domingo. 187 Pero él estaba tirado con avispas en su ropa. 188 Se acabó.

189 No recuerdo que pasó después. 190 Tal vez fue a hablar *con los niños.* 191 Entonces fue ella a regañarlos. 192 Lo que sea. 193 Pero entonces ellos se enojaron y se dispersaron. 194 Se fueron por su camino. 195 ¿Quién sabe a quienes encontraron? 196 Pero les dijeron que no fueran por el camino de la izquierda, porque allí estaba el pájaro de pico orgulloso. 197 Los viejos les dijeron que no fueran por ese camino. 198 Pero los jóvenes no los obedecieron. 199 Siguieron por el camino de la izquierda.

---

182 «Lo nis nisa. 183 Lo nis nisa», rnii ga' lez zuba' ma tub la' dzu.

184 Ii pro nis biñ bel rtub laa bez mi yad nu mam tanta' nu ricy ma. 185 Du ub bez zi'l bdu' ga' zi ze' nañ shab Ach. 186 Guzii ga'm nu nas Ach guziim. 187 Ii mi ze' ca bez yu' nañ shab mi mbish mi. 188 Orze' ni zi'l.

189 Nde' mnit lagya lac. 190 O ti byam bya niim. 191 Byam gucoo num de fiñ ze'. 192 ¿Lac? 193 Tees orze' la nu guzi lagy deñ nu brush las ñi. 194 Za laañ orze'. 195 Orze' nu ti cyu bdzeel ñi raj. 196 Orze' nu mnii dem gugy mi ñii nu cue' chañ nez yaa reg, gun ze' zub chigyiñ ru' le'. 197 Mnii ga' dem looñ. 198 Ze' de fiñ ze' wangyeñ ñi. 199 Za laa deñ nez yaa reg.

200 There they encountered a serpent. 201 They removed one of the serpent's eyeballs. 202 That eye became the moon. 203 The left eye became the moon. 204 The right eye became the sun. 205 But I forget how it happened. 206 Why did maggots hatch on the moon? 207 Maggots hatched on the moon causing it to look like a rabbit. 208 Maggots hatched *on the moon*. 209 That is what they say. 210 I forget how else it goes. 211 But this is what happened when sun came up, they say.

200 Entonces allí encontraron una serpiente. 201 Entonces le sacaron un ojo a la serpiente. 202 Entonces, eso se volvió la Luna. 203 El ojo izquierdo de ese animal, se convirtió en la Luna. 204 Y el ojo derecho se convirtió en el Sol. 205 Pero no recuerdo cómo. 206 ¿Por qué brotaron gusanos en la luna? 207 Brotaron gusanos en la luna para que parezca un conejo. 208 Los gusanos brotaron. 209 Eso es lo que decían. 210 Se me olvidó qué sigue. 211 Pero dicen que esa es la manera como salió el sol.

200 Orze' ze' byap ñi serpient. 201 Orze' nu blooñ tub urlo serpient ze'. 202 Orze' nde' byac ñi beey. 203 Urlo reg ma ze', nde' byac ñi beey. 204 Ze' urlo bee ma, nde' byac ñi doo güidz. 205 Par nde' mnit lagya nu lac mod. 206 ¿Lagu nu guucha' bya' lo beey ze'? 207 Bya' gucha' ma lo beey ze' nu gal na bich na ca. 208 Nde' bya' guch ma. 209 Nde' rnii ga' dem. 210 Par nde' mnit lagya laca' zir mod rnii nu nde'. 211 Tees ni mod guca' nu briiba' doo güidz rnii ga' dem.

11

Lovers

When I was learning Zapotec I discovered that an innocent comment like "That sure is an ugly dog" could elicit an angry response. "Are you alluding to me?" my companion might say. Because that is one way Zapotecs insult each other. A similar technique is used in the following discourse between a young man and a young woman to tell of their love for each other.

This text was given to me by Alvaro Marcial in 1989. He wrote it in practical orthography.

El amor de dos jóvenes

Cuando estaba aprendiendo el zapoteca descubrí que un inocente comentario como: "Ése sí que es un perro feo" puede provocar una enfurecida respuesta. "¿Te estás refiriendo a mí?", podría decir mi compañero, porque esa es la forma como los zapotecas se insultan uno al otro. Una técnica parecida se usa en el siguiente diálogo entre un joven y una señorita al decirse su amor uno al otro.

Este texto me lo dio Álvaro Marcial en 1989. Lo escribió en ortografía regular.

1 A young man said to a young woman,

"Today I saw a pigeon all alone. 2 Its color was quite pretty. 3 Its bill and feet were red. 4 And it had already shed the feathers with which it hatched. 5 I want to get it so much it hurts. 6 But what should I do to get it to keep."

7 Then the young woman said,

"I also saw a dove in the mountains today. 8 It was sitting on a plant that flowers. 9 The feathers had also finished coming out on its head. 10 And I also liked its color a lot. 11 There was a white patch on its neck. 12 If I were to get it, I would make a cage to put it in. 13 I would put *the cage* on the edge of the mat on which I sleep so that it could sing to me late into the night."

1 Un joven le dijo a una muchacha:

—Hoy vi una paloma que estaba solo. 2 Su color era muy bonito. 3 Su pico y sus pies eran rojos. 4 Y ya se le habían caídos las plumitas que trajo al nacer. 5 Me gustaría tanto tenerlo que hasta tengo dolor. 6 Pero ¿qué, debo hacer para poseerlo? —dijo.

7 La joven le dijo:

—Yo también vi un palomo en las montañas hoy. 8 Estaba posada en una planta de flores. 9 Ya le habían terminado de salir las plumas de la cabeza. 10 Y me gustaron bastante sus colores también. 11 Tenía una mancha blanca en el cuello. 12 Si la pudiera tener, haría una jaula para ponerla. 13 La pondría a un lado del petate en que duermo para que me cantara hasta altas horas de la noche —dijo ella.

Tub yu feñ nu tub fiñ feñ rniiy nu rca dey losa'y

1 Tub yu feñ nay rab yu tub fiñ feñ:

«Dzi na bzaca tub culumbu ub zi. 2 Cyit ñuu coloor ma. 3 Nunu nu ña cyuru' ma, nu gyi' ma. 4 Nunu bi blazh mne' ma de doob nu guch nu ma. 5 Na rziñ lañ añ ne nu rlagya nu gad ma ne. 6 Par lac gyicya nu gad ma gane», nay.

7 Orze' na fiñ feñ ze":

«Ni' zi'l ya bzaca tub begy logyi' dzi na. 8 Zub ma lo tub ya gyee. 9 Nunu ni' zi'l bi blazh briib doob cyug ma. 10 Nunu ni' dzi bet lagya coloor ma. 11 Ri tub nu cacy yeñ ma. 12 Benu bi guud ma ne, orze' zaa tub ya ligy nu cui ma. 13 Orze' zuuba ma ru' da' nu rdasa nu gul ma lo gudze za zily la» nañ.

12

The Vampire

Zapotecs believe that there are people living among them who are vampires. It is not clear how they become vampires. One man told me that they are born with a hair in their heart. The hair makes them do the things they do. Another man told me that they are able to do the things they do because they know magical words. No explanation was offered as to how people learn these words, but there is a widespread belief that there are books one can study to learn such words.

Vampires prey on people at night. They drink their blood and cause them to develop a sickness called *bi dañ* 'evil air'. When people become sick, if they dream they are fighting with someone, they may have *bi dañ*. One lady, after such a dream, told me that when she woke up she had teeth marks on her leg. That proved a vampire bit her. Vampires especially like the blood of babies. The main symptom for a baby is sudden death. If when a baby goes to sleep at night it is well, and if in the morning it is dead with a bruised neck, it is said to have died of *bi dañ*.

The cure for *bi dañ* is a special herb medicine. People also put holy water, garlic, or chile on their bed. The Vampire text was given to me in 1973 by a man in early twenties. It is composed of two short stories. The first one is the tale of a man who spent the night at the home of the vampire. He was a witness to what she did. The second one is the story of a woman who was caught red—handed flying through the air in the form of a turkey. The stories were offered to me as proof that vampires really do exist. I have several versions of these stories. I include information from those versions and from talking to my advisors in footnotes.

El vampiro

Los zapotecas creen que allí hay gente que vive entre ellos que son vampiros. No es muy claro cómo se convirtieron en vampiros. Un hombre me dijo que nacen con un pelo en el corazón. Ese pelo hace que hagan las cosas que hacen. Otro me dijo que pueden hacer las cosas que hacen porque saben palabras mágicas. No hay explicación de cómo la gente aprende estas palabras, pero hay la creencia popular de que existen libros que uno puede leer para aprenderlas.

Los vampiros atacan a la gente en la noche. Les chupan la sangre y les causan una enfermedad que se llama *bi dañ* o "aire malo." Cuando la gente se enferma, si sueñan que están peleando con alguien, puede ser que tengan *bi dañ*. Una señora, después de un sueño así, me dijo que cuando despertó tenía marcas de dientes en la pierna, lo que prueba que un vampiro la chupó.

A los vampiros les gusta especialmente la sangre de los nenes. El síntoma principal en los bebés es la muerte repentina. Si un bebé está bien en la noche cuando se duerme y en la mañana amanece muerto con un moretón en el cuello, se dice que murió de *bi dañ*.

El remedio para *bi dañ* es una medicina especial de hierbas. Algunos ponen también agua bendita, ajos, o chiles en su cama.

El texto del vampiro me lo dio en 1973 un hombre como de 20 años. Se compone de dos historias cortas. La primera es la historia de un hombre que pasa la noche en la casa de un vampiro. Fue testigo de lo que el vampiro hizo. La segunda es la historia de una mujer que fue atrapada volando en forma de guajolote. Estos cuentos me los dieron para probar que los vampiros realmente existen. Tengo varias versiones de estos cuentos. Incluyo información de las dos versiones y de la obtenida en las pláticas con mis colaboradores en las notas al pie de la página.

1 There once was a man *who* 2 went to the house of a companion. 3 That companion's wife was a vampire. 4 Whatever errand was the man going on? 5 Anyway he slept at the house of the person who was a vampire.

6 They all lay down to go to sleep. 7 When it was late at night, the woman began to act strangely. 8 Her husband was already laying there a sleep. 9 The man who was spending the night in their house was quietly laying there. 10 He was spying on the woman. 11 "Why is she acting this way?" he said *to himself*. 12 He began to spy on her.

13 She began to act strangely. 14 She was combing her hair. 15 She was putting corn cobs in the fire. 16 She was walking about acting strangely.

17 "Why is she acting this way?" he wondered.

18 He began to spy on her.

1 Hace tiempo había un hombre. 2 Él fue a la casa de uno de sus compañeros. 3 Y la esposa de aquel compañero era vampiro. 4 ¿Quién sabe a que fue aquella persona? 5 Pero se quedó a pasar la noche en la casa de la persona que era vampiro.

6 Y se acostaron para dormirse. 7 Cuando ya estaba bien oscuro, la mujer empezó a comportarse muy extraño. 8 Y su esposo ya estaba dormido. 9 Mientras tanto, la persona que se había quedado a pasar la noche en la casa de aquellas personas estaba despierto. 10 Estaba espiando a la mujer. 11 "¿Por qué se está comportando muy extraño?" se dijo a sí mismo. 12 Y empezó a espiar a ella.

13 Ella empezó a comportarse tan extraño. 14 Se puso a peinarse. 15 Echaba los olotes al fuego. 16 Ella andaba comportándose muy extraño.

17 —¿Por qué se comporta así —pensaba él.

18 Empezó a espiar a ella.

Byee

1 Gulas bzu tub mbecy. 2 Guay yu' tub losa'y. 3 Yu ze' nac mñaay byee. 4 ¿Ti la riñ gua mbecy ze'? 5 Orze' ptaas yu yu' mbecy nu nac byee ze'.

6 Orze' gucua dey nas yu. 7 Ornu becheñ, becheñ nap zi'l, orze' brugyi' shiñ ricy biñ mñaa ze'. 8 Ze' ñgyeem bi mbish yu nas yu. 9 Orze' ze' mbecy nu beche yu' de yu ze', yu ze' ri mbish yu. 10 Psiiñ yu ni biñ mñaa ze'. 11 «¿Lagu shiñ ricy mi?» nay. 12 Orze' brugyi' rsiiñ yu ni mi ze'.

13 Orze' brugyi' shiñ ricy mi. 14 Rzaam beg rzaam toom. 15 Rgu'm yaan rgu'm lo boo. 16 Shiñ ricy mi rded mi.

17 «¿Lagu ni ricy mi?» rsa' lagy yu.

18 Orze' brugyi' rsiiñ yu nim.

19 She thought that he had gone to sleep. 20 She looked at him as he lay there. 21 He was laying there very quietly. 22 He was laying there with the blanket over his head. 23 He was looking at her with only one eye.

24 She began to test her husband to see if he was asleep. 25 She jumped over him. 26 She jumped over him three times. 27 After that, she went outside the house. 28 She got a clay pan. 29 She made a cross with two pieces of pitch pine, and put it on top of *the clay pan*. 30 She set fire to the tips of all the pitch pine she had made into a cross and put on top of the clay pan. 31 She put her feet on the edge of the clay pan. 32 She ascended *into the air*[1] and 33 flew away.

---

[1]The vampire assumes the form of an animal and flies through the air. People who see them fly through the air at night describe them as a white light with a tail like a comet.

19 Ella pensaba que aquella persona ya estaba dormido. 20 Miró al que estaba acostado ahí. 21 Pero él estaba despierto. 22 Estaba tapado con la cobija hasta la cabeza. 23 La estaba mirando con un solo ojo.

24 Entonces ella se puso a comprobar si su esposo ya se había dormido. 25 Se saltó por encima de él. 26 Se saltó tres veces por encima de él. 27 Después de eso, salió afuera. 28 Había tomado una cazuela. 29 Hizo una cruz con dos pedazos de ocote, y la puso sobre la cazuela. 30 Encendió todas las puntas de *los pedazos* de ocote que había cruzado sobre la cazuela. 31 Entonces puso los pies sobre la cazuela, 32 y se voló.[1] 33 Se fue.

---

[1]El vampiro toma la forma de un animal y vuela por el aire. La gente que los ve volando en la noche los describe como una luz blanca con una cola como la de un cometa.

19 Rsa' lagy mi nu bi gush pcaal mbecy ze', rsa' lagy mi. 20 Orze' bgüiim lo mbecy nu mbish ze'. 21 Ze' yu ze' ri mbish yu. 22 Yu' tooy nergyich mbish yu. 23 Tub zi urloy rgüiiy lom.

24 Orze' brugyi' ricy mi preb ben a bi nas ñgyeem. 25 Orze' blaag mi ich yu ze'. 26 Chon tir blaag mi ich yu ze'. 27 Orze' blazh ze', orze' bruum ich yu'. 28 Orze' guud tub casuel nim. 29 Orze' briib cruuz mi cyup la' gyegy ru'ñ. 30 Gaze' nu pcaam gyi too dela gyegy nu briib cruuz mi ru' casuel ze'. 31 Orze' bzuub la gyi'm ru' casuel ze'. 32 Wes nañ lam. 33 Zam.

34 The man who was spending the night at her house went to spy on her to see where she was going. 35 Now when he arrived at a cross, she was there with *other vampires*. 36 She was playing with a baby.[2]

37 Then he returned to her house. 38 Soon after that, she arrived home. 39 When she arrived, her clay pan had already been set out. 40 Wherever did she get the clay pan from? 41 She vomited *the baby's blood* into the clay pan. 42 After that, she made a meal *of it*. 43 She ate it. 44 She prepared it. 45 She put all of the things that go in a meal into it. 46 She ate *it*. 47 "She ate it," said the man who witnessed it.

34 Y la persona que se había quedado a pasar la noche en la casa de ella fue a espiarla a dónde se iba. 35 Al llegar él donde están *unas* cruces, ahí estaba ella con otras compañeras suyas. 36 Estaba jugando con un bebé.[2]

37 Después regresó a la casa de ella. 38 Al poco rato de eso, ella llegó a la casa 39 Ya había llegado, ella tenía ya una cazuela. 40 ¿Quién sabe de dónde sacó la cazuela? 41 Entonces vomitó *la sangre de bebé* en la cazuela. 42 Después de eso, hizo una comida *con aquello*, 43 y se lo comió. 44 Lo preparó. 45 Le echó todo lo que se le echa a la comida. 46 Y se lo comió. 47 "Ella lo comió" dijo la persona que vió.

---

[2]She had gone to the house of the baby. She cast a deep sleep on its parents. Then she took the baby to the cross where she tormented it before drinking its blood. People describe the vampire's tormenting the baby by throwing it up into the air and catching it. If it misses, the baby may suffer bruising, or even a broken neck. Those are the two main symptoms of *bi dañ* in a baby.

[2]Ella fue a la casa del bebé. Hace que los papás se queden profundamente dormidos. Entonces lleva al bebé a la cruz, donde lo atormenta antes de tomarse su sangre. La gente describe el tormento que el vampiro le da al bebé diciendo que lo tira al aire y lo recibe. Si no lo recibe, el bebé puede sufrir heridas, hasta que puede que se quiebre el cuello. Estos son los dos síntomas principales de *bi dañ* en un niño.

34 Orze' gua mbecy nu beche yu'm ze' gua siiñ yu nim ca zam. 35 Orze' ornu bru'ñay lo cruuz, ze' yu'm nu losa'm. 36 Rgyit num mdoo.

37 Orze' yaa ga' yu ze' yu' mi ze'. 38 Ornu guchi nde', orze' brim. 39 Brim, orze' bi mbish tub casuel nim. 40 ¿Ti ca bloom casuel ze'? 41 Orze' guugy mi nañ casuel ze'. 42 Blazh ze', orze' bzaam comid. 43 Nde' bdow mi. 44 Bicy nap mi nde'. 45 Dela coz nu rzu' lo comid bdu'm lo nde'. 46 Bdow mi. 47 «Bdow mi», na mbecy nu bzaac ze'.

48 Once a person captured a vampire. 49 However did he do that? 50 Anyway, he saw the vampire coming in the sky. 51 She had become a tom turkey. 52 She was coming in the air. 53 Then he said the words of a prayer.[3] 54 "He said his prayers," they say. 55 Then that *animal* fell *to the ground.*[4] 56 Then he began to beat it. 57 Having beat it very much, it became a person.

58 "Don't beat me anymore. 59 That is all! It is over now," said the vampire.[5]

---

[3]*orsyoo* refers to words that people believe have power. They may be words from the church like Lord's Prayer, or the Hail Mary. Such words are thought to protect people from evil. Or they may be a secret form of black magic that only evil people know.

[4]In another version the man hit the turkey with a banana that had been blessed in the church causing it to fall to the ground.

[5]Some people tell me that beating a vampire causes it to cough up the hair in its heart. Then it will no longer be a vampire.

48 Cierta vez, una persona capturó a una nagual. 49 ¿Quién sabe cómo lo hizo? 50 Pero vió que la nagual venía en el aire. 51 Había convertida en un guajolote. 52 Venía en el aire. 53 Y se puso a rezar su oración.[3] 54 "Rezó su oración" dicen. 55 Entonces *ese animal* se cayó.[4] 56 Luego empezó él a azotarlo. 57 Al azotarlo tanto, se convirtió en persona.

58 —Ya no me azotes. 59 Con eso ya basta —dicía el vampiro.[5]

---

[3]*orsyoo* indica las palabras que la gente cree que tienen poder. Puede que sean palabras de algo religioso como la Oración del Señor o el Ave María. Se pupone que tales palabras protegen a la gente del mal. O puede que sean una forma de magia negra que solamente la gente diabólica sabe.

[4]En otra versión un hombre golpea a un guajolote con un plátano que ha sido bendecido en la iglesia, lo que hace que se caiga al suelo.

[5]Algunas personas me dicen que golpear a un vampiro hace que tosa y saque un pelo de su corazón. Entonces ya no vuelve a ser vampiro.

48 Tub tir tub mbecy bdub yu tub byee. 49 ¿Ti lac bicy yu raj? 50 Tees baa bzaac yu yad byee ze'. 51 Byac mi tub col. 52 Yad mi lo bi. 53 Gaze' nu bicy yu orsyoo. 54 «Mniiy orsyoo niy», na dey. 55 Orze' bet lag la coz ze'. 56 Gaze' nu brugyi' rgaaz yu ma. 57 Tanta' nu rgaaz yu ma na, orze' byac la ma mbecy.

58 «Cue' ga' gaaz ru ya. 59 Ni zi'l bi guc na», na byee ze'.

60 And the man who did that recognized who that person was. 61 Then he went to tell her husband. 62 Now when he arrived at the house, He beat her another time.[6] 63 That is why they say that animals become vampires, when they go to drink blood. 64 They remove their whole head and leave it at a cross, when they go about, they say.[7]

60 Y él que hizo aquello ya conocía a esa persona. 61 Entonces fue a decirle a su esposo. 62 A llegar a casa, ahí la azotó otra vez.[6] 63 Por eso dicen que los vampiros se convierten animales, cuando va a chupar sangre. 64 Se quitan las cabezas y las dejan *donde están algunas* cruces,[7] cuando iban.

---

[6]In this version of the story the woman was still living and the man who told it even named her. In another version I collected her husband killed her. She was a mythical character.

[7]The whole sequence of events might be hard to reconstruct from this text. When the vampire leaves its house it first goes to the cross where it meets other vampires. There it removes its head according to some people. According to others it exchanges its head with the head of another vampire of the opposite sex. Then it goes to the house of its victim. It may return to the cross with a baby. Before the sun comes up, it must return its victim to its house, and retrieve its head at the cross, and return home. Otherwise, it will be either headless, or with another person's head the next day.

[6]En esta versión de la historia la mujer viva todavía, y el hombre que me contó la historia me dio el nombre de la señora. En otra versión que coleccioné el esposo mata a su mujer. Ella era una persona mitológica.

[7]Toda la sequencia de eventos puede que sea difícil de reconstruir de este texto. Cuando el vampiro sale de su casa va primero a la cruz donde se encuentra con otros vampiros. Allá se quita la cabeza, de acuerdo con unas personas. Según otras cambia su cabeza con la cabeza de otro vampiro del sexo opuesto. Entonces va a la casa de la víctima. Puede que vuelva a la cruz con el bebé. Antes de que salga el sol debe devolver su víctima a la casa, quitar su cabeza de la cruz y volver a su casa. Si no lo hace así se queda sin cabeza o tendrá la cabeza de otra persona al día siguiente.

60 Nunu bi yu' lo la yu nu ni bicy ze' cyu mbecy nde'. 61 Orze' guay gua niiy lo ñgyee mi ze'. 62 Na ornu briy yu' na, ze' bgaaz yum tub tira'. 63 Nde' nu rnii dey nu bañcyug yac byee, ornu rza to'y reñ, rnii dey. 64 Nunu rbooy urtooy rzeeñ yu lo cruuz, ornu rzay rnii dey.

13

Zapotec Proverbs

This chapter is composed of forty-six Zapotec sayings. Where the meaning and function of a saying might be unclear, I have included the relevant information in a footnote. I divided the sayings into three groups: "Vices and Virtues, The Uncertainty of Life," and "Women and Marriage."

I owe most of the text in this section to Alvaro Marcial López. When he saw my initial collection, he became interested and took it over. He collected the majority of these sayings.

Proverbios zapotecos

Este capítulo se compone de cuarenta y sies dichos zapotecas. En las partes donde el significado y la función de un dicho no están muy claro, he incluido información relevante al caso al pie de la página. Dividí los dichos en tres grupos: Vicios y virtudes, La incertidumbre de la vida, y Las mujeres y el matrimonio. El texto de esta sección se debe especialmente a Álvaro Marcial López. Cuando él vio mi colección inicial, comenzó a juntar proverbios por su propia cuenta. Él recopiló la mayoría de estos dichos.

Vices and Virtues

1 How could the animal think I would not recognize it, when from far away it is apparent what it is like? Even in the corn gravy we recognize it. How much more *will we recognize it* in the soup?[1]

2 Children of lazy dogs turn out to be good hunters. The children of hunters turn out to be lazy.[2]

3 When a fast dog goes out, it will at least find a bone to eat. But the lazy dog doesn't even have excrement to eat.[3]

---

[1]Bad deeds can't be hidden.

[2]Just because a person's parents are hard working does not mean that he will be hard working.

[3]Lazy people don't have their basic needs met.

Vicios y virtudes

1 ¿Cómo puede pensar que no lo reconozco cuando desde lejos es aparente lo que es? Aun en el mole lo reconocemos, cuánto más en la sopa.[1]

2 Los hijos del perro flojo salen bueno para la cacería. Los hijos de los cazadores salen flojos.[2]

3 El perro ligero, cuando sale, encuentra al menos un hueso para comer. Pero el perro flojo, ni mierda consigue para comer.[3]

---

[1]Las malas obras no se pueden esconder.

[2]El que los papás de una persona sean muy trabajadores no quiere decir que la persona lo sea también.

[3]Gente flojo no tendrá para suplir sus necesidades.

Rishcyit ni mbecy Shcyeey

La na mbecy

1 ¿La rnii ga' too ma nu wayu' lo ma? Ze' zet la rabee la na ma. Mas gal lo niscub gyu' lon ma. Yegar lo nispit.

2 I'ñ che' zed druu guuz ma. I'ñ che' guuz druu zed ma.

3 Ze' che' dzach, ornu gruu ma, gyap ma mas ñuu rit nu gow ma. Tees che' zed ni gye' wagad gow ma.

4 The poor iguana. Because it does not like the rain, it does not want to get wet, it eats its own tail.[4]

5 People who are slow don't notice *what is happening* even when they are in danger. They experience what the crayfish experiences. Because there are crayfish who think that they *need* not be afraid, because they are so clever. They stay right by the water. Then flood water suddenly arrives, and carries them away.[5]

6 Don't show the egg to the chicken, because right now it is not thinking of laying.[6]

4 La pobre iguana por piensa mal de la lluvia, no quiere mojarse. Por eso come su misma cola.[4]

5 Las personas que actúan con lentitud, no se dan cuenta cuándo están en peligro. Les pasa lo mismo que a un cangrejo. Porque hay cangrejos que piensan que no tienen miedo, porque son muy listos. Pueden estar donde hay agua. De pronto, viene la inundación, y se los lleva.[5]

6 No enseñes el huevo a la gallina, porque por el momento no piensa en poner huevos.[6]

---

[4]People who refuse to work when the weather is bad do not have their needs met.

[5]People who are slow workers are in danger of starving, but they don't realize it.

[6]This is a warning not to fight.

---

[4]La gente que rehusa trabajar cuando el tiempo es malo nunca tendrá para suplir sus necesidades.

[5]La gente que es lenta está en peligro de morirse de hambre, pero no se da cuenta.

[6]Esta es una advertencia para no pelear.

4 Cuaa guch. Nu nac nu rzi ma gyey, walagy ma nu gyo' ma. Orze' laab ne ma row ma.

5 Mbecy nu ricy gul lagy, wagyicy cuen yu mas lo rishdzidz zuy. Yu ze' rzac yu gal nu rzac briz. Gun yu' briz rnii too ma nu wachib ma, gun lily zu ma. Orze' ri la ma mas ze' nu rzu nis. Orze' sij zi'l dri nis yu. Orze' rza nuñ ma.

6 Cue' rlyuur nguu lo gyid, gun na na la wagnii too ma shet ma.

7 When the bull enjoys work-ing, it licks the cord that ties its yoke.[7]

8 *If* a person fills his mouth with cornmeal, his saliva does not suffice to wetten it. He chokes.[8]

9 Be careful of slippery liquid, because it will lay you out along the roadside. Then dogs will lick your bottom.[9]

10 You will experience what the crow experiences. It stores the things that it will eat. Now when it seeks them, it doesn't find them.

---

[7]People who like to fight suffer the consequences.
[8]People who eavesdrop get more than they can handle.
[9]Drinking brings humiliation.

7 Cuando al buey le gusta tra-bajar, hasta lame su coyunda.[7]

8 La gente que tiene llena la boca de pinole, no tiene sufi-ciente saliva para mojarlo, y se ahoga.[8]

9 Cuidado con el líquido res-baladizo, porque te va a tirar a la orilla del camino. Entonces los perros te van a lamer el trasero.[9]

10 A ti te va a pasar como le pasa al cuervo: almacena cosas para comer, y cuando las busca, ya no las encuentra.

---

[7]A la gente que le gusta pelear sufre las consecuencias.
[8]La gente que escucha lo que no debe, oyen más de lo que debe.
[9]El tomar licor trae humillación.

7 Ornu tor gusht ni ma gyicy ma riiñ, orze' rle' la ma lo coyunt ni ma.

8 Mbecy nu rchaa la ru' nu yu' gyez uub, orze' wagagye nis yeñ yu sal ñi. Orze' rzub yu.

9 Cuidad nu nis cyudz, gun cyish ñi ru ru' gyernez. Orze' le' che' iiñ ru.

10 Ru zac ru gal nu rzac byac. Rgu' choow ma coz nu gow ma. Na ornu yub mañ, orze' wagyad ñi ni ma.

11 Be careful of the immoral woman because when you awaken, she will have already pulled down your pants.[10]

12 Don't torment weak men, just because they will not say anything. Be careful! There is a saying that people have *that goes like this*: Even if a dog is weak in the extreme, and even if it is bald in the extreme, if we step on its tail, it will surely bite us. *This is what* they say.

13 Be careful lest you act important in order to pass people up or go before them. Note what women do. They are already prepared. When leaf-cutter ants come out to fetch their hominy, all of the animals who come out first will have the fire of the torch put on top of them. This is what will happen to you if you do not see what you *really* are in the world.

---

[10]Immoral women rob men of all they have without their even being aware of it.

11 Ten cuidado con las mujeres rameras, porque cuando despiertes, ya te bajó el calzón.[10]

12 No atormentes a los hombres débiles, porque no dirán nada. Ten cuidado, porque la gente dice que, aun cuando un perro sea extremadamente débil, y sea muy calvo, si nos paramos en su cola, con seguridad nos va a morder, dicen.

13 Ten cuidado de no actuar como si fueras muy importante para poder pasar a otros o ir antes de ellos. Fíjate en lo que las mujeres hacen: se preparan *con teas de pino* para que, cuando las hormigas vengan a llevarse su nixtamal, les pongan la tea prendida encima a las primeras que lleguen. Esto es lo que te va a pasar si no te das cuenta de quien eres, en realidad, en el mundo.

---

[10]Mujeres inmorales le roban a los hombres todo lo que tienen sin que ellos se den cuenta.

11 Cuidad nu de biñ che', gun ornu cyish ru yaa, bi pshet tem carsuñ ru.

12 Cue' gyicy ras nur yu gyidz, gun a' niiy. Cuidad, gun mbish tub riidz nu rnii mbecy. Gun mas nu blaazh la che' gyidz, nunu mas blazh la ma nu byayagy ma, tees benu zuub gyi'n lo ne ma, orze' segur la cucua' ma ub na, rnii dey.

13 Cuidad nis gyicy ru gyel lily nir nu ded lor lo mbecy o nu char lo. Bdu' cuen coz nu ricy biñ mñaa. Bi zub lily mi. ornu griib byub nu cha gyii ma uub lich nim, orze' de bañ nu grib loga la cha gyi gyegy too ma. Ni gzac ru benu wagüiir lac zur gyishlombecy.

14 And there is also a saying that people have: "Don't get very far behind, because a mountain lion will come and eat those who get behind, because there is no one to protect them."

15 Why does the crab teach its babies to walk straight, when it walks sideways?[11]

16 Don't put on a shirt that is eight bars in width, because it will not fit you.[12]

17 Is it true that the cord around your waist is tight? Why do you want to take on the office of major mayordomo?

18 Why does the poor toad want to compare itself with a young bull? The only thing *they have in common* is a bloated abdomen.[13]

---

[11]Ambition is sinful.
[12]One shouldn't aspire to greatness.
[13]Proud people are ridiculous.

14 Y hay otro dicho de la gente: "No te quedes muy atrás, porque la gente que se queda atrás se las comerá un león. No habrá nadie para protegerlos."

15 ¿Por qué quiere la cangreja enseñar a su nene a caminar derecho, cuando ella misma camina chueco?[11]

16 No te ponga la camisa que mide ocho varas de ancho, porque no te queda bien.[12]

17 ¿Es verdad que tienes bien ceñido el cinturón? ¿Por qué quieres aceptar el cargo de mayordomo grande?

18 ¿Por qué quiere el pobre sapo compararse con un novillo, siendo que solo su panza es grande?[13]

---

[11]Ambición es pecado.
[12]Uno no debe aspirar grandeza.
[13]La gente orgullosa es ridícula.

14 Nunu ni zi'l mbish tub riidz nu rnii mbecy: «Cue' nu dzi gyiyeeñ ru gal ich la, gun de mbecy nu ryeeñ gal ich, gru'ña biidz gow ma yu. Orze' wad mbecy nu cay yu.»

15 ¿Lagu rlagya' be nu rlyuu ma ni mdoo ni ma nu li gza ma, se ub ma ni' chu rza ma?

16 Cue' gzur yaag nu yu' shuñ bar nu she nañ, gun wayap ru ñii.

17 ¿A lyar nicy ri duu nañ ru? ¿Lagu rlagy ru shet yaar mardom ily?

18 ¿Lagu rlagya' pro birgye' nu saap ma nobi? Ze' laab nañ zi'l ma ca'.

19 Do you really speak truthfully? Don't *allow* your foot to come out of the horses stirrup tomorrow or the next day.[14]

20 The poor buzzard. It tries to clean its mouth. But the stink will never leave its mouth, because its entire body stinks.[15]

21 The poor person. He experiences what a moth experiences *when* it casts itself into the hot coals.[16]

22 During the time when chickens cluck, they do not really want to lay *eggs*.[17]

---

[14]People's deceit catches them out.
[15]People cannot hide their hypocrisy.
[16]Bad people cannot help incriminating themselves.
[17]Braggers never do what they say.

19 ¿Es verdad lo que dices? No dejes que tu pie se salga del estribo de caballo mañana o pasado mañana.[14]

20 Pobre del zopilote. Trata de limpiar su pico. Pero su olor no se quitará de su pico, porque todo su cuerpo está lleno de olor.[15]

21 Pobre gente que le pasa lo que a la polilla. Ella misma se lanza al fuego.[16]

22 Cuando las gallinas cantan, en realidad no quieren poner huevos.[17]

---

[14]Las mentiras la van a alcanzar a la gente.
[15]La gente no puede esconder su hipocresía.
[16]Los malos no puedan evitar incriminarse.
[17]Los "echadores" nunca hacen lo que dicen.

19 ¿A lyar rishli rniir? Cue' zi orze' ina widz na gruu za gyi'r nañ strib ni ma.

20 Cuaa lyash. Ricy ma nu rgyiib ma ru' ma. Se nil waruu nu ti' ru' ma, gun dutuub la cuerp ma bzu la nu ti'.

21 Cuaa pro mbecy. Rzac yu gal nu rzac bigyid. Laab ub la ma rshet lag ma ub ma lo boo.

22 Gyid, tiem nu rul ru', walab nu rishli rlagy ma nu shet ma.

23 The bird that sings early in the morning is not the one that really has the fat.[18]

24 The dog that barks a lot is not really the one that bites. But the one that does not bark will surely bite.

25 Gnats enter the mouths of people who yawn.

26 People who spit into the air, when they look up, where it went, it falls right back into their mouths.[19]

27 Don't converse with him, because the edge of his gourd has broken. All while he is speaking, he only spills his honey on his chest.[20]

---

[18]People who say they have a lot never have much.

[19]People who gossip get gossiped about.

[20]Excessive speech is unbecoming.

23 El pájaro que canta en la mañana, no es el que de veras está gordo.[18]

24 El perro que ladra mucho no es en realidad el que muerde. Pero el que no ladra, es seguro que muerde.

25 Las moscas entran en la boca abierta.

26 La persona que escupe hacia al cielo, y cuando mira por donde se va la saliva, entonces le cae en su misma boca.[19]

27 No platicas con él, porque se rajó la orilla de su jícara. Mientras él platica solamente derrama la miel en su pecho.[20]

---

[18]La gente que dice que tiene mucho, nunca tiene.

[19]De la gente que anda chismeando, también se chismea.

[20]Demasiado hablar es chocante.

23 Chigyiñ nu rul ru' or napor, walab nu rishli ricy cup ma za.

24 Che' nu dzi rshi, walab nu rishli cucua' ma. Se bañ nu wacshi, ma ze' segur la cucua' ma.

25 Mbecy nu rshaa ru', yu ze' rzu' be'y ru'y.

26 Mbecy nu rne' nis yeñ par baa, na ornu güiiy ca par gash ñi, orze' laab ru'y gyet lag ñi.

27 Cue' go nur yu re riidz, gun bla' ru' ig niy. Dub laa lat nu roy riidz, lyush zi'l yu pshuy dziñ niy.

The Uncertainty of Life

28 Cats do not cover up their excrement every time.[21]

29 Affliction is like wealth. When it arrives, it arrives with a companion at a time we would not suspect.

30 Even if a dog has money it will dance. When it doesn't have money, it dances because it wants to get it.

31 Don't yearn for old age, because you get it for free.

---

[21]Business ventures are uncertain.

La inseguridad de la vida

28 Los gatos no ocultan su excremento siempre.[21]

29 La desgracia es como la riqueza. Cuando llega, llega con su compañero en el tiempo que no se espera.

30 Aún el perro, si tiene dinero, baila. Pero cuando no tiene dinero, baila porque quiere tenerlo.

31 No desees la vejez, porque la tendrás gratis.

---

[21]Aventurarse en negocios es inseguro.

Cyup ridz zun gyishlombecy

28 Bidz walab de byaj la soow ma too ñgye' ma.

29 Gyel zi nañ gal na gyel nap. Ornu ru'ñañ, orze' nu losa'ñ dru'ñañ tiem nu a̱' sa' lagy la na.

30 Benu gad tiñ mas gal che̱' gulgyi' ma. Na ornu sac tiñ, orze' rulgyi' la ma rlagy ma gad ñi.

31 Cue' zaab lagy ru gyel gush, gun leew la rad ñi.

32 People who have good luck, reach the edge of the wilderness slowly. But people who have bad luck, experience what the dung beetle experiences. The excrement is piled up at its door. Then it rolls down hill again. This is what bad luck is like

33 Notice the way it is with a meal. There isn't even one of them that doesn't have hair in it. Even if the women are very careful when they make it, they do not succeed. A hair will surely appear in it when the bowls are put out.

Women and Marriage

34 There is a hole that goes right through the mind of a woman. But the road in the mind of a man makes many turns.[22]

---

[22]Women are simple minded. Men are capable of deep thought.

32 La gente que tiene buena suerte llega lentamente a la orilla del desierto. Pero a la gente que tiene mala suerte le pasa lo que al escarabajo: el excremento se amontara en su puerta, y luego rueda hacia abajo otra vez. Así es la mala suerte.

33 Mira lo que pasa con la comida: no hay una sola en la que no se encuentra un pelo. Aún cuando las mujeres tengan mucho cuidado al prepararla, no pueden evitarlo. Un pelo aparecerá, con seguridad, cuando se ponga el plato en la mesa.

Las mujeres y el matrimonio

34 Hay un agujero que va a través de la mente de las mujeres. Pero el camino en la mente de los hombres da muchas vueltas.[22]

---

[22]Las mujeres tienen la mente vacía. Los hombres son inteligentes.

32 De mbecy nu cyit na suert ni, dze dze zi'l rshuub dey gal ru' ngush. Ze' de mbecy nu shiñ na suert ni, rzac dey gal nu rzac bañ rtub gye'. Bi rshuub bi rshuub la gye' ze' nu zub ro' ma. Rdudubañ par gyoow. Ni ricy de suert shiñ na.

33 Bdu' cuen mod nu rac nu comid. Warusu ni tub ñi nu waruu zac gyich loñ. Mas tona' la cuidad gyicy biñ mñaa ornu rzaam ñii, tees wagyicy mi gan. Waded la gruu zac tub gyich loñ ornu chu' gya'n.

Biñ mñaa

34 Biñ mñaa li laa ya gyegy nañ shcab nim. Ze' yu gyeey dzi ryach nez nañ shcab niy.

35 A chicken cannot set its feet on the roosters back.[23]

36 Women who do not have the intelligence they should have are like a hot griddle. If we throw a drop of water on it, it is not apparent where it went. Just like what a hot griddle does, so do they with the things of their husbands. As soon as they get a thing it is gone.

37 Women who lack intelligence, enjoy looking at a machete that shines. But intelligent women prefer to look at a machete that is filthy.[24]

38 Her *children* seem very pretty to her even though they be ugly.[25]

---

[23]Women should not dominate men.
[24]Intelligent women are more interested in good workers than good lookers.
[25]Women are not impartial about their children.

35 Una gallina no puede poner sus patas encima del gallo.[23]

36 Las mujeres que no ponen la mente donde deben son como un comal caliente. Si tiramos una gota de agua en ella, no es aparente a dónde va. Como hace la comal caliente, así hacen ellas con las cosas de sus esposos. Tan pronto como reciben algo, desaparece.

37 A las mujeres tontas les gusta mirar el machete que brilla. Pero a las mujeres inteligentes, les gusta más ver el machete sucio.[24]

38 Sus hijos le parecen muy bonitos, aunque sean feos.[25]

---

[23]Las mujeres no deben dominar al hombre.
[24]Las mujeres inteligentes se interesan más en los buenos trabajadores que en los guapos.
[25]Las mujeres no son imparciales con sus hijos.

35 Wac tub gyid zub gyi' ma ich ngüel.

36 De biñ mñaa nu sac shcab ni lugaar niñ, nam gal nu na rily zig. Shet lag na tub ndzuj nis loñ. Wacabee la ca zañ. Gal nu ricy la rily zig, ni ricy dem nu de coz ni ñgyeem. Sa rad ñi sa zañ.

37 Biñ mñaa nu sac shcab, yet lagy mi nu rgüiim lo mandzicy nu ryal lo. Ze' de biñ mñaa nu yu' shcab ni, yet zir lagy mi güiim mandzicy nu gu' bid lo.

38 Cyit la na nim rziim, mas shiñ na nim.

39 People who are partial hit their hands in excrement.[26]

40 When my *daughter* Jacinta gets a husband, she will go to a home where smoke comes from. She will not go there where smoke does not come from.[27]

41 If we take notice, from far away the heifer calf that will give milk is apparent.[28]

42 When a rock rolls, only one goes. But as it goes along, it becomes two.[29]

43 Birds go about with their companion. Rocks lie there with others of their kind.[30]

---

[26]It is wrong to be partial in choosing a spouse.
[27]Women should not marry into lazy families.
[28]It is apparent which women will grow up to be hard workers.
[29]Marriage is natural.
[30]Marriage is natural.

39 La gente que es parcial se ensucía las manos en excremento.[26]

40 Mi hija Jacinta, cuando tenga esposo, va a ir a donde sale humo. No va a donde no salga humo[27]

41 Si nos fijamos bien, desde lejos se conoce la ternera que da leche.[28]

42 Cuando rueda una piedra, va solo una. Pero en el camino, se vuelven dos.[29]

43 Los pájaros andan con sus compañeros. Las piedras están puestas con sus compañeros.[30]

---

[26]Está mal ser parcial al escoger un cónyuge.
[27]Las mujeres no se deben casar con alguien cuya familia es floja.
[28]Es aparente qué mujeres crecerán y serán buenas trabajadoras.
[29]El matrimonio es natural.
[30]El matrimonio es natural.

39 Mbecy nu rcui, lo gye' cyi yaay.

40 Chiint ne̱, ornu gad ñgyeeñ, ze' nu driib dzeeñ chañ. Wayañ ze' nu wactiib dzeeñ.

41 Benu du' cuen na, zet la rabee la na terner nu cuic lech.

42 Gyita', ornu dudub ñi, orze' tub ziñ zañ. Tees za gaañ, orze' gyac cyup ñii.

43 Chigyiñ nu losa' ma rded ma. Gyita' nu losa'ñ mbish ñi.

44 Getting wives is just like buying animals. There are people who buy robust animals. Later, because they do not have any luck, they will not have them for long. In a moment or two they become thin. But if people have luck, even though they buy a frail animal, in a moment or two it will become wholesome for them

45 "Are you afraid for us to leave your father? Haven't you noticed the work *that the insect who makes* cocoons does? It does not have a machete. It does not have any possessions. But it makes a very pretty house. Now speak," she said to her husband.

44 Buscar una esposa es como comprar un animal: Hay quienes compran animales robustos. Despues, porque no tienen suerte, no los tienen por mucho tiempo. En un instante o dos se queda delgado. Pero si tienen suerte, aun cuando compren un animal débil, en un instante o dos puede convertirse en algo bueno para ellos.

45 —¿Tienes miedo de que dejemos a tu papá? ¿Te has fijado en lo que hace el capullo? No tiene machete. No tiene posesiones, pero hace una casa muy hermosa. Ahora, habla —le dice a su esposo.

44 Par nu gad mñaan, gal gaal la nañ nu nu rzii mbecy bañcyug. Yu' dey rziiy bañ yalagy. Na despuees par nu sac suert niy. Wazuu yaa tuñ lay ma. Tub cyup zi'l gyarit ma. Tees benu mbecy nu ricy cup suert, mas bañ gyidz ziiy, tub cyup zi'l gyanap ma niy.

45 «¿A dzi rdzib ru nu gruun lo uz ru? ¿A wacu' cuen ru riiñ nu ricy gyid cuag? Sac mandzicy ni ma. sac ni tub la suu ma. Tees cyit na yu' ma rzaa ma. Na mnii ben», nañ rab ñi ñgyeeñ.

46 "Do you think I will not
have anything to eat if you abandon me. I *will have* more than I
need. Look at the ants. At times
they cannot be sustained by eating the crumbs that fall from peo-
ples mouths onto the ground.
How much more me," she said. [31]

---

[31]A woman can live without a
husband.

46 —¿Crees que no voy a tener que comer si me abando-
nas? Pero quedará algo para mí.
Mira a las hormigas. A veces no
pueden comer las migajas que
caen de la boca de la gente, todo
lo que cae al suelo. Así me pasa
a mí —dice ella.[31]

---

[31]Una mujer puede vivir sin un
esposo.

46 «¿A rnii toor nu wad coz nu daw benu zaan ru ya? Par ya grusuba'
lañ. Güii de bree. Yu' tiem nu wagagyee ma nu gow ma de nguzh ru'
mbecy, de nu yet lag lo yu. Ze' yegar ya», nam.

14

Ashes

This folktale is a beautiful expression of a world view in which life is thought to be unintelligible and without meaning. A prevailing theme is that things are never as they seem. Ashes cook tortillas. Pine trees grow in oceans. And hummingbirds drink whole oceans. Zapotecs are preoccupied with illusion. Also note that the folktale begins with ashes and ends with ashes. To the Zapotec life is not a very happy state, but death is even worse. From beginning to end man's existence is as ashes. Not even God is thought to be benevolent. The church is burnt down. A very insightful assessment of Zapotec World view is presented in Kearney (1972).

This folktale was told to Claudio Martinez by his mother, Juana Antonio. He wrote it in practical orthography and gave it to me in 1977 because he wanted me to have a "Zapotec Poem." The style of the folktale is unique. It consists of a series of questions each of which is followed by an answer. Each answer determines the content of the following question. This is the only folktale of this type that I have found.

Cenizas

Este cuento es una bonita expresión de un punto de vista de un mundo en el que se piensa que la vida es inexplicable y sin significado. El tema predominante es que las cosas nunca son como parecen. Las tortillas se cuecen en ceniza. Los pinos crecen en los océanos. Y los chuparrosas se

213

toman toda el agua de los océanos. Los zapotecas se interesan en las fantasías. Es de notar también que el cuento comienza con cenizas y termina con cenizas. Para los zapotecas la vida no es un estado feliz, pero la muerte es aun peor. Del principio al fin la existencia del hombre es como cenizas. Piensan que ni aun Dios es bondadoso. La iglesia se quemó. Kearney (1972) nos presenta una valoración desagradable del punto de vista del mundo zapoteca.

Claudio Martínez escuchó este cuento de su madre, Juana Antonio. Él lo escribió y me lo dio en 1977 porque quería que yo tuviera un "poema zapoteca". El estilo de este cuento es único. Consiste de una serie de preguntas seguidas por sus respectivas respuestas. Cada respuesta determina el contenido de la siguiente pregunta. Éste es el único cuento de este tipo que he encontrado.

1 Where did mother-cloud go?[1]

2 She went to get ashes to cook tortillas for the black person to eat.

3 Where is the black person now?

4 He went *to defecate.*

5 Where is *his* excrement?

6 A turkey buzzard has already finished eating it.

---

[1]There are two problems with the translation of *bey*. The first has to do with the meaning of the word. It has been translated both as 'cloud' and 'moon' by different Zapotec speakers. The person who gave the text said that he is not sure what the word means. *bey* 'cloud' has low tone. This word has mid tone. *beey* 'moon' also has low tone and is laryngealized as well. I follow the translation of the person who gave the text. The second problem has to do with its relation to *ña'* 'mom'. The man who gave the text has suggested two possibilities. It could be a vocative: Where did mom go, cloud? Or it could be a compound. I chose the second possibility, because it is not a name. All names, coming from Spanish, have either high tone or falling tone. It is not a known nickname. One Zapotec speaker took it to be a possessor: the moon's mother. But this word for mother is not normally possessed. The man who gave the text rejected that translation.

1 ¿A dónde se fue mamá nube?[1]

2 La mamá se fue a traer cenizas para cocer tortillas que come el Negro.

3 ¿Y dónde está el Negro?

4 El Negro se fue a defecar.

5 ¿Y dónde están las heces?

6 Ya las acaba de comer el zopilote cabeza roja.

---

[1]Hay dos problemas en la traducción de la palabra *bey*. En primera parte, no está seguro qué significa la palabra. Se había traducido en 'nube' por unos hablantes de zapoteco, y en 'luna' por otros. La persona que me dio el texto no está seguro que quiere decir la palabra. *bey* 'nube' tiene tono bajo. Esa palabra tiene tono mediano. *beey* 'luna' también tiene tono bajo y su vocal es un laríngeo. Yo he traducido como la persona que me dio el texto. En segunda parte, no está seguro cómo relaciona *bey* con *ña'* 'mamá'. Posiblemente es un vocativo: ¿A dónde se fue mamá, nube? Pero todos los nombres tienen tono alto, o tono alto-bajo, porque vienen del español. No hay un apodo *bey* con tono mediano. Posiblemente *ña' -bey* es una palabra compuesta. Un hablante de zapoteco ha traducido *bey* como poseedor. Pero *ña'* siempre no ocurre con poseedor. Por eso la persona que me dio el texto rechazó esa solución.

Di'ñ nu gay gyit gow Cas

1 ¿Ca za ña' bey?
2 Ña' za gyiim di'ñ gay gyit gow Cas.
3 ¿Ca na Cas?
4 Cas zam chu'.
5 ¿Ca na chu'?
6 Chu' bi blazh bdow lyash ic ña.

7 Where is the turkey buzzard?

8 It is perching on a giant pine tree.

9 Where is the giant pine tree?

10 It is *growing* in the ocean.

11 Where is the ocean?

12 A humming bird has already finished drinking it.

13 Where is the humming bird?

14 It is sitting on the corner of the church building.

15 Where is the church building?

16 It has already burnt down.

7 ¿Y dónde está el zopilote cabeza roja?

8 El zopilote cabeza roja está en el pino grande.

9 ¿Y dónde está el pino grande?

10 El pino grande está en el océano.

11 ¿Y dónde está el océano?

12 Acaba de terminar de tomárselo el chuparrosa.

13 ¿Y dónde está el chuparrosa?

14 El chuparrosa está en la esquina de la iglesia.

15 ¿Y dónde está la iglesia?

16 La iglesia ya se quemó.

7 ¿Ca na lyash ic ña?
8 Lyash ic ña zub ma lo ya gyerdoo.
9 ¿Ca na ya gyerdoo?
10 Ya gyerdoo zub lo nisyudoo.
11 ¿Ca na nisyudoo?
12 Nisyudoo bi blazh go' chibi'.
13 ¿Ca na chibi'?
14 Chibi' zub ma scyiñ ni yu' wedz.
15 ¿Ca na yu' wedz?
16 Yu' wedz bi wic.

Los Zapotecos de San Lorenzo Texmelucan

San Lorenzo Texmelucan *shcyeey,* es un pueblecito zapoteca situado al suroeste de la ciudad de Oaxaca, en el distrito de Sola de Vega. Es un centro municipal y tiene otros seis poblados más pequeños, llamados rancherías, en su administración: Río Nube, Carrizal, Palo de Lima. Rancho de Talea, El Zuchil y El Arador. La gente que vive en todas estas rancherías cuando quiere hablar de San Lorenzo dice simplemente *gyedz* 'el pueblo', puesto que es el centro político y religioso para todos ellos. Van al pueblo a hacer su servicio comunitario y militar, a pagar impuestos, a arreglar asuntos legales, a la misa, a celebrar las fiestas católicas, a casarse, a ser bautizados y allá son enterrados.[1] Así que, San Lorenzo es el foco de la actividad comunal para toda el área que le rodea, y no es sorprendente que toda la gente de la municipalidad simplemente se refiere a sí misma como *mbecy gyedz* 'la gente de San Lorenzo'.

Los habitantes de San Lorenzo constituyen una unidad tanto lingüística como cultural. Lingüísticamente todos ellos hablan una variedad del zapoteca que se ha llamado en la literatura "Papabuco" (Upson and Longacre 1965; Harvey 1968; Rendón 1971, 1976). Otras comunidades en donde se habla Papabuco son: Santa María Zaniza, San Juan Elotepec, Santiago

---

[1]Cuando yo vivía en San Lorenzo, la única iglesia que había estaba en el pueblo. En años recientes se han construido iglesias en algunas de las rancherías.

Textitlán y Santiago Xochiltepec. El zapoteca de Texmelucan comparte un gran número de afinidades con las lenguas que se hablan en estas comunidades, pero son mutuamente ininteligibles. England (1978) reporta resultado de solamente 10% de comprensión del texto del zapoteca de Zaniza que se tocó en San Lorenzo Texmelucan. Otras lenguas zapotecas son todavía más distantes.

Casi todos los hablantes del zapoteca de Texmelucan viven en la municipalidad de San Lorenzo Texmelucan y no hay hablantes del español entre ellos, con la excepción de los maestros del gobierno. La mayoría de los que viven en esta área son monolingües: el zapoteca se usa en cada aspecto de la vida diaria.

La unidad cultural de la gente de San Lorenzo está reflejada en la distinción que ellos hacen entre ellos mismos: *mbecy shcyeey* 'la gente de San Lorenzo'; y todos los demás, los que ellos llaman *wan* 'Juan'. Esta última expresión contrasta con el nombre "Juan" porque denota a un miembro de una clase, más que a una identidad individual. Entre la gente que ellos llaman "Juan" hay también palabras características que los distinguen más de otros hablantes del Papabuco, *waan*, y para los chatinos, *chok*.

Los patrones sociales de la gente de San Lorenzo tienen muchas características que son similares a las encontradas en otras comunidades zapotecas. Los casamientos se contratan a través de los casamenteros *chigool*. Después de la celebración del compromiso *lagyez* (que literalmente es "cigarro"), el novio va a vivir con la familia de la novia para hacer servicio por ella. Eso no sucede con "Juan." Éste recibe a su esposa sin pagar.

Durante el tiempo que está haciendo el servicio por la novia el suegro del novio le da a su hija como esposa. También durante este tiempo ellos se casan en la iglesia católica, si ninguno de los dos tiene un cónyuge que viva de un matrimonio anterior. Después sigue una celebración por la boda *fandang*.

Cuando el servicio por la novia termina, los recién casados pasan a vivir con la familia del novio. Viven con la familia del hombre hasta que el siguiente hijo de la familia ha crecido. Entonces, el papá del muchacho, idealmente, dota a su hijo de casa y tierra, estableciendo así una nueva residencia para él. Entonces ya no se dice que el hombre está viviendo con su papá, y ya no se le considera bajo la autoridad del padre, pues "ha dejado a su padre."

El hijo menor permanece con su padre hasta que éste se muere y entonces hereda lo que queda de su riqueza. Así, la herencia se pasa típicamente de padre a hijos, siendo distribuida parte de ella mientras el padre vive. Las mujeres no heredan igual que los hombres como en algunas comunidades zapotecas. Un hombre puede dejar algo a sus hijas, pero lo más probable es que los hermanos o tíos se lo quiten.

Como en otras áreas es común que un hombre tenga *mñaa gyish* 'mujeres de la maleza'. Él considera que estas mujeres son tan propiedad suya como su esposa legal, aunque no se considera responsable de sostenerlas a ellas o a los hijos (llamados piel de su pie, *gyidlab*) que ellas le den.

El compadrazgo es una asociación voluntaria que existe en San Lorenzo en, más o menos, la misma forma que en otras comunidades zapotecas. Ravicz (1967) se refiere a las dos dimensiones de esta asociación como "compadrazgo" y "padrinazgo." El compadrazgo, que es la relación entre un hombre y los papás de su ahijado, se caracteriza por un respeto y ayuda mutua. El respeto se expresa en las formas especiales de dirigirse y referirse al compadre de uno. Al saludar al compadre uno debe decirle *compadre* 'compadre', y nunca debe referirse a él por su nombre de pila. Al hablar del compadre de uno, uno debe siempre decir *mbalya bed* 'mi compadre Pedro' y nunca decir simplemente "Pedro."

Como otros han notado, la relación no es simétrica. En ella, el padre del niño tiene cierta obligación hacia su compadre, el padrino de su hijo. Se dan ayuda mutua llevando a cabo labores juntos y ayudándose uno al otro cuando uno da una fiesta o construye una casa.

El padrinazgo, la relación entre el padrino y el ahijado, está caracterizado por el respeto y la obligación mutua. Cuando un ahijado se encuentra con su padrino lo saluda como si fuera su padre: *"shnur tat doo yaar caru'"* 'Hola, papá, dame tu mano para que bese' y se inclina ante él. El padrino contesta: *"shnup num ru"* 'Que Dios te bendiga' y extiende su mano para ponerla sobre la cabeza de su ahijado. El ahijado le lleva regalos a su padrino en Todos Santos. El padrino aconseja al ahijado cuando se va a casar y ayuda a su compadre con el gasto de la comida de la boda. Si el ahijado se muere, el padrino tiene parte también en la responsabilidad del entierro.

Como en otras comunidades zapotecas, la vida política de la comunidad se centra alrededor de un sistema de servicio voluntario, sin remuneración económica. Este sistema consiste en una serie de oficios graduados, políticos y religiosos, llamados cargos por los cuales se espera que pasen los hombres. A todos los hombres, desde la edad de 16 años, se les requiere dar servicio por un año, seguido por, cuando menos, un año de descanso. Siendo que sólo un hombre de cada familia da su servicio en un tiempo específico, este período de descanso varía de acuerdo al tamaño de la familia. Los cargos se catalogan de tal forma que, teóricamente, un hombre debe tomar cada cargo en orden de rango. Los cargos siguen el orden siguiente: *ga* 'topil', *jef* 'jefe', *mayoor* 'mayoral', *gulab* 'colaco', *bacyer* 'vaquero', y *mayordom* 'mayordomo'. Cuando una persona ha desempeñado el cargo de mayordomo ya no se le pide que desempeñe ningún cargo. Se dice entonces que él ha dejado de ser topil, y puede ser elegido a desempeñar un cargo en el ayuntamiento del pueblo.

Todos los servicios se desempeñan sin pago y se consideran difíciles. La expresión zapoteca para el ser nombrado a este cargo es literalmente "ser golpeado" (*dugyi*). De las personas que la gente elige por votación para ser las autoridades del pueblo se dice que *cub dey yu* 'lo capturaron'. El cargo de presidente del pueblo se considera ser el más difícil, siendo que el presidente no puede trabajar en sus campos por tres años porque tiene que sentarse diariamente en el palacio municipal a desempeñar las responsabilidades propias de su oficio. Así que, después de que una persona desempeña el papel de presidente, no se le pide hacer ningún trabajo para el pueblo. Se dice entonces que "el trabajo del pueblo lo pasó."

Además de los "cargos," hay el trabajo de la comunidad *riiñ gyedz*, en el que participa todo el que no está trabajando en algún cargo. Los primeros días de cada año *ña'n cub* todos toman parte en la limpieza de los caminos. Todos participan, también, en el trabajo de la milpa del pueblo *gyel riiñ*. La participación en los cargos y en las actividades comunales, como el trabajo para el pueblo y las fiestas católicas, refuerzan la unidad cultural de la gente de San Lorenzo y la distingue de "Juan."

Toda la gente de San Lorenzo se dedica a la agricultura. Viven en una área montañosa de Oaxaca que tiene una altitud de 1,250 a 1,875 metros. En las partes más bajas crecen maíz, frijol, plátano, piña, cítricos, caña de azúcar, mamey, aguacate, chile, tomate y café. En las partes más altas crecen maíz, frijol, calabaza y tomate. El maíz, el frijol y el azúcar morena que producen se consumen localmente. Las cosechas que producen más entradas monetarias son el plátano, la piña y el café.

A principios de la década de los 70 la única forma de vender estas cosechas era acarreándolas al mercado de Sola de Vega, ya sea cargadas en la espalda o en animales de carga, en una brecha que sube hasta ese pueblo. En años más recientes se han construido carreteras que van a cada uno de los pueblecitos. La gente tiene ahora más fácil acceso a los mercados de Sola de Vega y Oaxaca llevando sus productos en camiones de alquiler. Pero siendo que el viaje al mercado es indispensable para comprar cosas básicas necesarias e implementos para el campo, ropa, jabón, azúcar de arroz, maíz extra, etc., al hacer estos viajes, continúa usando los antiguos caminos para llevar sus productos a Sola de Vega.

Aunque hay una demanda general de trabajadores, casi no se puede encontrar personas que quieran trabajar por pago. Esto se debe parcialmente al valor negativo que ponen al hecho de trabajar dependiendo de otras personas, y parcialmente a una escasez general de capital. Las alternativas a tener ayuda pagada son similares a las que se presentan en cualquier lado en Oaxaca: intercambio de trabajo, lo que se llama *riiñ lo'* 'trabajo de cerca', cooperación en el cultivo *riiñ coz cyaal*, pago con trabajo por el uso de los animales, servicio por la futura esposa, adopción de un pariente cuando una pareja no tiene niños para ayudarles a manejar el rancho de la familia, y en ocasiones, pedir prestado un topil a las autoridades.

Además de las actividades agriculturales, hay otras formas secundarias de hacer dinero, tales como aventurarse en el mundo de los negocios *daljez*, criando y vendiendo animales y yendo a trabajar a otros lugares por períodos cortos *cha nap tiiñ.*

Como en otras comunidades indígenas mexicanas, hay sentimientos negativos hacia la acumulación de riquezas. Estos sentimientos se expresan de varias maneras. Los ricos nunca exhiben su riqueza en su forma de vivir, sino que adoptan el mismo estilo de vida que la mayoría de los miembros de la comunidad. Frecuentemente son objeto de críticas, brujerías y algunas veces de vandalismo por parte de sus vecinos. Algunas ocupaciones, como la de tendero, no se consideran apropiadas para la gente de San Lorenzo.

En 1972 no había tiendas en el pueblo. Con grandes dificultades dos personas empezaron a vender algo de mercancía en general. Sin embargo, fuera de en la venta de refrescos, cerveza, mezcal y ropa barata, no tuvieron mucho éxito, porque la mayoría de la gente prefiere ahorrar el dinero para ir de compras a Sola de Vega. En años más recientes comenzó a operar en el pueblo una tienda patrocinada por el gobierno que vende productos básicos. A los hombres que trabajan en la tienda se les nombra de la misma manera que se nombra a alguien para un cargo político. A estos no se les considera tenderos. Ésta es la forma como la gente de San Lorenzo participa y comparte en el panorama de su economía, reforzando así su identidad como "gente de San Lorenzo."

La gente de San Lorenzo ve el mundo lleno de seres caprichosos de todas clases, y potencialmente perjudiciales. Dos de estos tipos de seres sobrenaturales se distinguen con las palabras *ñgyoozh* 'dios' y *doo* 'hada'. El término "dios" se aplica al Dios de la iglesia católica, a Jesús, a los santos, la cruz y las vírgenes, que son además identificados con el término *gyishnazh.* El vocablo "hada" traduce una palabra que se refiere a un segundo tipo deá seres sobrenaturales. Al contrario de los espíritus, se piensa que tienen cuerpo. Algunas veces se refieren a ellos como a la "gente que no fue creada por Dios." Hay hada de la montaña *doo gyi'*, o Matlaziwa; hada local, *doo guyu'*, o chaneque; hada de los hongos halucinatorios, *doo be'y;* hada de la enredadera de campanillas, *doo gyee ñaa* o *doo lyucy;* hada del floripondio, *gyee yon;* hada del chamico, *doo gyech;* hada del trueno, *doo guzii* o cosijo; y el Sol, *doo güidz.* De estos seres, solamente el Sol es a veces llamado "dios."

En San Lorenzo se busca mantener armonía con estos seres sobrenaturales participando en las actividades de la iglesia católica, ofreciendo sacrificios *(chu' dey presen)* y asegurándose de la ayuda de varios "conocedores."

Siempre que esta armonía es alterada puede que vayan a un adivino. Hay tres clases de adivinos: el que dice la fortuna *(yu rboo cuen)*, el espiritista *(yu sin)*, y la persona que adivina usando cera y agua *(yu rboo nab lo nis za)*. Una persona enferma puede ir también a un hierbatero *(yu ricy guñaa)*, o a uno que saca todo lo sucio *(yu rboo toop)* que ha sido sobrenaturalmente incrustado en el cuerpo de la persona enferma. Hay también personas especializadas para ofrecer los sacrificios al hada local *(yu rgu' presen)*, que es la causa mayor de las enfermedades, y también en contrarrestar los efectos de la brujería *(yu rboo nab)*.

El ser humano es también visto como caprichoso y potencialmente dañino. La gente de San Lorenzo cree que la brujería está ampliamente extendida. Como en otras comunidades zapotecas, sin embargo, no hay médicos. Selby (1974) considera que el término zapoteca *tu'* 'brujo' se usa para la gente foránea, que como tal, es sospechosa. Se piensa que la brujería se lleva a cabo insertando elementos dañinos en una imagen de la víctima, imagen que se hace frecuentemente usando una pieza de su ropa. Esta imagen se esconde. La "cura" se efectúa por medio de un especialista que sabe cómo encontrar la imagen.

Otras influencias malignas que los hombres pueden ejercer son: el mal de ojo y el vampiro, o nagual *(byee)*. Estas dos influencias tienen una fuerza maligna, el aire, que se asocia con ellos. El mal de ojo, literalmente es "el aire en el ojo de una persona" *(bi lo mbecy)*. La enfermedad causada por el vampiro es llamada *bi dañ* 'aire perjudicial'. El aire puede ejercer una influencia maligna en la persona de varias y diferentes maneras. Puede meterse en la persona causándole dolor. Es la causa de los ataques epilépticos *(ricy ñi bi)*. Se cree que el aire de un muerto es perjudicial para las plantas y la gente. Las personas de San Lorenzo dicen que ellas no tienen espíritus protectores *(nan dey bañcyug)* como los chatinos y algunos de los otros grupos de zapotecas (Mac Laury 1970:23). En este aspecto se diferencian también de varias de las otras comunidades zapotecas.

En un bosquejo cultural de esta naturaleza no es posible tratar un patrón cultural en detalle, más bien hemos tratado de enfocar algunos de los patrones que caracterizan a la gente de San Lorenzo como una unidad cultural. Es por su participación en patrones comunes sociales, políticos, ecómicos y religiosos, como se muestra en este bosquejo, que ellos se ven a sí mismos como gente distinta a "Juan."

Appendix 1

The Archive

Each of the texts in this collection has been glossed according to a rigorous set of guidelines (Bickford 1997), and they will be submitted to an electronic archive of text materials being prepared by members of the Summer Institute of Linguistics and others. Plans are to distribute these materials on the internet. A sample of what is expected to be available from the archive appears below. The following information occurs for each Zapotec expression:

Transcription in practical orthography
Transcription in technical orthography
Transcription of tone: (H)igh, (M)id, and (L)ow
Morphophonemic transcription
Morpheme glosses
Word glosses
Literal translation

For more information contact the Linguistic Department of
The Summer Institute of Linguistics, Mexico Branch, PO Box 8987,
Catalina AZ 85738 (E-mail Linguistics_Mexico@sil.org).

Gu_doo		nu	tub	yu	feñ
gu_do²		nu	tub	yu	[ɸeñ]
H_M		Lʰ	HL	L	H
gu	do²	d/nu	tub	yu	[ɸeñ]
tuber	fairy	with	one	3m	young
tuber(sp)		and	a	man	young

The "Chichicamole" Tuber and a Young Man

1.1 Bzu	tub	yu	feñ.	2.1 Lac	orzé!	brusu
bzu	tub	yu	[ɸeñ]	lak	[or]ze'	brusu
Lʰ	HL	L	H	Lʰ	H.L	L.HL
gb-zu	tub	yu	[ɸeñ]	lak	[or] ≡ ze?	gb-ru² ≡ zu
C-stand(Ind)	one	3m	young	how?	CB	C-step.foreward
There.was	a	man	young	however	*	Came.foreward

There once was a young man. It came about that

tub	yu_bel	rlagy	yu	gow	yuy.	3.1 Tanta!
tub	yu_bel	rlagʸ	yu	gow	yuy	[tant]a?
L	L_H	M	L	Lʰ	H	H.L'
tub	yu bel	r-(a) ≡ lagʸ	yu	k-(d)ow	yu-yu	[tant]-(g)a?
one	3m aged	H-want	3m	P-eat	3m-3m	so.much-Rep
a	old.man	wants	man	will.eat	he.him	much

an old man wanted to eat him. So (the young man)

nu	laab	rishdzidz	rded	yu.	4.1 Gaze!_nu
nu	la²b	rišjiǰ	rded	yu	gaze?_nu
l	HF	L.H	M	L	L.H_L
nu	la²b	rišǰ ≡ ǰiǰ	r—ded	yu	gaze? nu
Comp	be.true	danger	H—cross	3m	then Comp
*	is.true	dangerously	goes.about	he	then

lived in constant danger.

mnii_tooy	nu	nap	zir	benu	ub_lay	cut	yu
mni²_to²y	nu	nap	zir	benu	ub_lay	kut	yu
HF_M	L	L	H	H.L	M_'L	H	L
gb-ni² to²-yu	nu	nap	zir	ben≡nu	ub la -yu	k-(d)u²t	yu
C-say head-3m	Comp	good	more	if	self Emp-3m	P-kill	3m
he.decided	that	good	more	if	himself	will.kill	he

He decided that it would be better if he killed

ub_yu,	4.2 gun	cuaa		zir	yu	benu	gow	yu_bel
ub_yu	gun	kʷa²		zir	yu	benu	gow	yu_bel
L_L	H	M		H	L	H.L	Lʰ	H_H
ub yu	gun	kʷa²		zir	yu	be≡nu	k-(d)ow	yu bel
self 3m	because	be.unfotunate	more	3m	if	P-eat	3m	aged
he himself	because	Is.unfortunate	more	he	if	will.eat	old.man	

himself, because he would be worse off if the old man ate (him).

Apéndice 2

El archivo de español

Cada uno de los textos de esta colección han sido interpretados de acuerdo a un juego riguroso de guías (Bickford 1997), y serán asentadas en archivo electrónico de materiales de textos que están siendo preparados por miembros del Instituto Lingüístico de Verano y por otras personas. Se planea distribuir estos materiales en el Internet. Una muestra de lo que se espera que este disponible en los archivos aparece a continuación. La siguiente información se da para cada expresión zapoteca.

Adaptación técnica con tono
Transcripciones morfofonémicas
Glosas de morfemas
Glosas de palabras
La traducción

Para mas información: The Linguistic Department, The Summer Institute of Linguistics, P O Box 8987, Catalina AZ 85739, E U A (Correo electronico: Linguistics_Mexico@sil.org).

		nu	*tub*	*yu*	*feñ*
Gu_doo		nu	tub	yu	[ɸeñ]
gu_do?		Lʰ	HL	L	H
H_M		d/nu	tub	yu	[ɸeñ]
gu	do?	con	uno	3m	joven
tubérculo	duende	y	un	hombre	joven
chichicamole					

El chichicamole y el joven

1.1 *Bzu*	*tub*	*yu*	*feñ,*	2.1 *Lac*	*orze!*	*brusu*
bzu	tub	yu	[ɸeñ]	lak	[or]ze'	brusu
Lʰ	HL	L	H	Lʰ	H.L	L.HL
gb-zu	tub	yu	[ɸeñ]	lak	[or] ≡ ze?	gb-ru? ≡ zu
C-estar.de.pie(Ind)	uno	3m	jóven	¿como?	LO	C-presentarse
hubo	un	hombe	jóven	pues	*	se.presentó

Había una vez un joven

brusu	*tub*	*yu_bel*		*rlagy*	*yu*	*gow*	*yuy.*
burus	tub	yu_bel		rlagʸ	yu	gow	yuy
L.HL	L	L_H		M	L	Lʰ	H
gb-ru? ≡ zu	tub	yu	bel	r-a) ≡ lagʸ	yu	k-(d)ow	yu-yu
C-presentarse	un	3m	de.mayor.edad	H-quere	3m	P-comer	3m-3m
se.presentó	un	anciano		quiere	él	comerá	él.a.él

y también un abuelo que quería comérselo.

3.1 *Tanta!*	*nu*	*laab*	*rishdzidz*	*rded*	*yu.*
[tant]a?	nu	la?b	rišjiǰ	rded	yu
H.L'	L	HF	L.H	M	L
[tant]-(g)a?	nu	la?b	rišǰ ≡ ǰiǰ	r-ded	yu
tanto-Rep	Comp	estar.cierto	peligro	H-atravesar	3m
mucho	*	es.verdad	en.peligro	anda	él

Por tanto, andaba siempre en peligro.

4.1 *Gaze!_nu*   *mnïi_tooy*   *nu*   *nap*   *zir*   *benu*

    gaze?_nu   mni²_to²y   nu   nap   zir   benu

    L.H_L   HF_M   L   L   H   H.L

    gaze?   nu   gb-ni² to²-yu   nu   nap   zir   ben≡nu

    entonces Cmp   C-say cabeza-3m   Comp   buen   más   si

    entonces   decidió   que   bien   más   si

       Por eso pensaba que sería mejor si

    ub_lay   *cut*   *yu* *ub_yu,*   4.2 *gun*   *cuaa*   *zir*

    ub_lay   kut   yu ub_yu   gun   kʷa²   zir

    M_'L   H   L   L_L   H   M   H

    ub   la-yu   k—(d)u²t yu ub   yu   gun   kʷa²   zir

    mismo Emf-3m P-matar 3m mismo 3m   porque Estar.desgraciado más

    sí.mismo   matará   él sí.mismo   porque desgraciado.de   más

       se matara, porque sería peor

Índice

Prólogo.   xi

1. Los siete tipos de lluvia   2
   Un hombre de San Lorenzo es tragado por un cocodrilo que lo lleva
   al otro lado del séptimo océano donde se encuentra con el
   fabricante de la lluvia.

2. Matlaziwa   28
   Un hombre de San Lorenzo se encuentra en la montaña con una
   hada que seduce a los hombres.

3. El chichicamole y el joven   48
   Con la ayuda de un bulbo venenoso un joven cambia el propósito de
   un viejo que quería comérselo.

4. El zorrillo   58
   Un zorrillo le pide a un león de la montaña que sea su compadre, lo
   que trae como consecuencia trágicos resultados.

5. Pedro engaña al rey   65
   El tramposo Pedro Urdemalas demuestra que su inteligencia es
   superior a la del rey.

6. El hombre tonto 78
Un hombre simple y tonto prueba que es más sabeduría que su
hermano listo.

7. Lucecita 99
Lucecita usa su sabiduría femenina para ayudar a su inepto esposo
tenga éxito.

8. Cuerposulal 136
Un hombre va al otro lado del séptimo océano a rescatar a su esposa
de las garras de Cerposulal que es una personificación de la muerte.

9. El mundo de los muertos 155
Un hombre va al mundo de los muertos a traer de vuelta a su
esposa que había muerto.

10. Una vieja encontró al Sol y a la Luna 172
Una anciana se encuentra con dos huérfanos que se convierten en
los que llevan al Sol y a la Luna en su viaje por el cielo.

11. El amor de dos jóvenes 189
Un joven y una señorita se refieren a su amor que se profesan
mutuamente al hablar de pájaros bonitos.

12. El vampiro 192
Un hombre de San Lorenzo pasa la noche en la casa de una mujer vampiro.

13. Proverbios zapotecos 199
La sabiduría zapoteca se representa en expresiones tradicionales cortas
acerca de la vida, los vicios, las virtudes y las relaciones humanas.

14. Cenizas 213
Una poeta zapoteca presenta su punto de vista acerca del mundo.

Los zapotecas de San Lorenzo Texmelucan 217

Apéndice 2: El archivo de español 227

Índice 231

Referencias 233

References

Alcina Franch, José. 1972. Los dioses del Panteón Zapoteco. Anales de Antropología 9. Universidad Nacional Autónoma de México.

Bickford, J. Albert. 1997. A rich model for presenting interlinear text. Summer Institute of Linguistics Electronic Working Papers 1997–003, June 1997 [online]. Available: http://www.sil.org/silewp/1997/003 [1997, June 6].

de la Fuente, Julio. 1949. Yalalag: Una villa Zapoteca Serrana. México: Museo Nacional de Antropología.

Egland, Steven, Doris Bartholomew, and Saúl Cruz Ramos. 1978. La inteligibilidad interdialectal en México: Resultados de algunos sondeos. México: Instituto Lingüistico de Verano.

Harvey, Herbert R. 1968. Chatino and Papabuco in the historical sources. International Journal of American Linguistics 34:288–89.

Horcasitas, Fernando and Douglas Butterworth. 1963. La Llorona. Tlalocan: Revista de Fuentes para el Conocimiento de las Culturas Indígenas de México 4:204–24.

Kearney, Michael. 1972. The winds of Ixtepeji: World view and society in a Zapotec town. New York: Holt, Rinehart, and Winston.

MacLaury, Robert Ethan. 1970. Ayoquesco Zapotec: Ethnography, phonology, and lexicon. M.A. thesis. University of the Americas. Puebla, Mexico.

Nader, Laura. 1969. The Zapotec of Oaxaca. Handbook of Middle American Indians: Ethnology, Part 1 7:329–59. Austin: University of Texas Press.

Parsons, Elsie Clews. 1936. Mitla: Town of souls and other Zapotec-speaking pueblos of Oaxaca, Mexico. University of Chicago Press.

Ravicz, Robert. 1967. The Compadrinazco. The Hand Book of Middle American Indians 6:238–52. Austin: University of Texas Press.

Rendón, Juan José. 1971. Relaciones externas del llamado idioma Papabuco. Anales de Anthropología 8:213–31.

———. 1976. Estudio socio-lingüístico de cinco comunidades zapotecas en el distrito de Sola de Vega, Oaxaca. Anales de Anthropología 13:137–60.

Selby, Henry A. 1974. Zapotec deviance. Austin: The University of Texas Press.

Speck, Charles H. 1984. The phonology of the Texmelucan Zapotec verb. International Journal of American Linguistics 50:139–64.

Speck, Jane. 1986. Leyendo y escribiendo el zapoteco de San Lorenzo Texmelucan. Instituto Lingüístico de Verano. México.

Upson, B. W. and Robert E. Longacre. 1965. Proto-Chatino phonology. International Journal of American Linguistics 31:312–22.

Whitcotton, Joseph. 1977. The Zapotecs: Princes, priests, and peasants. Norman: University of Oklahoma Press.

www.ingramcontent.com/pod-product-compliance
Lightning Source LLC
Chambersburg PA
CBHW071854270326
41929CB00013B/2223